THE OAKWOOD PRESS

# The Essent ~~~
## to Swiss
## Heritage and
## Tourist Railways

*by*
*Mervyn Jones*

THE OAKWOOD PRESS

© Oakwood Press & Mervyn Jones 2007

British Library Cataloguing in Publication Data
A Record for this book is available from the British Library
ISBN 978 0 85361 659 7

Typeset by Oakwood Graphics.
Repro by pkmediaworks, Cranborne, Dorset.
Printed by Cambrian Printers Ltd, Aberystwyth, Ceredigeon.

# About the Author

Mervyn Jones began his interest in railways in the early 1950s spending much of his free time as a youngster at Preston railway station.

That was all left behind when he joined the British Police Service. Over the following 35 years he served in the Lancashire, Merseyside, Hampshire, West Midlands and Cheshire forces, retiring from the latter as Chief Constable towards the end of 1997. Since then he has travelled the world extensively on behalf of the United Kingdom's Foreign and Commonwealth Office teaching developing governments how to cope with natural and man-made disasters. On one occasion he taught in (Outer) Mongolia travelling there and back with his wife by the Trans-Siberian and Trans-Mongolian railways.

He is the holder a Master of Science degree in Social Policy from Cranfield University, is a Serving Officer of the Order of St John, a recipient of the Queen's Police Medal for Distinguished Service and the Police Long Service Medal. He lives with his wife, Caroline, half the year at their home on the North Wales, Shropshire and Cheshire borders and the other half in the south of France between Avignon and Nîmes.

His last railway publication was *The Essential Guide to French Heritage and Tourist Railways*, also published by Oakwood Press, in 2006. He is currently researching, photographing and writing his next guide on another European country's railways.

*Front cover:* E3/3 No. 8523 was built in 1915 by SLM at Winterthur and is now owned by the Compagnie du Train à Vapeur de la Vallée du Joux (*see entry 23*). It is seen here on 9th July, 2006 leaving Le Pont in the Jura heading for Le Brassus on the Franco-Swiss border.
*Author*

*Title page* Rhätische Bahn's electric and steam-driven rotary snowplough (*Schneeschleudern*) clears the way at the Bernina Hospiz station.
*Rhätische Bahn/swiss-image.ch*

*Rear cover:* On 12th October, 2006 Gornergratbahn's Bhe 4/8 No. 3043 follows Bhe 2/4 No. 3014 down the hill towards Riffelalp and eventually Zermatt.     *Author*

Published by The Oakwood Press (Usk), P.O. Box 13, Usk, Mon., NP15 1YS.
E-mail:     sales@oakwoodpress.co.uk
Website:   www.oakwoodpress.co.uk

# Contents

# Introduction

This guide is intended not only to appeal to railway enthusiasts but to holiday-makers and travellers who are attracted to the idea of visiting Switzerland and wish to see this beautiful country from an interesting perspective. This guide lists a total of 117 locations throughout Switzerland where heritage and tourist railways and related activities can be found. Of these, the author has identified 93 railways and/or routes, the situation at the beginning of 2007 being that all but two were fully active. One in Western Switzerland has unfortunately closed but hopes are kept alive that perhaps one day, phoenix-like, it will rise again. The other is an active development project to restore a line in Eastern Switzerland from the town of Etzwilen to Singen just over the border in Germany. Also listed are nine museums including the outstanding Swiss Transport Museum in Luzern (Lucerne). A further 15 locations have been identified where items of related railway or transport interest can be found. Some of these include organizations which have preserved rolling stock which is stored and often on display. Moreover, in some instances, material is in full working order and has been approved for excursions on the Swiss Federal Railway [Schweizerische Bundesbahnen (SBB)] tracks or those of other railway networks.

Many of the railways identified here travel on routes, long and short, invariably through outstandingly beautiful countryside. A small number of others operate on purpose-laid track in country amusement parks, thus offering something for all the family, young and old.

Ballenberg-Dampfbahn's 1926-built steam locomotive No. 1068 on charter to the UK's Railway Touring Company approaches Meiringen on 3rd February, 2007.    *Author*

# Acknowledgements

The author wishes to acknowledge the help, support, advice and, indeed, friendship, he has received from many quarters during the research for and the writing of this guide. One organization, however, which deserves special mention is *Union des chemins de fer historiques de Suisse* (HECH) which, as will be seen later, is the key organization in Switzerland looking after the interests of heritage and tourist railways. Incidentally, in the German language the organization is known as *Verband Historischer Eisenbahnen Schweiz* and in Italian as the *Unione dei treni storici della Svizzera*. The organization can be contacted c/o Hugo Wenger, Etzelstrasse 3, CH-8635 Dürnten, Switzerland or by e-mail through the website www.hech.ch This site, written in French and German (and in the course of being written in Italian) proved to be an excellent starting point, as were the individual websites of many of the locations identified. The author is particularly indebted to them all for the assistance and advice provided as well as, not least, for the up-to-date information about the activities of many of their members running tourist and heritage railways.

Important sources of information in compiling this guide have been by making visits to many of the railways and museums and learning at first hand about their history and current operations. Discussions enjoyed with organizers, enthusiasts and travellers, who were always found to be willing to share their valuable knowledge, proved most fruitful.

Other sources of information found to be important in compiling this guide were the many websites that have been written and published on Swiss heritage and tourist railways. The author, therefore, is indebted to the webmasters of HECH and other sites visited. Whilst all copyright (*les droits d'auteur*) has been respected, it is acknowledged and appreciated by the author how useful these sites have been in compiling up-to-date information for this guide. Most of the photographs were taken by the author or his wife; however, Rhätische Bahn in conjunction with swiss-photo.ch provided some superb pictures mostly taken by Peter Donatsch.

The author also wishes to express his appreciation to the UK's Swiss Railways Society, of which he is a member. The officers of the Society have been particularly helpful as has been their quarterly magazine, *Swiss Express*.

Finally, the author wishes to give special thanks to his wife, Caroline, who supported him throughout the project in many, many ways.

A Gornergratbahn train heads for Riffelberg on 12th October, 2006. Notice the helicopter above which is ferrying buckets of concrete for a building project near to the summit of the Gornergrat mountain.                                                                                   *Author*

# Switzerland
# The country, its people
# and administration

The Swiss flag proudly displayed at the stern of the MV *Schwyz* as it leaves the landing stage at Vitznau close to the Rigi Bahn station (*see entry 93*).                    *Author*

Switzerland, located in the centre of Western Europe, is also known as the *Confoederation Helvetica* hence the international road vehicle designation 'CH'. Helvetica is derived from the Latin word 'Helvetier' which was the name of the people who lived in this part of Europe before it became modern-day Switzerland. The national flag is a white cross on a red background. The Swiss are very proud of their flag which seems to be flown just about everywhere. Switzerland does not have an official national flower but the Edelweiss has assumed such status albeit on an unofficial basis. The capital of the country is Bern, located towards the north-west corner of the country.

### History

The creation of the country that we know today as Switzerland began in 1291 when three cantons - Schwyz, Uri and Unterwalden - formed an alliance against their powerful neighbour the Hapsburgs. In the 14th century, the cantons of Bern, Glarus, Luzern, Zug and Zürich also joined the Confederation. The Hapsburgs attempted to destroy this alliance in a series of battles but were defeated leading directly to Switzerland's independence in 1499. In the early 16th century the Confederation embarked on a policy of territorial expansion, notably in Locarno and Lugano in Italy's Lombardy region, but were subsequently defeated by the French and Venetian forces at the Battle of Marignano in 1515.

In the very late 18th century, Napoleon invaded Switzerland and abolished the Confederation, which by then consisted of 13 cantons, and replaced it by establishing the Helvetic Republic. This Republic was short-lived and the Confederation, happily for the Swiss, was restored in 1803. However, the country remained under French control until the defeat of Napoleon at the Battle of Waterloo in 1815. More cantons later joined the Confederation although unity was difficult to achieve given that there were significant divisions on the grounds of religion. Many of these differences were not overcome until a new constitution was drawn up in 1848, thus creating a formal union of cantons governed by a Federal Assembly and centred in what became the Swiss capital, Bern.

The last invasion that Switzerland experienced took place in 1857 when the Prussians attempted to annex Neuchâtel. The Swiss Army was sent to the border on the River Rhine where it successfully repelled the invaders.

World Wars I and II followed but Switzerland kept its neutrality and was not drawn into the conflicts surrounding them. When the European Community was formed, Switzerland rejected the idea of membership and has continued to do so even though opinion within the country, on whether or not to join, is still divided. Switzerland became a member of the United Nations as recently as 2002 although it was one of the first countries in 1920 to join its predecessor organization, the League of Nations which chose at that time to establish its international headquarters in Geneva.

*Geography*

Switzerland geographically is a small country having 41,300 sq. km (15,950 sq. miles) making it just under one-sixth of the size of the United Kingdom. Two-thirds of Switzerland's relief is mountainous or hilly, which, as will be seen, in the late 19th century presented special challenges to the engineers building railways and roads.

There are three distinct geographical areas. The Jura Mountains which are located in the north-west; Mittelland's central plateau; and the Alps, which is the largest region to the south and to the east. The highest mountain in Switzerland is the Dufourspitze with an altitude of 4,634 m (15,200 ft). Other well-known mountains include the Eiger at 3,970 m (13,025 ft) the Mönch at 4,099 m (13,448 ft) the Jungfraujoch at 4,158 m (13,642 ft) and the Matterhorn at 4,478 m (14,672 ft).

Switzerland has international frontiers with five other countries, i.e. Italy (741 km) France (572 km) Germany (363 km) Austria (165 km) and Liechtenstein (41 km).

The principal rivers in Switzerland are the Rhine (375 km in length in Switzerland), the Aar (295 km), the Rhône (264 km), the Reuss (158 km), the Linth/Limmat (140 km), the Saane/Sarine (128 km), the Thur (125 km) and the Inn (104 km). Switzerland is drained in four different directions, i.e. into the North Sea via the Rhine, the Mediterranean Sea via the Rhône, the Adriatic Sea via the Rivers Po and the Adige and, finally, into the Black Sea via the Danube.

Switzerland is a country well known for its lakes. The main ones are Lake Geneva, also referred to as Lac Léman or Lac de Genève, (581.3 sq. km in area), Lake Constance, also known as Bodensee, (541.1 sq. km), Lake Neuchâtel, also referred to as Lac de Neuchâtel or Neuenburgersee, (218.3 sq. km), Lake Maggiore (212.3 sq. km), Lake Lucerne, named in Swiss German as the Vierwaldstättersee, (113.7 sq. km), Lake Zürich, referred to also as the Zürichsee, (90.1 sq. km), Lake Lugano (48.7 sq. km), Lake Thun, known locally as Thunersee, (48.4 sq. km), Lake Biel, referred to

The Matterhorn in all its glory as seen from a carriage on the Gornergratbahn (*see entry 54*).
*Author*

The landing stage alongside Montreux's colourful promenade with MV *Chablais* (its livery promoting a Nestlé product) taking passengers on board prior to crossing to Bouveret. *Author*

as Lac de Bienne or Bielersee, (39.6 sq. km), Lake Zug or Zugersee (38.3 sq. km), Lake Brienz or Brienzersee (29.8 sq. km), Lake Walen, or Walensee or Lake Walenstadt, (24.1 sq. km), and finally, Lake Murten, or Lac Morat or Murtensee, (23 sq. km). Lake Geneva is the largest freshwater lake in Western Europe, containing some 89 trillion litres. It is fed by the River Rhône, which rises at the world-famous glacier in the Furka Pass and flows westwards between the mountains in the Valais canton to enter the lake near Villeneuve. Eventually it exits the lake at Geneva as the Rhône once again and flows on into France. It is estimated that it takes 17 years for the water to travel from the Rhône glacier at Furka to Geneva. The lake is only 14 km wide at its broadest point but it is deep, plunging to a maximum depth of 310 m.

### Climate

The weather in Switzerland varies enormously. The highest rainfall, with approximately 260 cm per year, is at Rochers-de-Naye, a mountain near to Montreux. More rain falls in the western part of Switzerland invariably caused by clouds coming over France from the Atlantic. Parts of the Alps in the south also receive their fair share of rain. Lugano in the canton of Ticino, for example, receives something in the order of 175 cm per year. If the winds blow in clouds from the south, they are blocked by the Alps and rain falls. This sometimes has the effect of causing dry warm weather to the north often accompanied by strong winds. This event is known as Foehn or Föhn and many people claim that they get headaches under such conditions, an experience not dissimilar to the impact that the Mistral wind has on people in the southern Rhône valley. However, one benefit these conditions bring is that visibility often is extremely good. To the east in the Engadin and to the south-west in Valais there is little rain comparatively. Scuol in Graubünden receives only about 70 cm in a year and Staldenried in Valais as little as 53 cm.

A restaurant close to the summit of the Piz Bernina. This location 'enjoys' snow all the year round.                                                                                        *Author*

The average amount of sunshine per year is 1,700 hours and some villages in Valais even claim that they are exposed to as much as 2,300 hours of sunshine in a year - because of this kind climate kiwis, peaches, figs and tomatoes grow in abundance. The warmest parts of Switzerland tend to be in the cantons of Ticino and Valais and, in particular, the town of Montreux where palm trees line the promenade alongside Lake Geneva. Ticino enjoys almost 300 sunny days each year with a daily average temperature in July of over 26°C.

It is a myth for people outside the country who imagine that Switzerland is as cold as the polar regions, for that is a long way from the truth. In the plain, temperatures can rise as high as 30°C in summer, and even in the mountains, the sun is hot. In winter, temperatures rarely drop below minus 5°C in the whole country, except, understandably, on the very tops of the mountains. Air temperature and the altitude, of course, determine the form precipitation takes. Switzerland enjoys more than a fair share of snow particularly in the mountains helpfully aiding the winter sports tourism industry. The mountainous character of Switzerland is also responsible for spectacular differences in the weather among different regions. It is very common to move from a cold, cloudy and rainy landscape to a beautiful clear blue sky with hot sun in just a few minutes.

## Government

Administratively, Switzerland's Confederation (*Eidgenossenschaft*) comprises the following institutions:

*Bundesversammlung* (Federal Assembly) is the legislative authority and comprises two houses, the *Ständerat* or *kleine Kammer* (small chamber) and the *Nationalrat* or *grosse Kammer* (large chamber). Both houses meet in the *Bundeshaus* in Bern.

The *Bundesrat* is the executive authority and is made up of seven members who are elected by a combined assembly of both chambers. One of the members is responsible for the Environment, Transport, Energy and Communications. The Transport portfolio includes the national responsibility for the motorways and the railways.

Switzerland consists of 23 *Kantone* (cantons or states), three of which are in fact divided into half-cantons - Unterwalden, Basel and Appenzell. Each canton consists of a number of *Bezirke* (districts) which in turn are further divided into *Gemeinden* (municipalities). The cantons are responsible for education, transportation and social institutions; the districts, for education and the judiciary; and, the municipalities for local services such as electricity, water, the fire brigade, the police, local transportation, schools and taxation. The latter can vary significantly between municipalities, a most obvious visual example on a visit to Switzerland being the variation in the price of petrol and diesel at the fuel stations. There are 2,929 municipalities in total. A municipality with more than 10,000 citizens is called a *Stadt* (town) and a smaller one a *Dorf* (village).

The cantons listed in their official order are: Zürich (ZH), Bern or Berne (BE), Luzern or Lucerne (LU), Uri (UR), Schwyz (SZ), Unterwalden (UW) being divided into Obwalden (OW) and Nidwalden (NW), Glarus (GL), Zug (ZG), Freiburg or Friburg (FR), Solothurn (SO), Basel (BA) being sub-divided into Basel Stadt (BS) and

Basel Land (BL), Schaffhausen (SH), Appenzell (AP) being sub-divided into Appenzell Ausserrhoden (AR) and Appenzell Innerrhoden (AI), Sankt Gallen (SG), Graubünden (GR), Aargau (AG), Thurgau (TG), Ticino (TI), Vaud (VD), Valais or Wallis (VS), Neuchâtel (NE), Genève (GE) and Jura (JU). Switzerland's vehicle registration plates include the cantonal abbreviation indicating the 'home' location of the registered owner.

The largest canton geographically is Graubünden (7.105 million sq. km) and the smallest Zug (239,000 sq. km). Zug is also reputed to be the richest of all of the cantons.

### Population

The total population of Switzerland, including foreign nationals granted residential status, is 7.5 million which is about an eighth of that of the United Kingdom. In terms of language, 65 per cent regularly speak German (most common in Mittelland, Bernese Oberland, Valais, northern and north-eastern Switzerland), 18 per cent French (predominantly in western Switzerland), 12 per cent Italian (mainly in Ticino), 1 per cent Romansch (found in south-eastern Switzerland) and 4 per cent other languages. English is a common second language. In respect of religion, almost 48 per cent are Roman Catholic, just over 44 per cent are Protestant and 8 per cent follow other faiths.

Zürich canton has the greatest population with 1.2 million and Uri the least with just short of 36,000 residents. The greatest concentration of foreign nationals resident in Switzerland is in the Geneva canton with 37.6 per cent being non-Swiss.

### Economy

About two-thirds of the area of Switzerland is covered with forests, lakes and mountains but the country has no mineral resources of its own. Consequently, mineral resources have to be imported, processed and sold on within the country and, in some instances, exported. The service industry is the most important part of the economy. Although farming is important the products of Swiss farmers do not meet the needs of the population, so Switzerland has to rely on importing goods from other countries. The economy is defined in three sectors. The primary sector is agriculture (*Landwirtschaft*) employing less than 10 per cent of the population. The second sector is industry (*Industrie*), trade (*Gewerbe*) and handicrafts (*Handwerk*) and employs about 40 per cent of the population. This sector includes people employed in the machine and metal industries, watch making and textiles. Many of these products are exported but, some would argue, not as profitably as they could be given that the Swiss franc is expensive and Switzerland is not a member of the European Union (EU). The third sector, employing more than 50 per cent of the population, is the service industry (*Dienstleistungssektor*) focused on banking, which is the most important, insurance and tourism. An efficient transportation system, especially the rail network, is key to the success of the latter.

## Currency

As has already been said, Switzerland is not a member of the European Union and therefore retains its own currency - the Swiss franc - abbreviated in this guide on the ISO terminology as CHF. At the time of first publication of this book (March 2007) the Swiss franc was worth 41½ pence GBP. It is not uncommon to be able to make purchases using euros, especially in those places close to EU country frontiers.

## Transportation

The entire rail network amounts to 5,312 km of which 2,143 km belongs to privately run railway companies. There are 98 km of rack/cogwheel railways, 60 km of funicular routes and 905 km of suspended cable cars. There is a total of 71,297 km of roads of which only 1,734 km are trunk roads. Locally, there are 1,202 km of bus routes, 330 km of trolleybus routes and 187 km of tramways. Nationally, bus companies operate over a total length of 16,339 km of which more than 63 per cent is fulfilled by the nationally run Post Bus services. There are 1,244 km of navigable waterways. Switzerland enjoys the greatest number of rail journeys per capita at 34 compared with 23 in Austria, 20 in Germany, 15 in France, 11 in Spain and just nine in Italy.

A Post Bus awaiting passengers at the bus station in Meiringen on 3rd February, 2007
*Author*

# A Brief History of Swiss Railways

The year 2007 is Switzerland's 160th anniversary of the opening of its first own railway operation when a line was constructed from Zürich to Baden, Aargovia. Compared with neighbouring European countries, Switzerland was late joining in on the development of their own railways. For example, both France and Germany had built lines of several thousand kilometres in the 1830s and 1840s. Ironically, Switzerland's first railways were not Swiss at all. In mid-1844, Alsace Railways began running services between St Louis and Basel on Swiss territory. A year later, in the December, the French built and opened the first station in Switzerland in Basel. However, it was not until two years later that Switzerland opened its first Swiss-owned railway.

Earlier in 1836, some enterprising members of the Zürich Chamber of Commerce commissioned a feasibility study for the construction of a railway to Basel, 82 km away. It was intended that the line would follow the rivers Limmat, Aare and Rhine. However, the project had to be abandoned when the half-cantons - Basel-Stadt and Basel-Landschaft - refused to support the idea. At the same time, because of a downturn in interest for railway ventures, the much-needed financial support was not forthcoming. The plans were archived. Six years later some Zürich businessmen tried again. This time they focused on a northern connection, which after debate with the affected cantons, led to the building of the Zürich to Baden line. The line was formally opened on 7th August, 1847. Again, progress in further expansion of Switzerland's railways was very slow as evidenced by the sad fact that this line remained the only exclusively Swiss line for the following seven years.

The Zürich to Baden railway line was known from the outset as the 'Spanisch-Brötli-Bahn' (Spanish Bun Railway) because of a particular Baden culinary delight – a tasty bun which was made of slightly puffed yeast pastry and was a particular favourite of local inhabitants. The first locomotive that ran on this line was named 'Limmat'. The original has long gone but just after the end of World War II, to mark the centenary of the railway, a true replica was built and run again on the line. Fifty years later *Limmat* enjoyed another outing for its next major anniversary. The locomotive, even though a replica, is fast becoming a vehicle of historic interest in its own right. It is kept on permanent display in the Swiss Transport Museum at Luzern (*see entry 96*).

In 1848, a change was made to the Swiss Constitution which brought an important benefit for the future running of railways across the boundaries of the various cantons of Switzerland. In that year, Switzerland converted from being a Federation of Cantons to being a Federal State. This was an important change for a number of reasons, not least of all that cantonal border controls were abolished and trade could follow free of customs duties. Had this not happened at the time that it did, then it would have further reinforced parochial attitudes within some cantons towards 'federal' activities including, of course, general transportation schemes including rail networks.

The postal system and telegraphy were two examples of where the Federal State immediately took control but it chose at that time not to assume responsibility for the development of the railways. This failure no doubt contributed to the slow start in the development of the Swiss Railway network. The fundamental questions to be addressed by the Swiss were: who was to build the railways and who was to operate them - the individual cantons or private companies? Other questions such as which routes to build and so on were secondary at that time.

In 1849, some in the Federal Assembly thought that the State should take a leading role and instructed the Federal Council to draft a Bill for the development of a future federal railway. Advice was needed so the Swiss authorities turned for help to the birthplace of railways, Great Britain. Two British experts were engaged, Henry

*Limmat* - the 60-year-old replica of the locomotive which operated on the first Swiss railway service, 'The Spanish Bun Train'.     *Author*

Swinburne and Robert Stephenson, the son of George Stephenson the legendary locomotive and railway pioneer. Over two years Swinburne and Stephenson undertook their studies travelling extensively throughout Switzerland at the end of which they wrote a proposal. They thought that a main line should be built from Basel to Luzern which would be crossed at Olten by a lowland line from Morges to Zürich, on to Winterthur and Lake Constance and then down to Chur. Basel and Lake Constance were key to the plan especially as the international rail links to France and Germany were already located there. Branch lines it was proposed would link to Bern, the Swiss capital. There was some good sense in their proposals as construction costs for bridges and tunnels would be minimised in that the intended routes would follow river valleys. Unfortunately for the plan the Britons had not fully understood Swiss politics because objections came from every direction. Bern citizens were particularly vociferous given that the capital city was intended to be on a branch line. Those from Zürich complained that they did not have the direct link to Waldshut (and therefore Germany). People from Geneva said they would have to use a steamboat to get to Morges before they could join a train. Ticino citizens saw themselves being cut off from the rest of Federation as it was thought too expensive to build a line from Lugano to Bellinzona. All these objections led to the rejection of Swinburne and Stephenson's proposals and the abandonment, at that time, of the idea of the Federation taking the lead role in establishing the country's railway network.

In 1852, the Federal Government voted to leave the construction and operation of the railways to the cantons. It was expected that the cantons would likely engage private enterprise to meet their requirements, which they did. Amazingly, in spite of the initial slow start, numerous lines were built very quickly and whilst the individual cantons gained local benefits, a rational national network linking the cantons failed to happen.

Towards the end of the decade railway entrepreneurs began to recognise the problems caused by the lack of coherence. Drastic action followed in the form of mergers or takeovers of the numerous railway companies. More rationalisation followed in 1870 and again in the 1880s leading eventually to the formation of five large networks, i.e. the 'Jura-Simplon' railway (JS), the 'Schweizerische Centralbahn' (SCB), 'Schweizerische Nordostbahn' (NOB), the 'Vereinigte Schweizerbahnen' (VSB) and 'Gotthardbahn' (GB). In just three decades, the network had grown to a length of 2,500 km.

By the early 1890s, those who supported the idea of nationalizing the railways were gathering forces and gaining more supporters. However, the big problem was how the Federal Government would finance the purchase of the private railway companies at what was a time of economic difficulty. The Government published its purchase plans in 1897 and later the Swiss people were invited to vote on whether the country should have a National Railway. Almost 68 per cent voted in favour. On 1st January, 1902, the first Swiss Federal Railway (SBB) train arrived at Bern station at two in the morning to the welcoming applause of many railway workers who had turned out at such an early hour.

The formation of the SBB brought in growing expansion of the network with extra routes and an expanded infrastructure with more viaducts, bridges, tunnels and stations. Perhaps the greatest impact that SBB had in the early years of the 20th century, before the onset of hostilities in 1914, was to opt for electrification. A programme of building electric power stations was embarked upon - the Ritom was the first to open in 1920, followed by the Gotthard (at Amsteg) in 1924, the Vernayaz in 1927 and the Etzal was finally completed in 1937. All these constructions led to SBB being self sufficient in electricity until after the end of World War II.

'White coal' a term applied to electricity supplies for railway traction developed at a pace in the early years after the end of World War I. It started with the use of Direct Current but given the low voltages involved it was found only to be suitable for tramways and short branch lines. Three-phase current followed but it also had its problems so it was not until Single-Phase Alternating Current came along that the difficulties were resolved. Having said that, it is remarkable that so many differing systems and power ratings were introduced some of which are still being used today. Those choices always had a potential problem for denying interconnectivity in the network. However, given the ingenuity of modern locomotive constructors, such as Switzerland's Stadler, for example, a situation now exists where modern traction can switch to differing power systems without having to stop and change locomotive. A good working example of this is found in trains running out of Switzerland using alternating current and into Italy with its direct current.

In spite of many plans to build more Alpine crossings only one existed at the end of the 19th century - the Gotthard - which had been opened to traffic as early as May 1882. A proposal for another crossing that eventually did meet with success was that made by the Jura-Simplon railway company. They gained approvals and financial support from the Swiss and Italian governments to build the Simplon tunnel. The first 'tube' was opened in 1906 and a second followed in 1922 making them the longest tunnels in the world at that time. This success inspired the building of other tunnels, for example, Neuchâtel and Moutier in the direction of Thun, Hasle-Rüegsau to Thun, Neuchâtel to Bern, two other Jura tunnels and the Grenchenberg. Perhaps the crowning glory was the Lötschberg tunnel which was opened in 1913. Sadly, this achievement had been marred by a tunnel collapse five years before which had taken the lives of 25 Italian construction workers.

After the end of World War II and until the present day, significant investment has continued with the objective of not only maintaining but also developing Switzerland's rail services. The quality of the trains has steadily improved with better seating and better visibility for passengers. Timetables offer regular and frequent services on an extensive network, which, with value-for-money fares, encourages travellers and commuters alike to choose to use rail services as an alternative to road traffic options. Similarly, the movement of freight by rail rather than by road is taken very seriously indeed, actively encouraged by successive Swiss Governments both at cantonal and national levels. Perhaps this is best summed up by Moritz Leunberger, a Federal Government minister and in 1997 the Head of the Swiss Transport and Energy Department who in a Foreword to the book *The Swiss Railways Saga* (*see Bibliography*) wrote:

In no other country of Europe are railways used as frequently and widely as in Switzerland. And no other transit country along the alpine wall transports a higher share of the goods on rails. Whoever analyzes today's Swiss railway network, will realise that our ancestors made good decisions. Thanks to their wise foresight, a railway network was built which almost fully survived, while in many other countries it shrank to a skeleton of important mainlines. Proud railway figures are more than just a decoration of carefully kept statistics. They are disguised performance. The railway performance protects air and soil, preventing pollution and noise.

After 160 years of continuing development, Switzerland can be justifiably proud of its railway heritage.

# Rack/Cogwheel Systems

Switzerland, because of the mountainous nature of its terrain, needed a system which would allow trains that could not rely on normal adhesion alone to negotiate steep gradients of which there are a great many in the country. This was why the invention of the various rack/cogwheel systems played a crucial part in bringing railways to otherwise inaccessible locations. There is no other country in the world where there are as many in use. There are four, perhaps five, main types of rack/cogwheel systems.

The Riggenbach system was invented by Niklaus Riggenbach and is the oldest form of rack railway/cogwheel system. It is formed by steel plates or channels connected by round or square rods at regular intervals. The Riggenbach system was the first devised but suffers from the fact that its fixed rack is much more complex and expensive to build than the other, later designs. Incidentally, this system is sometimes also referred to as the Marsh system, because of simultaneous invention by an American inventor of that name who was the builder of the Mount Washington Cog Railway in the United States of America.

The Abt system was devised by Roman Abt, a Swiss locomotive engineer. Abt at this time was working for a rack/cogwheel railway which used the Riggenbach design which he thought could be improved. The Abt rack features steel plates mounted vertically and in parallel to the rails, with rack teeth machined to a precise profile within them. These engage with the locomotive's pinion teeth much more smoothly than the Riggenbach system. Two or three parallel sets of Abt rack plates are used, with a corresponding number of driving pinions on the locomotive, to ensure that at least one pinion tooth is always engaged securely. Today, the majority of rack/cogwheel railways in Switzerland use the Abt system.

A memorial to Niklaus Riggenbach on a wall at Vitznau station on the Rigi Bahn. *Author*

The Riggenbach rack rail on the Rorschach-Heiden Bahn.      *Author*

The cog engaging the double rack teeth of the Abt system on the Aigle-Leysin railway.  *Author*

The rack teeth of the Strub system on the Jungfraubahn. *Author*

The Strub system was invented by Emil Strub and is similar to the Abt system but uses just one wide rack plate welded on top of a flat bottomed 'T' shaped rail. It is the simplest rack system to maintain and as a consequence has become increasingly popular in use.

The Locher system was invented by Eduard Locher and involves teeth cut in the sides rather than the top of the rail. It is engaged on each side of the rail by two cogwheels on the locomotive. The system allows steeper gradients to be negotiated than the other systems, whose teeth could otherwise 'jump' out of the rack. It is used in only one location in Switzerland, the Pilatus Railway (*see entry 92*) which at 48 per cent has the steepest gradient of any rack railway in the world.

A fifth system is one devised by the Von Roll company, a Swiss aerial tramway and industrial manufacturing company. It was later taken over by the Austrian manufacturer Doppelmayr in 1996. The system is similar to that of Roman Abt's except that the teeth in the single blade are cut to suit the gear design either of the Riggenbach or the Strub cogwheels. Because of its simplicity, the Von Roll rack replaces Riggenbach or Strub racks in new or renewed installations, thus avoiding the greater expense of replacing the cogs on existing steam-driven or electric powered locomotives and rail cars.

Some rail systems are known as 'rack-and-adhesion' because they use the cog drive only on the steepest sections where normal adhesion would fail. Elsewhere on the route they operate like any other adhesion only type traction. Routes or railways that operate on such combined systems in Switzerland are: the Brünig Bahn, Chemins de fer Legère de Riviere, Luzern-Stans-Engelberg, Bernese Oberland Bahn, Aigle-Ollon-Monthey-Champéry, Aigle-Leysin, Bex-Villars-Bretaye, Martigny Châtelard, Matterhorn Gotthard Bahn, Appenzellerbahn, Furka Cogwheel and the Rorschach-Heiden Bahn.

However, railways operating on steep gradients are obliged to operate by rack/cogwheel only. This means that the locomotive's wheels freewheel and,

A preserved powered rail car from the Pilatus railway illustrating the Locher system. One of the two horizontally-mounted cogwheels can be seen painted in a silver colour. This rail car is on permanent display in the Swiss Transport Museum in Luzern (*see entry 96*).
*Author*

despite appearances to the contrary, do not contribute in any way to the propulsion of the train. The railways that run solely on rack/cogwheel systems in Switzerland are: the Brienz-Rothorn Bahn, Schynige-Platte Bahn, Wengeralpbahn, Jungfraubahn, Gornergratbahn, Ferrovia Monte Generoso, Pilatus Bahn, Rigi Bahnen, Rheineck-Walzenhausen Bahn and the Montreux Glion Rochers-de-Naye railway.

Originally, almost all of the rack/cogwheel railways were powered by steam-driven locomotives. These had to be extensively modified to work effectively. Unlike a diesel- or electric-powered locomotive, the steam locomotive only works when its source of power - the boiler - is level or fairly close to it. A working locomotive's boiler requires water to cover the boiler tubes and firebox at all times. If it does not, fusible plugs in the firebox crown will melt causing failure, sometimes catastrophic. In order that such steam locomotives succeed, the boiler, cab and general superstructure of the locomotive have to be tilted forward so that when climbing the gradient they become horizontal.

As a consequence, locomotives of this design, for opposing reasons, cannot function on level track. It is necessary, therefore, that the entire line, including inside the maintenance sheds, is kept on a gradient. These difficulties with steam traction, particularly the cost of building and running such locomotives, was one of the main reasons why rack/cogwheel railways were among the first to be electrified. Most of today's rack railways operate on electricity but not all, for example, the Brienz Rothorn Bahn (*see entry 51*). The observer will also notice that rack/cogwheel locomotives, for safety reasons, always push their passenger carriages up gradients and lead them down. The reason for this being that the locomotives are fitted with powerful brakes, often including hooks or clamps which can give maximum grip to the rack rail. Some locomotives are also fitted with automatic brakes that are applied should the speed get too great. Often there is no coupler between the locomotive and first carriage of the train as gravity will always rule the day. The maximum speed of trains operating on a rack/cogwheel railway rarely exceeds 25 km/h.

# Getting the best out of this Guide

To assist the reader in orientating him or herself relative to what is on offer and perhaps for planning a visit or visits to Switzerland, the railways and other locations identified in this guide have been organized in a number of ways. Firstly, on a **national basis** (*see entry 1 on page 23*); secondly, those railways passing through **more than one region** (*entries begin at page 29*); and, thirdly, those **crossing international frontiers** (*entries begin at page 39*). The fourth grouping identifies those railways distributed on a **regional basis**, i.e. Western Switzerland including Geneva (*entries begin at page 49*); Mittelland, Bernese Oberland and Valais Region including Bern (*entries begin at page 90*); Northern Region including Zürich (*entries begin at page 129*); Central Switzerland and Ticino (*entries begin at page 139*); and, finally, Eastern Switzerland including Graubünden (*entries begin at page 160*).

All five regions in Switzerland have something to offer the railway enthusiast, the traveller and the family holiday-maker. Within each region the entries have been organized in three thematic sections. Firstly, there are the railways and/or their routes; secondly, museums; and, thirdly, items of related railway or general transport interest. The book examines railways of all gauges and types. It does not detail, though, funiculars and cable cars, of which there are a great number in Switzerland. Having said that, where such a facility adjoins a railway and is relevant to it, a brief description is given.

The guide, hopefully, has avoided becoming over detailed about the material which is held, in favour of listing, where known, what may be seen and indicating where more information may be found. However, some comprehensive lists have been provided for some of the larger operations where the information has fallen easy to hand. Those who want even more detail will invariably find that a good starting point is the organization's website. There are many of these for Swiss Railways, which, experience has shown, contain a wealth of information. To assist in this respect, websites and e-mail addresses, where they exist, are provided. Websites are a very helpful means of obtaining current information but it is worth noting that some have not always been regularly maintained or have been given a new address (URL) leaving the web browser or search engine at a loss. Similarly, some e-mail addresses are not always effective. At the time of going to print all the websites and e-mail addresses have been checked, found to be active and to be what they purported to be. Incidentally, where a website is listed, shown in brackets immediately after is the language or languages in which the information is written, i.e. German (de), French (fr), Italian (it), English (en), Dutch (nl), Japanese (jp) and Spanish (es).

Each entry also identifies the location by town or city, its canton and proximity to a major regional centre of population. Route directions are not provided but a grid reference drawn from the *Michelin Map No. 729 - Switzerland* is given. Consideration was given to including GPS references but from the author's experience it is just as easy to enter the destination rather than provide data which have huge potential for error. Contact details such as addresses, telephone and fax number are listed. It will be noted that the numbers given are shown in a format as if one is dialling from within Switzerland. If dialling from abroad start the call with the international dialling code - in the UK it is 00 - followed by the code for Switzerland which is 41; then drop the first digit - the 0 - then follow it with the number. For example, the number in Switzerland for Chemin de Fer-Musée Blonay-Chamby is 021 943 21 21 but if calling from the UK dial the following: 00 41 21 943 21 21. Other information provided includes dates of opening, hours of operation, examples of the charges levied and train journey times which normally are for a single direction unless otherwise indicated. The year in brackets after the entry indicates when the information was obtained.

Steam locomotives HG 3/4 No. 3 and G2 2/2 No. 105 (*right*) being prepared for the day's operations close to the Chamby depot/museum.                                    *Author*

Every attempt has been made to ensure that all the information in this guide is correct and up-to-date, but it is important to render a health warning. Before travelling any distance in Switzerland to any of the locations listed herein, it is wise, in order to avoid disappointment, to check the state of current operations. There are many factors in heritage and tourist railway operations, short of closure or suspension, which can alter the availability of a service, not least the changing condition of many of the ageing locomotives and other rolling stock. Also, much of the Swiss preserved railway material can and does move around the country so if one wishes particularly to see something, it is wise to check beforehand where it is.

Foreign languages can sometimes present a barrier to some in gaining more information. Therefore to assist those who may have some understanding of German, French or Italian (but not Romansch!) a glossary of the more common railway terms has been included.

Finally, for planning all journeys within Switzerland, it is worth noting that all tickets, timetables, fares and special offers are available at manned railway stations, travel agencies, or via Rail Service on telephone 0900 300 300 (CHF 1.19 per minute) or by way of SBB's website which is helpfully accessible in any one of four languages (de fr it en).

The author is always keen to keep the information correct and up-to-date. By the nature of things, this guide has limitations in that it can only provide a 'snapshot' of what the state of affairs was at a particular time. The source material for this book was gathered towards the end of 2006 and the beginning of 2007. Much of the information contained herein will not change, well at least, not significantly. Other detail, however, will alter; operating dates of the Heritage Railways, timetables, tariffs, rolling stock, company names and so on. Having said that, if this publication is used as it's intended, as a guide, then it is hoped that the contents will have relevance for some time to come. Operating dates for the preserved railways are a good example: whilst precise dates have been given for 2007, next year and beyond they will obviously change, but it is the author's experience that whilst that is true the pattern of activity often remains the same. To help in this regard the author offers two ideas. Firstly, contributions are invited if any inaccuracies are identified in this book, changes are found to have been made to the operating circumstances or new facilities have become available. Such information can be sent to the author who can be contacted by e-mail at swiss@rail-guides.eu or c/o Oakwood Press. The second idea the author has is to provide a website. One such site has already been written supporting *The Essential Guide to French Heritage and Tourist Railways*, i.e. www.rail-guides.eu That site will be extended to embrace this guide as well as others which are presently in the planning stage.

# Switzerland's National Railway

**1  Swiss Federal Railways - in Swiss German - Schweizerische Bundesbahnen [SBB] in Swiss French - Chemin de fer Fedéraux [CFF] in Swiss Italian - Ferrovie Federali Svizzeria [FFS]**

Re 4/4 460 No. 116-7 locomotive seen here at Landquart on 3rd October, 2006.    *Author*

*Introduction:* SBB is Switzerland's national rail carrier. The 2005 statistics contained in the Annual Report of the Schweizerische Bundesbahnen indicate that SBB operated on 3,163 km of track. In 2005 the company carried 275,900,000 passengers accompanying 321,000 items of luggage and 482,000 bicycles with 95.7 per cent of passenger trains arriving less than five minutes late. Freight transported amounted to 56,150,000 net tonnes with 90.3 per cent of freight trains arriving less than 31 minutes late. Overall a total of 28,330 persons are employed by the SBB Group. A total of 3,645 GWh of electricity was generated or purchased for use on the network with 75.4 per cent coming from renewable energy sources. It is worth noting that 100 per cent of the SBB network is electrified which compares with Italy 69.4 per cent, Austria 62.5 per cent, Germany 55.7 per cent. and France 50.1 per cent. Operating revenues in Switzerland in 2005 amounted to CHF 7,088,000.

*Gauge:*  The track has been all standard gauge since 1st January, 2005 when the only narrow gauge in the SBB network - the Brünig Line - became part of die Zentralbahn company (*see entry 95*). The maximum gradient on the SBB network is 2.6 per cent.

*Infrastructure:*  There are a total of 1,137 level crossings, 13,642 points (in the USA referred to as switches), 31,231 signals, 307 tunnels with a total length of 259 km, 5,873 bridges/viaducts with a total length of 87 km. Notable bridges are the Reuss on the Turgi-Brugg line (75.6 m and built in 1855), Goldach on the Goldach-Mörschwil line (77.1 m in 1856), the Reuss on the Ebikon-Luzern line (143.6 m in 1918), Kessiloch West on the Zwingen-Grellingen line (55 m in 1925), Ponte Diga on the Melide-Maroggia-Melano line (81.7 m in 1965), St Adrian on the Watchwil-Arth Goldau line (94.6 m in 1897) and the Aare bridge on the Olten-Olten-Hammer line (105.2 m in 1927). There are 804 SBB stations, the busiest of which are Zürich with a daily average of 300,000 passengers, Berne - 145,000, Winterthur - 122,000, Basel - 120,000, Geneva - 85,000, Lausanne - 65,000 and Luzern - 62,000. The longest tunnel is the Simplon II at 19.82 km, the longest bridge/viaduct is Hardturm on the Zürich HB - Zürich Oerlikon route at 1.26 km, the highest bridge (77 m) is the Intschiereuss on the Amsteg-Silenen-Gurtnellon line and the station at the highest altitude is at Airolo (1,141 m above sea level). The busiest location for trains per day is near Zürich with 636 per day.

A SBB-Regio service train heading for the end of the standard gauge line at the attractive village of Buttes, seen in the background on 20th October, 2006. *Author*

An SBB standard gauge train led by Re 4/4 460 No. 049-0 from Bern arrives alongside Platform 5 at Interlaken Ost on 10th October, 2006. To the right can be seen a narrow gauge GoldenPass carriage awaiting its return to Montreux via Zweisimmen. To the left the headlights belong to a Zentralbahn SPATZ train about to depart for Meiringen. *Author*

An SBB ICN train (RABDe 500 series) departing from Bern station on 14th October, 2006. *Author*

**Traction and Rolling stock:** There are 449 main line locomotives of which only three are diesel-powered. There are 274 shunting vehicles/tractors of which 229 are run on diesel. SBB owns 10,769 freight wagons and has a further 7,372 privately owned within the fleet. The electricity power utilised throughout the network is 15,000V 16.7Hz. Locomotives operated on the SBB network:

Re 4/4 II Nos. 11101-11349
Re 4/4 III Nos. 11350-11370
Ae 6/6 Nos. 11403-11520
Re 6/6 Nos. 11601-11689
Re 420 Nos. 186, 276 and 310
Re 421 Nos. 371-397

Re 450 Nos. 000-014
Re 460 Nos. 000-118
Re 481 Nos. 001-006
Re 482 Nos. 000-049
Re 484 Nos. 001-018
Re 620 Nos. 033-087

Electric-powered rail cars:

TGV 112
RBe 4/4 Nos. 1404-1406
RABDe 500 Nos. 000-043
RABDe 510 Nos. 000-017
RABe 520 Nos. 000-016
RABe 521 Nos. 001-030

RABe 523 Nos. 001-012
RBe 540 Nos. 006-079
Bem 550 Nos. 000-004
RBDe 560 Nos. 000-083 and 100-132
RBDe 561 Nos. 000-005
RBDe 562 Nos. 000-005

Non-powered rail cars:

Bt 50 85 26-33 Nos. 900-999
Bt 50 85 26-34 Nos. 900-914
Bt 50 85 28-94 Nos. 900-989
Bt 50 85 26-94 Nos. 900-939
Bt 50 85 29-34 Nos. 900-983

Bt 50 85 29-35 Nos. 900-934, 950-955 & 960-965
Bt 50 85 82-33 Nos. 910-939, 951-955, 960-992
Bt 50 85 82-34 Nos. 900-905
Dt 50 85 92-33 Nos. 920-939

NB: A useful website to visit to learn more about the changing scene in rolling stock in Switzerland (and elsewhere in Europe) is www.railfaneurope.net

**Preservation:** SBB plays an important role in safeguarding Switzerland's railway heritage. Items of historic interest safeguarded are shown in the Appendix on page 187.
**Contact details:** SBB, Hochschulstr 6, CH-3030 Bern - Telephone: 051 220 11 11. E-mail: off the Kontakt page of the main website.
**Website:** www.sbb.ch (de fr it en)
**Operating dates:** Daily services throughout Switzerland run all the year round. For timetables and routes, consult www.sbb.ch/travel This site also provides the useful facility to book hotels and flights. The website also identifies any journey on any railway in Switzerland and not just SBB.

A 'double-decker' carriage of an SBB train having just arrived at Wil station on 5th October, 2006.          *Author*

SBB 'double-decker' restaurant car at Interlaken Ost station on 10th October, 2006.          *Author*

Train activity at Zürich HB on 4th February, 2007. In the foreground is Re 4/4 460 No. 094-6 bringing in an Inter-Regio train from Luzern. Behind is Re 4/4 II No. 11127 entering the station with a ZVV service and in the background an ICN train.                    *Author*

*Tariff:* Fares apply according to journey taken and obviously are too numerous to list here. There are five rail passes which allow travellers in Switzerland discounted fares. The passes are: the Swiss Pass which allows for unlimited travel throughout the train, bus and boat Swiss Travel System network, including on trams and buses. This pass also offers discounts on many mountain railways, cable cars and museums. It is valid consecutively for 4, 8, 15, 22 days or one month. The Swiss Flexi Pass offers the same advantages as the Swiss Pass but allows the traveller to choose the days on which they wish to use the pass. The Flexi Pass is valid for one month and can be used for 3, 4, 5, 6 or 8 days within that month. The Swiss Transfer ticket is ideal for short stays or holidays spent in one specific location, consisting of a return ticket from the Swiss border or one of Switzerland's airports to the destination. It is valid for one month but cannot be purchased in Switzerland. The Swiss Card offers the same advantages as the Swiss Transfer Ticket but with the added benefits that the visitor can travel by train, bus, boat and on many privately owned mountain railways for half the normal price, again valid for one month. The Swiss Half Fare Card allows for the unlimited purchase of train, bus, boat and some cable car tickets at half price within the one month validity. The Swiss Half-Fare Card is especially beneficial to motorists. With all these passes children from 6 to 16 years inclusive travel free with a Family Card if accompanied by at least one parent. Examples of prices as at December 2006 for an adult were: Swiss Pass (4 days) CHF 250; Swiss Flexi Pass (4 days) CHF 292; Swiss Transfer ticket (2nd class) CHF 124; Swiss Card (2nd class) CHF 178; and, Swiss Half Fare card CHF 99.

*Comments:* Latest train schedules can also be found on www.switzerland.com Rail package tour details can be obtained from Railtours Suisse SA, Chutzenstr 24, CH-3000 Bern - Telephone: 031 378 00 00 or on the website www.railtour.ch However, by far the best website to learn information about services and fares in English is www.sbb.ch/en

*Some sample routes and timings:* Geneva (Cornavin) to Milan, a distance of 368 km with a travelling time varying between 3 hours 45 minutes and 4 hours 32 minutes; and, Zürich to Chiasso, a distance of 242 km with a journey time varying between 3 hours 23 minutes and 3 hours 48 minutes. These variations are according to the train service selected and not caused by delays of which there are very few in Switzerland.

## Museum

## 2  Heritage Foundation [SBB Historic]

The SBB model railway exhibition and small museum close to Interlaken's west station.

*Author*

*Location*:  Bern, the capital city of Switzerland in the north-west of the country.
*Canton*:  Bern (BE).
*Contact details*:  SBB Historic (Historical Heritage Foundation SBB) Bollwerk 12, CH-3000 Bern 65. The offices of SBB Historic are located next door to Bern railway station. Telephone: 051 220 25 11 Fax : 051 220 40 99. E-mail: info@sbbhistoric.ch
*Website*: www.sbb-historic.ch
*History:* Swiss Federal Railways, under its trading name SBB AG, founded the SBB Heritage Foundation, a non-profit making organization, in the Spring of 2001. It adopted a number of roles with tasks that include collecting, maintaining, conserving, informing, documenting and archiving the memorabilia of Swiss railway history. This material is accessible not only to SBB employees but to academics as well as the general public.
*Comments:* There are five main venues for SBB Historic. Firstly, there is the Library at Bern station which is open to the general public (*see entry 67*). Secondly, the Swiss Transport Museum in Luzern which displays much of SBB Historic's material (*see entry 96*). Thirdly in Winterthur the archives of the former Swiss Locomotive and Engine works (SLM) are kept (*see entry 79*). Fourthly, in Estavayer-le-Lac, a huge and exclusive collection of railway lamps is on show in the local museum (*see entry 38*). Finally, the fifth venue, at Interlaken, is the Bahn-Treff where model railways and other items of railway history are on display (*see entry 66*).

# Switzerland's Trans-Regional Railways

### 3 Rhätische Bahn - The Glacier Express

Ge 4/4 III No. 651 *Fideris*, an example of the principal traction for the Glacier Express services, stands at Samedan station close to St Moritz on 6th October, 2006.     *Author*

**Locations & cantons:**  From Zermatt in Valais to Chur or to Davos or St Moritz in Graubünden.

**Michelin map references:** M5 and N5.

**Route:** Zermatt (alt. 1,604m) to Visp to Brig to Andermatt (alt. 1,436m), over the Oberalp Pass (alt. 2,033m) to Disentis (alt. 1,130m), to Chur, or via Landquart to Davos (alt. 1,540m), or to St Moritz (alt. 1,775m) via Filisur. The total distance is 291 km.

**Journey time:**  7 hours 51 minutes to St Moritz or 7 hours 59 minutes to Davos.

**Gauge:**    Narrow (metre) operating by a combination of adhesion and rack/cogwheel. The Abt rack/cogwheel system is employed in three locations: the Matter valley between Stalden and Zermatt which has a maximum gradient of 12.5 per cent; on the climb up the Oberalp Pass (11 per cent); and, in the Goms (between Andermatt and Brig) with gradients of up to 9 per cent.

**Traction:**  Electric-powered 11,000V 16.7Hz.

**Rolling stock:**  Electric-powered locomotives: Ge 4/4 III operating up to 2,400 kW; the Ge 4/4 II at 1,700 kW; and, the Ge 6/6 II at 1,776 kW. However, other Ge locomotives substitute from time to time.

**Near to here:**  At Zermatt the Gornergrat railway (*see entry 54*); at Realp the Furka Cogwheel Steam railway (*see entry 53*), at Andermatt the Matterhorn Gotthard Bahn (MGB) service through the Schöllenen-Schlucht valley to Göschenen (*see entry 59*).

**Places to see:**    There are 91 tunnels and 291 bridges including the famous Landwasser viaduct near Filisur. The tallest structure at a height of 85 m on the journey is the Solis bridge over the River Albula.

**Contact details:** Rhätische Bahn AG (RhB), Bahnhofstrasse 25, CH-7002 Chur Telephone: 0812 886 100 Fax: 0812 886 101. E-mail: contact@rhb.ch or…
Matterhorn Gotthard Bahn (MGB), Nordstrasse 20, CH-3900 Brig Telephone: 027 927 77 77 Fax: 027 927 77 79. E-mail: info@glacierexpress.ch

An afternoon Glacier Express from Andermatt crossing the Furkareuss II viaduct near Hospental and heading for the Furka base tunnel at Realp on 30th September, 2006.

*Author*

Ge 4/4 I No. 601 leads the morning Glacier Express from Davos Platz on 4th October, 2006. Here it is seen running through the Landwasser valley between Frauenkirch and Glaris heading for Wiesen.                                                                                                     *Author*

**Website**: www.rhb.ch or www.glacierexpress.ch
**Operating dates**:  From late May to late October with four services per day in each direction, i.e. one to and from Chur, one to and from Davos Platz and two to and from St Moritz. From mid-December to mid-May there is just one service per day to and from St Moritz (2007).
**Tariff**: Seat reservations must be made before travelling. An adult 2nd class single ticket costs CHF 129 and 1st class CHF 215. Children from 6 to 16 years travel at 50 per cent of the adult fare. Children under 6 (who do not require a seat) travel free. In summer to these fares must be added a surcharge for the St Moritz journey of CHF 68 which includes a 3-course lunch delivered to the seat or without lunch CHF 30. The surcharges applied to the Chur and Davos Platz routes are CHF 53 with lunch and CHF 15 without. In winter the surcharge is CHF 9 without lunch for the only route then running, i.e. to and from St Moritz (2007). Lunch can be taken in the restaurant car by prior reservation. A rail bar is available throughout the journey where hot and cold beverages, sandwiches, snacks and souvenirs can be purchased. Smoking is not allowed on any Glacier Express trains.
**History**:  The first train services which carried the name the Glacier Express began in 1930, hauled by electric traction, the journey in those days taking 11 hours. Up until the early 1980s the train service only ran in the summer months because of the adverse winter conditions on the passes. However, all that changed in 1982 when the Furka base tunnel was opened (15.4 km in length). The tunnel, together with the acquisition of improved locomotives developed in the 1980s and 1990s, has meant that the journey time has been cut to less than eight hours. The railway line or lines over which the Glacier Express travels, however, trace their origins back to 1890 when a Dutchman - Jan Holsboer - and his supporters opened the section of line between Landquart and Davos (LD). Four years later the LD company set the goal of building a cantonal rail network and at that time re-named itself the Rhätische line (RhB). In 1896, Chur and Thusis were added and two years later work began on the Albula extension to St Moritz which was eventually opened in 1903. Further expansion followed in the early decades of the 20th century - Davos to Filsur (1909), Disentis/Mustér (1912) and Bever/Scuol/Tarasp (1914). The network became electric-powered in 1922. Other

A Ge 4/4 III leads a Glacier Express train out of the tunnel close to Filisur on to the spectacular Landwasser viaduct heading for Tiefencastel. *Rhätische Bahn/swiss-image.ch*

A restaurant car for a Glacier Express seen at Landquart on 3rd October, 2006.  *Author*

important players in the development of the line at its western end were BVZ Zermatt-Bahn and the Furka-Oberalp railway (FO) and their founding companies. Brig and Gletsch came on the network in 1914 but World War I intervened delaying further progress for the building of the line over the Furka and Oberalp passes. It was not until 1926, therefore, that the first trains were able to cross these passes but, as has already been said, only in the summer months. The section from Visp to Zermatt was built and opened in 1891 and was electrified in 1929 and this service began all-year operations in 1933. Work began on the final section from Visp to Brig in 1928 and which was opened to traffic in 1930 thus providing the opportunity in that same year to introduce the Glacier Express connecting Zermatt with St Moritz. At this time the two contributing companies were operating differently-powered locomotives. At the eastern end (RhB) electric-powered 'Krokodils' (Crocodiles) were being used (*see page 158 for a photograph*) and in the west H/G 3/4 steam locomotives were operated. The latter were sent to Vietnam in 1947 but, fortunately for steam enthusiasts, they were repatriated in the early 1990s. They now provide a tourist steam service over the Furka Pass (*see entry 53*).

**Comments:** The Glacier Express now operates with both panoramic coaches built by the Swiss manufacturer Stadler, both in 1st class (36 seats) and 2nd class (48 seats) as well as with conventional coaches. The panoramic coaches are obviously superior not only for their better viewing prospects but also they are air-conditioned. They also offer a route commentary by way of head phones in the German, French, English, Italian, Chinese and Japanese languages. Conventional coaches, on the other hand, offer 36 seats in 1st class and 56 seats in 2nd class; however, they are not air-conditioned but for photographers the windows can be opened unlike the windows in the panoramic coaches. A route commentary is available but by carriage loudspeakers and only in German, French and English. A 'Certificate of the Journey' is also available as a souvenir. Rhätische Bahn also operates other services including the Bernina Express from St Moritz, or Chur or Davos Platz to and from Ticino in Italy (*see entry 6*) to which a journey on the Glacier Express can be linked.

**Further reading:**  *Glacier Express* by Klaus & Ilona Eckert (*see Bibliography*).

## 4 GoldenPass Panoramic Services [GP] operated by the Montreux-Oberland-Bahn [MOB]

Here at Montreux is the Panoramic lead carriage on the GoldenPass service to Zweisimmen. The driver is located behind the smaller window above the passengers.

*Author*

*Location:* Montreux, 30 km south-east of Lausanne on Lake Geneva.

*Canton:* Vaud (VD).

*Michelin map reference:* E6.

*Nearest main line station:* Montreux.

*Route:* Montreux (alt. 395 m) to Gstaad to Zweisimmen (alt. 941 m), to Spiez (alt. 595 m), to Interlaken (alt. 567 m), to Brienz, over the Brünig Pass, to Sarnen, to Luzern. (NB: The Panoramic coaches only travel as far as Zweisimmen.) The total distance is 75 km.

*Journey times:* The journey to and from Montreux and Zweisimmen takes 2 hours 1 minute. A further 59 minutes can be added for the Zweisimmen and Interlaken Ost link and a further 1 hour 56 minutes for the Interlaken Ost and Luzern connection.

*Gauge:* Narrow (metre) adhesion only. The maximum gradient on this route to and from Montreux and Zweisimmen is 7.3 per cent.

*Traction:* Electric-powered (900V DC).

*Rolling stock:* Panoramic railway coaches used on this route are constructed by the Swiss motorbus coachwork builder Ramseier Jenzer of Bern. Locomotives: GDe 4/4 Nos. 6001-6004 and Ge 4/4 Nos. 8001-8004. Electric-powered rail cars: Be 4/4 Nos. 1001, 1002, 1003 and 5001-5004, BDe 4/4 Nos. 3001-3002, 3004-3006 and, finally, ABDe 8/8 Nos. 4001-4004. Non-powered rail cars: Ast Nos. 116-117, Arst Nos. 151-152 (the GoldenPass Panoramic 'Grande Vue' VIP service), ABt Nos. 3301-3302 & Nos. 5301-5304. Historic material includes: BCFe 4/4 No. 11 and ex-CIWL coaches Nos. Ars 101 and As 102.

One of the original blue/white liveried trains of the Montreux-Oberland-Bahn leaving Les Avants above Montreux on 17th October, 2006. *Author*

*Near to here*: Brienz-Rothorn Bahn (*see entry 51*), the Brünig Pass (alt. 1001 m) route (*see entry 84*).

*Places to see*: The GoldenPass train leaves Montreux and rises above Lake Geneva and enters a tunnel at Jaman emerging into the Alpine mountains and valleys attaining a maximum height at Enmosec of 1,274 m before arriving at Zweisimmen. Passengers can continue on the GoldenPass service to Interlaken and Luzern but not in the panoramic coaches.

*Contact details*: Rail Center GoldenPass, rue de la Gare, CH-1820 Montreux 1. Telephone: 0900 245 245 or 0840 245 245. E-mail: www.mob.ch

*Website*: www.mob.ch

*Operating dates*: Daily, all the year round. The first service from Montreux to Zweisimmen leaves at 0536 and the last at 2145 hours. In the opposite direction the first train leaves at 0430 and the last at 2051 hours. The GoldenPass Panoramic departs Montreux at 1045, 1345 and 1545 hours and leaves Zweisimmen at 0828, 1028, 1305 and 1628 hours.

*Tariff*: An adult 2nd class single ticket from Montreux to Zweisimmen costs CHF 29 and a return CHF 58. An adult 1st Class single is CHF 48 and return CHF 96 (2006).

*History*: Montreux-Oberland-Bahn (MOB) is one of the oldest electric-powered railway lines in Switzerland with the line between Montreux and Zweisimmen first commencing operations over a period between 1901 and 1905. In 1912 the Zweisimmen-Lenk line was introduced. From the outset the Montreux-Oberland-Bahn took its railway seriously. For example, very early in its development dining and saloon coaches were operated. However, all did not bode well as a direct consequence of the Depression in the early 1930s. The Golden Mountain Pullman Express service of 1931 was hit hard by the economic crisis and drastic measures had to be taken to survive. This included selling off rolling stock; the saloon coaches, for example, built especially for this train service, were purchased by the Rhätische Bahn in 1939. Happily, they have survived and are still in regular use today. The successor to that early luxury train is the Panoramic Express, later the Super Panoramic Express of 1985 and the Crystal Panoramic Express of 1993. The service sets out from Montreux station alongside the SBB standard gauge tracks and also the departure point for the rack and pinion 800 mm gauge railway to Rochers-de-Naye (*see entry 33*). It then winds its way up through the vineyards above Lake Geneva, through Chamby as far as Les Avants. After running through the tunnel under the Col de Jaman (1,512 m) it reaches the Saane Valley where it follows the river of that name upstream. Leaving the French-speaking Canton of Vaud it then enters the German-speaking Canton of Bern. After reaching Gstaad it climbs the Saanenmöser Pass which, at 1,279 m, is the highest point on the journey. Thereafter, it drops 333 m down to the town of Zweisimmen.

*Comments*: Montreux-Oberland-Bahn, by way of its GoldenPass services, was the world's first railway to utilise panoramic trains and, at the time of writing, the company still remains Switzerland's only line to offer special seating on its GoldenPass Panoramic 'Grande Vue' VIP service, of which there are three trains running in both directions each day. These allow some fare paying passengers - 'the VIPs' - to sit at the front of the train under the driver's compartment and share the train driver's view of the route ahead. The company also offers a luxury service - the GoldenPass Classic - featuring Compagnie Internationale de Wagons Lits & des Grands Express Européens (CIWL) coaches (*see next entry*) and the Train du Chocolat (*see entry 19*). GoldenPass Services, as a result of various mergers, now oversees the activities of the following: Montreux-Oberland-Bahn (MOB), Transports Montreux-Vevey-Riviera (MVR), VSA Travels and Car Services, garage-parking services at Montreux station and the Rochers-de-Naye botanical garden at La Rambertia including its rack railway. Apart from the direct trains between Montreux and Zweisimmen, described above, and between Montreux and Lenk, there are hourly MOB services operating on the Montreux-Les Avants, Gstaad-Zweisimmen and Zweisimmen-Lenk routes.

GoldenPass train from Luzern bound for Zweisimmen descending the 12 per cent gradient from Brünig station to Meiringen on 4th February, 2007. The traction is Zentralbahn's HGe 4/4 No. 101965-2 leading the way down the Riggenbach rack. *Author*

## 5 GoldenPass Classic

The interior of one of the 1912-built *Belle Époque* coaches of the former Compagnie Internationale de Wagons Lits et des Grands Express Européens (CIWL). Inset is the distinctive CIWL coat of arms carried on each carriage. *Author*

*Location:* Montreux, 31 km east-south-east of Lausanne.
*Canton:* Vaud (VD).
*Michelin map reference:* E6.
*Operated by:* GoldenPass Services.
*Nearest main line station:* Montreux.
*Route:* Montreux-Zweisimmen, a total distance of 75 km.
*Journey time:* 2 hours 1 minute.
*Gauge:* Narrow (metre) by adhesion only.
*Traction:* Electric-powered (900V DC).
*Rolling stock:* *Belle Epoque* coaches (ex-Compagnie Internationale de Wagons Lits & des Grands Express Européens) hauled by an electric locomotive from either the GDe 4/4 or Ge 4/4 classes.
*Contact details:* Rail Center GoldenPass, rue de la Gare, CH-1820 Montreux 1. Telephone: 0900 245 245 or 0840 245 245. E-mail: mob@mob.ch
*Website:* www.mob.ch (de fr en)
*Operating dates:* Two services per day to and from Montreux and Zweisimmen departing Montreux at 0845 and 1445 hours and returning from Zweisimmen at 1228 and 1737 hours.
*Tariff:* An adult 2nd class single ticket from Montreux to Zweisimmen costs CHF 29 and a return CHF 58. A 1st class single is CHF 48 and return CHF 96 (2006).
*Comments:* This train began in May 2005 and was built on the idea of the 'Orient Express' service. In addition to the 1st class *Belle Époque* coaches there are 2nd class coaches as well as a wine-tasting cellar coach. A cold terroir dish can be taken in 1st class or in the wine-tasting coach by prior reservation.

A Bernina Express negotiating the outstanding circular viaduct at Brusio.

# Switzerland's Railways crossing International Frontiers

## 6 Rhätische Bahn - Bernina Express

A Bernina Express circling the Lago Bianco on a cold October day in 2006.    *Author*

*Locations*:  Chur and Tirano (Italy).
*Canton*:  Graubünden.
*Italian Region*:  Lombardy.
*Michelin map reference*:  M5 and O7.
*Nearest main line stations*:  Chur or Tirano.
*Routes*:  Three routes - Chur, Davos or St Moritz to Tirano in Italy via Pontresina and Poschiavo. The overall distance travelled is 130 km.
*Journey time*:  Chur to Tirano takes 4 hours 14 minutes; the return journey takes 4 hours 23 minutes.
*Gauge*:  Narrow (metre) and, perhaps surprisingly, operating by adhesion only over a maximum gradient on the route of 7 per cent.
*Traction*:  Electric-powered (11,000V 16.7Hz) from Chur, Davos and St Moritz to Pontresina and 1,000V DC from Pontresina to Tirano.
*Rolling stock*:  The following locomotives are deployed: Ge 4/4 III Nos. 641-649, Ge 4/4 II Nos. 611-631, Ge 4/4 I Nos. 601-610, Ge 6/6 II Nos. 701-707 and, finally, Gem 4/4 Nos. 801 & 802 (the latter is diesel/electric). Electric-powered rail cars used are Abe 4/4 Nos. 41-46 & 51-56.
*Places to see*:  Glorious scenery can be enjoyed throughout the route in all seasons and especially in the snow. The passenger carriages of the Bernina Express with their

A midday Bernina Express negotiating the Montebello curve on its journey to Tirano in Italy. The Mörteratsch glacier is in the background.                    *Caroline Jones*

panoramic roofs facilitate the viewing of the mountain peaks. The Mörteratsch glacier is a magnificent sight from the well-know Montebello curve. Disappointingly, the glacier, like many others in Switzerland, is receding as a consequence of global warming. It is a sad fact that it was not many years ago that one could descend from the train and walk about 100 metres to edge of the glacier – it is now a hike of more than three km. The viaduct near to Brusio station (107 m in length) forming a complete circle is magnificent and not to be missed. The route has a considerable amount of railway architecture to see: from Landquart to Thusis the line passes over 43 bridges, but, surprisingly for Switzerland, does not pass through a single tunnel; from Thusis to St Moritz, 109 bridges are crossed and more than 26 per cent of the journey is spent in the 42 tunnels and galleries; and, finally from St Moritz to Tirano there are 47 bridges and 13 tunnels. Overall, there are 20.6 km of tunnels and 4.1 km of bridges or viaducts of which the longest is 220 m.
*Contact details*: Rhätische Bahn, Bahnhofstrasse 25, CH-2002 Chur. Telephone: 081 254 91 04. E-mail: contact@rhb.ch
*Website*: www.rhb.ch
*Operating dates*: Daily throughout the year; in winter (October to May) there are two services per day - one to and from Chur and the other to and from St Moritz. In summer (May to October) the same as for the winter services but with an extra service to and from Davos Platz. The times of departure and arrival vary slightly between winter and summer so check first, but in any case prior booking is essential if travelling on the train rather than just observing from the track side.
*Tariff*: An adult 1st class return for Chur-Tirano is CHF 182 (2nd class CHF 148) and an adult 1st class return for St Moritz - Tirano is CHF 90 (2nd class CHF 54) (2007).
*History*: The Bernina Pass route to Tirano, was built in the early years of the 20th century and opened in 1906 as a tourist railway at a time of rapidly increasing tourism in the country. In the beginning, its service was restricted to the summer season but because it was necessary to consider the interests of the outlying Puschlav valley, the service became an all year round operation in 1910. For several decades the Bernina route represented the only viable connection in winter between the Puschlav and other parts of Switzerland. Of course, that meant, as it does so even today, that considerable effort has to be expended to keep the line open even under the most adverse of weather conditions. The Bernina line crosses the Alps from north to south attaining altitudes of more than 2,000 m - the train climbs, for example the Piz Bernina at an altitude of 4,049 m. One interesting fact about this railway is that for its traction it does not take advantage of a rack/cogwheel system. Rather it operates by adhesion only even though its maximum gradient is quite steep in some places at 1 in 14 (7.14 per cent) made all the more challenging by the existence of snow and ice for a significant part of the year. In the last few decades, the transportation of goods across the Bernina Pass has become very important both for the profitability of running the railway and the economy of the canton. Today, not only are the tourist trains running the route but numerous goods trains carrying fuel oils, petrol, fodder, grain and many other goods. The infrastructure of the railway has constantly been improved especially after the Rhätische Bahn took responsibility for the route in 1943. However, to be fair to its predecessor company, in the 1930s the track on the plateau of the Bernina Pass plateau was re-laid in a number of locations to afford better protection from inevitable snow-drifts and avalanches. In recent years, the electrical installations, originally put in between 1908 and 1921, and the rolling stock have all been renewed.
*Comments*: The Trenino Rosso is the Italian equivalent of this service (*see entry 11*).

## 7 Cisalpino AG [CIS]

The 1104 hours Cisalpino service departing Zürich HB for Milan and Trieste on 4th February, 2007.                                                    *Author*

*Location*:  Bern, in the canton of Bern (BE) and various major cities in Switzerland and Italy.

*Michelin map reference*: G5.

*Operated by*: SBB-CFF-FSS and Trenitalia in partnership with the catering company, Cremonini.

*Routes*: Cisalpino operates a total of 51 train services every day on the following routes: Zürich to Venice, Zürich to Genoa/Livorno, Zürich to Trieste, Schaffhausen to Milan, Bellinzona to Milan, Basel/Lucerne to Milan, Basel/Lucerne to Venice, Basel/Bern to Milan, Geneva to Milan and Geneva to Venice. It is intended that services will be extended further south commencing in 2009. Cisalpino trains will then travel from Zürich to Rome, a distance of about 865 km, in what is hoped to be about seven hours.

*Journey times*: Some sample timings: Basel to Florence in 8 hours 18 minutes, Zürich to Milan in 4 hours 26 minutes and Luzern to Venice in 7 hours 17 minutes.

*Gauge*: Standard by adhesion only often using tilting trains (pendolinos).

*Traction*: Electric-powered (15,000V 16.7Hz in Switzerland and 3,000V DC in Italy).

*Rolling stock*:  Probably the best well-known is the Cisalpino Pendolino. The locomotives and carriages were designed and built by Fiat Ferroviaria Savigliano and belong to the new generation of ETR 470-type tilting trains. 'Pendolino' comes from the German word *pendeln*, which literally means 'to swing to and fro'. This is the secret of the train's extra speed. By the carriages tilting they can travel faster through bends, making for significant savings in journey time on the winding routes over the Lötschberg, Gotthard and Simplon passes. Another advantage of this design is that the one train can work with two different power supplies, for Italy direct current and for Switzerland alternating current, thus allowing for non-stop through services. ETR 470 train interiors were the work of the celebrated Italian designer Giorgetto Giugiaro, each train offering up to 475 passengers comfortable seats either in 1st and 2nd classes. Cisalpino also operate conventional trains. These are the EC Cisalpino, EC 354/355 'Canaletto' and the EC 382/383 'Cinque Terre'. From 2008, Cisalpino will introduce 14 new ETR 610 tilting trains to be built by Alstom Ferroviaria. As well as their avant-garde Giugiaro design, these new trains will travel at speeds up to 250 km/h on high-speed stretches of track. This will allow for journey times from Basle to Milan, for example, to be cut by up to an hour.

**Contact details:**  Cisalpino AG, Parkterrasse 10, Postfach 5757, CH-3001 Bern. Telephone: 058 580 85 00 Fax: 058 580 86 61. E-mail: info@cisalpino.com

**Website:**  www.cisalpino.com (it fr de en)

**Operating dates:**  Daily frequent services all the year round.

**Tariff:**  Some sample adult 2nd class fares including the compulsory Cisalpino surcharge: Geneva to Milan - CHF 94, Bern to Milan - CHF 85, Brig to Venice - CHF 84, Zürich to Florence - CHF 125, Zürich to Genoa - CHF 92 and Bern to Stresa - CHF 74 (2005).

**History:**  Cisalpino AG was founded on 23rd November, 1993 as a collaborative venture by the Italian FS (Trenitalia) and SBB (Swiss Federal Railways).

**Comments:**  The headquarters for Cisalpino AG is in Bern. The trains are maintained in Milan by Italian State Railways (FS). Staff on Cisalpino trains is drawn both from Italian State Railways and from Swiss Federal Railways. The company Cremonini, whose headquarters is in Rome, operates the dining car services.


## 8  Chemin de fer Martigny-Chatelard [MC] (into France) sometimes referred to as the Mont Blanc Express

**Location:**  Martigny, 38 km south of Montreux.

**Canton:**  Valais (VS).

**Michelin map reference:**  F7.

**Operated by:**  Transports de Martigny et Régions.

**Nearest main line station:**  Martigny.

**Route:**  Martigny to Châtelard and on to Chamonix and finally St Gervais-les-Bains (La Fayet) in the Haute-Savoie department of the Rhône-Alpes region of France. The distance from Martigny to Châtelard is 21 km and Martigny to St Gervais is approximately 70 km.

**Journey time:**  Martigny to Chamonix takes 90 minutes.

**Gauge:**  Narrow (metre) operating by a combination of adhesion with the Strub rack/cogwheel system. The maximum gradient on this route is 20 per cent.

**Traction:**  Electric-powered (830V DC).

**Rolling stock:**  Electric-powered rail cars: BDeh 4/4 4-8, BDeh 4/4 501, BDeh 821-822/823-824. Non-powered rail cars: Bt 601-602 and BDt 63-68. This line also preserves the following of historic interest: ABFeh 4/4 No. 15, Bt No. 51 and BFZt No. 74.

**Near to here:**  Trains Touristiques d'Emosson (*see entry 42*).

**Places to see:**  Mont Blanc (alt. 4,808 m). The route crosses Le Trient gorge looking down on a staggering drop of 426 m (1,400 feet) to the valley floor.

**Contact details:**  TMR SA, rue de la Poste 3, Case postale 727, CH-1920 Martigny. Telephone: 027 721 68 40 Fax: 027 721 68 59. E-mail: pascal.may@tmrsa.ch

**Website:**  www.tmrsa.ch

**Operating dates:**  Daily services; consult the SBB timetable on www.sbb.ch/en/index or the French timetables www.ter-sncf.com/rhone_alpes/V2/carte_horaires/index.asp

**Tariff:**  An adult 2nd class single ticket between Martigny and the border at Châtelard costs CHF 16.80 (2006).

The Mont-Blanc Express, with Mont Blanc in the background, heading for Martigny in 2005.                                                                              *Author*

*History*:  Four years before the Martigny-Orsieres railway was built in 1910, the rail link between Martigny and Châtelard had been opened. There had been many requests over the previous 15 years to the Federal authorities for permission to build the railway by the authorities in the two towns, there being much debate as to which was the most appropriate route. Eventually approval was given in 1900 to build the Martigny-Vernayaz-Salvan-Finhaut-Châtelard route. The 'Martigny-Châtelard, ligne du Valais à Chamonix' railway company was formed and work commenced in November 1902 and concluded four years later.

*Comments*:  In 2006 this railway route celebrated its 100th anniversary. Leaving Martigny and crossing a challenging landscape, the Mont Blanc Express climbs to a maximum altitude of 2,480 m at Salvan. It was here that Marconi successfully first tested his wireless telegraphy. Shortly after here the train arrives at Marécottes, renowned for its alpine zoo. On the train goes to Trétien, passing through the magnificent gorges of the Tr  ège and arriving at Châtelard, where the steepest funicular in the world is located. In a little over 10 minutes the funicular raises the traveller almost 500 m to an altitude of 1,821 m. From there a small *panoramique* train and another small funicular take the traveller to the Emosson dam; from there are breath-taking views of the Mont Blanc. Once over the French border the train soon arrives at Chamonix, a world-famous alpine resort and access to the so-called 'Roofs of Europe' i.e. l'Aiguille du Midi (3,842 m), La Mer de Glace (Montenvers, 1,913 m), and the Mont Blanc tram service taking one to the Nid d'Aigle, 2,380 m. The Martigny-Orsières (MO) railway also runs from Martigny (*see entry 26*).

## 9 Ferrovie Autolinee Regionali Ticinesi [FART] (into Italy) and is also known as the Centovalli Railway

A Centovalli Be 4/6 crossing the steel viaduct with its dramatic drop near to the village of Intragna not far from Locarno. *Author*

*Location*: Locarno.
*Canton*: Ticino (TI).
*Michelin map reference*: K7.
*Operated jointly by*: The Italian Vigezzina (SSIF) and the Swiss Centovallina (FART).
*Nearest Swiss main line station*: Locarno.
*Route*: Locarno to Domodossola (in Italy).
*Distance*: 17 km in Switzerland and 32 km in Italy.
*Journey time*: 1 hour 43 minutes.
*Gauge*: Narrow (metre) operating by adhesion only on a maximum gradient of 6.1 per cent.
*Traction*: Electric-powered as follows: Locarno-S.Antonio-Bignasco (5,000V 26Hz); Tramway Locarno (800V 26Hz); and, Locarno-Domodossola (1,200V DC).
*Rolling stock*: The most current vehicles are Be 4/6 Nos. 51-56, Ae 4/6 No. 57 (FART) and Be 4/6 Nos. 61-64 (SSIF). Even today there are still some of the original ABFe 4/4 Nos. 11-18 (today's ABDe 4/4) on duty. As a historic exhibit the ABFe 4/4 No. 17 is preserved.
*Places to see*: Outstanding steel viaducts crossing tributaries of the River Melazza. There are seven bridges in Switzerland and 25 in Italy. As far as tunnels are

Centovalli's Ae 4/6 No.57 crossing the stone-constructed viaduct after Intragna heading for Domodossola on 1st October, 2006.                                                                 *Author*

concerned there are 22 in Switzerland and 11 in Italy. The steel viaduct near Intragna is awe-inspiring - if one is lucky one may see individuals bungee-jumping off the viaduct!

**Contact details:**  Ferrovie Autolinee Regionali Ticinesi, via Franzoni 1, CH-6601 Locarno.  Telephone: : 091 756 04 00 Fax : 091 756 04 99 or Società Subalpina di Imprese Ferroviarie, Via Mizzoccola 9, I-28037 Domodossola Italy. E-mail: fart@centovalli.ch

**Website:**  www.centovalli.ch

**Operating dates:**  Daily hourly services in both directions from about 0800 to 1900 hours.

**Tariff:**  An adult 2nd class ticket costs CHF 39 (2007).

*History*:  This railway was founded in 1907. From very early on local politicians had agreed plans to create railway connections into the valleys of the Tessin thus linking the two neighbouring countries from Domodossola in Italy to Locarno in the Swiss Tessin. However, it took almost a quarter century for this goal to be achieved with the two companies involved being troubled a number of times with financial problems. The Italian section of the operation almost went bankrupt several times and it was necessary on a number of a occasions for the Swiss to intervene with financial help. Financial problems  continued in the operation of the railway until quite recently when a new law was enacted in Italy which allowed for better national support for the smaller railway lines. It has not just been financial difficulties that this railway has had to face. In August 1978, the greatest disaster in the history of the railway was caused by a violent storm when, within just one night, the Italian part of the line was destroyed. Four bridges had to be completely re-built to restore services. Although the necessary financial support was immediately forthcoming, it still took more then two years to re-build the whole line before normal operations could resume.

*Comments*:   An international railway travelling through the superb scenery of the Centovalli, which literally means the 'Valley of the 100 Valleys'. The line from Domodossola in Piedmont to Locarno in Ticino is the shortest rail connection from the Valais canton in Switzerland (via the Simplon tunnel) and the Swiss Tessin (Ticino). Until the opening of the Furka base tunnel it was the only viable connection between the two Swiss cantons during the winter months.


### 10  Treni Regionali Ticino Lombardia [TILO]

*Location*:  Chiasso, on the Swiss/Italian border near Lugano.
*Canton*:  Ticino (TI).
*Michelin map reference*:  K8.
*Operated jointly by*:  TILO SA, a collaboration between SBB CFF FFS and Trenitalia.
*Routes*:  In Switzerland: a) S1 route - Chiasso north to Mendrisio, Lugano, Bellinzona, Biasca and Airolo (distance - 125 km); b) S2 route - Bellinzona to Locarno (20 km); and, c) S3 route - Bellinzona to Luino (41 km). In Italy: d) R route - Chiasso south to Como San Giovanni, Sergno, Monza to Milan Porta Garibaldi or Milan Centrale (64 km); and, e) S9 route - Seregno to Milan San Cristoforo (34 km).
*Journey times*:  a) S1 - 1 hour 20 minutes to Biasca; b) S2 - 25 minutes; c) S3 - 58 minutes; d) R - 1 hour 10 minutes; and, e) S9 - 52 minutes (2007).
*Gauge*:  Standard by adhesion only.
*Traction*:  Electric-powered (in Switzerland - 15,000V 16.7Hz and in Italy - 3,000V DC).
*Rolling stock*:  TILO operate 10 E464s, 13 RBDe 560s and 19 RABe 524s Nos. 001-019 Flirt's (Fast Light Innovative Rail Transport) built by Stadler (*see entry 116*).
*Contact details*:  TILO SA, Corso San Gottardo 73, Casella Postale No. 1147, CH-6830 Chiasso, Svizzera. Telephone: 05 12 27 65 42 Fax: 05 12 27 96 12.  E-mail: info@tilo.ch
*Website*:  www.tilo.ch (it)
*Operating dates*:  Daily - on all routes hourly services from early morning to late evening.
*Tariff*:  An adult 2nd class single: b) S2 route - CHF 7.80; and, c) S3 route - CHF 13.40. For R, S1 & S9 routes, fares can be learned on local enquiry (2007).
*History*:  TILO was formed on 12th December, 2004.
*Comments*:  S1 route takes the traveller up the most beautiful Leventina valley almost to the St Gotthard tunnel/pass. The S2 route hugs the shores of Lake Maggiore for 26 km.  Both journeys are not to be missed either by train or by car.

## 11  Rhätische Bahn - Trenino Rosso (from Italy into Switzerland)

Whilst strictly speaking this is not a Trenino Rosso service, it is on the route and is using identical traction and carriages as it negotiates the summit near to the Piz Bernina on 6th October, 2006.                                                                                                  *Author*

*Locations*: Tirano and St Moritz.
*Italian Region*: Lombardy.
*Swiss Canton*: Graubünden (GR).
*Michelin map reference*: O7 and N6.
*Nearest main line station*: Tirano - Italian (FS) Railways.
*Route*: From Tirano (alt. 429 m) in Italy to Poschiavo (alt. 973 m) to Pontresina (alt. 1,773 m), arriving at its final destination St Moritz (alt. 1775 m), a total distance of  57 km.
*Journey time*: 2 hours 22 minutes from Tirano to St Moritz and 2 hours 27 minutes for the return journey.
*Gauge*: Narrow (metre) by adhesion only.
*Traction*: Electric-powered - 1,000V DC from Tirano to Pontresina and 11,000V 16.7Hz from Pontresina to St Moritz, Chur and Davos.
*Rolling stock*: As for the Bernina Express (*see entry 6*).
*Places to see*: Climbs the Ospizio Bernina (alt. 2,253 m) the highest point on the journey where it passes the Lago Bianca and later, before reaching Pontresina, the Mörteratsch glacier.
*Contact details*: Rhätische Bahn, Bahnhofstrasse 25, CH-2002 Chur. Telephone: 081 254 91 04. E-mail: tirano@rhb.ch or poschiavo@rhb.ch
*Website*: www.rhb.ch
*Operating dates*: On Tuesdays to Sundays from 10th-26th December, 2006 and from 28th December, 2006 to 11th March, 2007. It probably will be similar dates in future years. Train No. 970 leaves Tirano at 0849 and arrives at St Moritz at 1111 hours. Train 975 leaves St Moritz at 1444 and arrives in Tirano at 1711 hours.
*Tariff*: An adult return ticket costs CHF 48.60. Group discounts (for 10 persons or more) are available on prior application (2007).
*Comments*: This service is the Italian inspired version of the Bernina Express.

# Switzerland's Railways by Region

## Western Switzerland (including Geneva)

This region, as its name indicates, is situated in the west in Switzerland and has an international boundary with France. It has five cantons: Jura (JU), Neuchâtel (NE), Vaud (VD), Fribourg (FR), and Geneva (GE). Its principal cities and towns are Geneva, Neuchâtel, Fribourg, Lausanne and Montreux. It has 26 railways and/or routes, two museums, five items of related transport interest and one discontinued railway. French is the principal language spoken in the region.

### Railways

**12 Aigle-Leysin [AL]**

The Aigle-Leysin non-powered rail car No. Bt 352 standing at the temporary 'platform' in the town of Aigle. A new terminus for the three rail services which run from Aigle is in the course of construction and it is hoped will be fully operational in 2008.     *Author*

*Location*:  Aigle, 17 km south of Montreux.
*Canton*: Vaud.
*Michelin map reference*: E7.
*Operated by*: Transports Publics du Chablais (TPC).
*Nearest main line station*: Aigle.
*Route*:  Aigle (alt. 404m) to Leysin (alt. 1,451m) a total distance of 6.2 km. There are four tunnels - Drapel (455 m), Rennaz (154 m), La Roulaz (18 m) and Leysin (233 m), three stations and five halts.
*Journey time*: On average it takes 28 minutes each way.

*Gauge*: Narrow (metre) operating on the Abt rack/cogwheel system for 5.164 km of the route. The maximum adhesion gradient is 3.2 per cent and the maximum rack gradient is 23 per cent.
*Type of traction*: Electric-powered (1,500V DC).
*Rolling stock*: Electric-powered rail cars: ARSeh 2/4 No. 201 (1946), BDeh 2/4 Nos. 202-203 (dating from 1946 to 1993), BDeh 4/4 Nos. 301-302, BDeh 4/4 Nos. 311-313. Five non-powered rail cars (built between 1966-1993), seven goods wagons (1900 to 1913), two B2 carriages (dating from 1900 and 1955) but both out of service and two tank wagons both of 1908 vintage but out of service. There is also a 1915-built He 2/2 (*véhicule historique*) and a 1949 Te 2/2 locotracteur which is out of service.
*Contact details*: Transports Publics du Chablais SA, rue de la Gare 38, CH-1860 Aigle. Telephone: 024 468 03 03 Fax: 024 468 03 31. E-mail: info@tpc.ch
*Website*: www.tpc.ch
*Operating dates*: 36 trains run every day at approximately half-hour intervals from 0500 to 2300 hours
*Tariff*: CHF 10.40 each way. Group rates and multipass cards are available (2006).
*History*: The concession to build the line was granted in June 1892. For a brief résumé of the development of this line and the three other local lines read the history section of the Transports public du Chablais (*see entry 18*).
*Comments*: Trains run through the beautiful vineyards overlooking Switzerland's Rhône valley. The climate here is renowned for being extremely mild.


### 13  Aigle-Ollon-Monthey-Champéry  [AOMC]

One of AOMC's BDeh's - this one No. 502 standing at its depot near Ollon on 16th October, 2006.                                                                                    *Author*


*Location*: Aigle, 17 km south of Montreux.
*Canton*: Vaud VD).
*Michelin map reference*: E7.
*Operated by*: Transports Publics du Chablais [TPC]
*Nearest main line station*: Aigle.
*Route*: Aigle (alt. 404 m) to Ollon to Monthey to Champéry (alt. 1,049 m), a total distance of 23.1 km. There is one tunnel at Troistorrents (length 193 m), six stations and 20 halts on the route.

*Journey time:* 1 hour 2 minutes each way.

*Gauge:* Narrow (metre).

*Traction:* Electric-powered (850V DC) operating by adhesion and the Strub rack/cogwheel system for 3.659 km of the route. The maximum adhesion gradient is 6.5 per cent and the maximum for the rack/cogwheel gradient is 13.5 per cent.

*Rolling stock:* Electric-powered rail cars: BDeh 4/4 Nos. 501-503 & 511-514 variously built between 1954 and 1987, Be 4/4 Nos. 101-105 built between 1966 and 1985, Beh 4/8 Nos. 591-592, two 2001-built electric-powered double rail cars, five non-powered rail cars of 1966 to 1987 construction, 10 goods wagons built between 1908 and 1920, two of which are out of service.

*Contact details:* Transports Publics du Chablais SA, rue de la Gare 38, CH-1860 Aigle. Telephone: 024 468 03 03 Fax: 024 468 03 31. E-mail: info@tpc.ch

*Website:* www.tpc.ch

*Operating dates:* Daily with a total of 56 services between Aigle and Monthey and 46 between Monthey and Champéry operating from 0520 to 2358 hours.

*History:* For a brief résumé of the development of this line and the three other local lines read the history section of the Transports public du Chablais (*see entry 18*).

*Tariff:* Aigle to Champery CHF 12.40 each way and Monthey to Champery CHF 7.80 each way. Group rates and multipass cards are available (2006).

## 14  Aigle-Sépey-Diablerets [ASD]

Even though the BDe 4/4 rail cars of the Aigle-Sépey-Diablerets railway have to negotiate gradients of up to 6 per cent in all weathers including  snow, they manage to do so without the aid of a rack/cogwheel system.  Here, No. 402 has not long left the maintenance depot at Aigle and is heading for Le Sépey on a bright October day in 2006.

*Author*

*Location*: Aigle, 17 km south of Montreux.
*Canton*: Vaud (VD).
*Michelin map reference*: E7.
*Operated by*: Transports Publics du Chablais (TPC).
*Nearest main line station*: Aigle.
*Route*: Aigle (alt. 404 m) to Le Sépey to Les Diablerets (alt. 1,157 m). The total distance travelled is 22.3 km. There are six tunnels - Grand-Hôtel (6,119 m), Verchiez (16 m), Vanel (28 m), Plambuit (39 m), Dard (202 m) and Joux-au-Craz (40 m). There are two stations and 10 halts.
*Journey time*: 48 minutes each way.
*Gauge*: Narrow (metre) by adhesion only with a maximum gradient of 6 per cent.
*Traction*: Electric-powered 1,500V DC.
*Rolling stock*: Electric-powered rail cars: two 1913-built BDe 4/4 (both *véhicules historiques*), four 1987-built BDe 4/4 Nos. 401-404, five passenger carriages two of which were constructed in 1913 and are classified as *véhicules historiques*, four non-powered rail cars (1966-2000 build), 15 goods wagons all built in 1913, one service wagon and one chasse-neige.
*Contact details*: Transports Publics du Chablais SA, rue de la Gare 38, CH-1860 Aigle. Telephone: 024 468 03 03 Fax : 024 468 03 31. E-mail: info@tpc.ch
*Website*: www.tpc.ch
*Operating dates*: Daily with a total of 28 services between 0619 and 2155 hours.
*Tariff*: An adult single ticket costs CHF 10.40. Group rates and multipass cards are available (2006).
*History*: For a brief résumé of the development of this line and the three other local lines read the history section of the Transports public du Chablais (*see entry 18*).
*Comments*: Probably the best of three routes out of Aigle, the area being noted for its wine production. The track loops round Aigle's magnificent château before heading up the most attractive valley of the Grand Eau.

### 15 Bex-Villars-Col de Bretaye [BVB]

*Location*: Bex, 25 km south of Montreux.
*Canton*: Vaud (VD).
*Michelin map reference*: F7.
*Operated by*: Transports publics du Chablais (TPC).
*Nearest main line station*: Bex.
*Route*: Bex (alt. 427m) to Villars to Col de Bretaye (alt. 1,820 m), a total distance of 17 km. There is one tunnel at Fontannaz-Seulaz (1,182 m), three stations and 10 halts.
*Journey time*: Bex to Villars 40 minutes and Villars to Col de Bretaye a further 18 minutes.
*Gauge*: Narrow (metre) by adhesion for a maximum gradient of 6 per cent and also operating on the Abt system rack/cogwheel for 7.3 km of the route with a maximum gradient of 20 per cent.
*Traction*: Electric-powered (650V DC).
*Rolling stock*: Two electric-powered locomotives: HGe 4/4 No. 31 built in 1953 and No. 32 built in 1964; electric-powered rail cars: two Be 2/2s, built in 1915 one of which is out of service, Be 2/3 Nos. 15-16 (both 1948 construction), BDeh 2/4 Nos. 22-26 (variously built between 1940 & 1945), BDeh 4/4 Nos. 81-83 (1976-1987), Beh 4/8 Nos. 91-93, two electric-powered double rail cars (2000 and 2001), three

BDeh 4/4 No. 83 of the Bex-Villars-Bretaye railway approaches the station at Villars. To this point the trains have travelled from the town of Bex by adhesion only but from here passengers heading for the Col de Bretaye are obliged to change train to one operating on the Abt rack/cogwheel system. *Author*

passenger carriages (1953-1999), six non-powered rail cars (1964-1987), one 1898-built locotracteur Te 2/2 and 20 goods wagons, most dating back to the first decade of the 20th century.

***Contact details***: Transports Publics du Chablais SA, rue de la Gare 38, CH-1860 Aigle. Telephone: 024 468 03 03 Fax : 024 468 03 31. E-mail: info@tpc.ch

***Website***: www.tpc.ch

***Operating dates***: Daily with 32 scheduled services from 0600 to 2200 hours.

***Tariff***: Bex to Villars CHF 7.80 each way and Villars to Col de Bretaye CHF 16.20 each way. Group rates and multipass cards are available (2006).

***History***: The three concessions to build this railway were granted between 1897 and 1911. The Bex to Bévieux section was opened in 1898, the Bévieux to Gryon in 1900, the Gryon to Villars in 1901, the Villars to Chesières in 1906 and the final section to Col de Bretaye in 1913. For a brief résumé of the development of this line and the three other local lines see the history section of the Transports public du Chablais (*see entry 18*).

## 16 Bière-Apples-Morges Railway [BAM]

***Location***: Morges on Lac Léman, 13 km west of Lausanne and 50 km north-east of Geneva.

***Canton***: Vaud (VD).

***Michelin map reference***: C6.

***Operated by***: Transports de la région Morges-Bière-Cossonay.

***Routes***: a) Morges to Apples to Bière; and, b) Apples to L'Isle - Mont-la-Ville. The distances are for, a) 17.4 km, and for, b) 10 km. The total distance covered by the network is 30 km.

On 17th October, 2006, Be 4/4 No. 14 approaching Apples station temporarily halting track maintenance work.                                                                    *Author*

*Journey times*: a) 28 minutes and b) 14 minutes.
*Gauge*: Narrow (metre) by adhesion only for a maximum gradient of 3.5 per cent.
*Traction*: Electric-powered (15,000V 16.7Hz).
*Rolling stock*: In addition to the fleet of Be 4/4s there is restored stock available for private hire functions including a 1943-built BDe 4/4 with 40 seats, a 1925-built voiture à bogies AB25 with 60 seats, 12 of which are in first class and an 1898-built two-axle coach which has been converted into a bar.
*Contact details*: Direction MBC, en Riond-Bosson 3, CP-232, CH-1110 Morges 2. Telephone: 021 811 43 43. E-mail: info@lesmbc.ch
*Website*: www.lesmbc.ch (fr)
*Operating dates*: Daily with 22 services per day to and from Bière and Morges between the hours of 0545 and 0026. There are 16 services per day each way between Apples and L'Isle-Mont–la-Ville operating from 0618 to 0019 hours.
*Tariff*: Local fare structure applies (2006).
*History*: This railway was founded in 1895.
*Comments*: In addition to operating the railway services (BAM) the company runs bus services locally (TPM) and regionally (MBC). Excursions described as BAM Saveur are also regularly offered, usually on Saturdays, throughout the year. The trip includes a meal and costs CHF 91 per person (2006). The countryside through which this railway runs, from Lac Léman to the foot of the Jura, is most beautiful.

## 17 Blonay-Chamby, Museum Railway
## (Chemin de Fer-Musée Blonay-Chamby) [BC]

*Location*: Blonay, 24 km east of Lausanne and 6 km north of Montreux.
*Canton*: Vaud (VD).
*Michelin map reference*: E6.
*Nearest main line stations*: Blonay or Chamby.
*Route*: Blonay to Chamby, a distance of 3 km.
*Journey time*: 15 minutes.
*Gauge*: Narrow (metre) by adhesion only.
*Traction*: Steam- and electric-powered.
*Rolling stock*: There 10 steam-driven locomotives, three of which are in regular use:
a 1913 HG 3/4 built by SLM at Winterthur and previously used on the Brig-Furka-
Disentis line (BFD) and later on the Furka-Oberalp Bahn (FO), a 1901 G 3/3 also built
by SLM at Winterthur and previously used on the Brünig line and later the Bière-
Apples-Morges line (BAM), and a 1918-built G 2 x 2/2 built by MBG, Karlsruhe and
previously used in Germany on the Haspe-Voerde-Breckerfeld line and later on the
Zell- Todtnau, Black Forest line. There are three electric-powered locomotives, two
of which are operational: Ge 4/4 No. 75 built in 1913 by SLM at Winterthur and 1935
Te 2/2 No. 926 built by Strassenbahn Zürich. There are 13 electric-powered rail cars,
five of which are operational: a 1909-built BCFeh 4/4 used previously on the
Monthey-Champéry-Morgins route (MCM) and later on the Aigle-Ollon-Monthey-
Champéry line (AOMC), a 1905-built BCFe 4/4 operated on the Montreux-
Oberland-Bahn (MOB), a 1914-built Ze 2/2 from the Rheintalische Strasserbahn
(RhSt), a 1914-built Ce 2/2 from the Stadtische Strassenbahn in Berb (SSB) and
finally a 1903-built BCe 4/4 from the Chemin de Fer Electriques de la Gruyère
(CEG). There are 19 passenger carriages dating back to 1890, 14 are in regular use.
There is one 1903-built fourgon originally operated on the Chemin de Fer Electriques
de la Gruyère and still in regular use, as well as 14 goods wagons, eight of which are
still operational. There are also three service vehicles and three draisines.
*Near to here*: The Train de Pléiades leaves from Blonay station (*see entry 31*). Trains
of the Chemin de fer Legère de Riviere, formerly known as Chemins de Fer
Électriques Veveysans (*see entry 32*), arrive and depart frequently at this station to
and from Montreux.
*Contact details*: Chemin de Fer-Musée Blonay-Chamby, Case Postal 366 CH-1001
Lausanne. Telephone: 021 943 21 21 Fax: 021 943 22 21. E-mail: info@blonay-
chamby.ch
*Website*: www.blonay-chamby.ch
*Operating dates*: May to October at weekends and on Thursday and Friday
afternoon from 1st July to 26th August. There are special events throughout the year
including at Easter. At the weekends 34 of the journeys utilise electric-powered
traction. There are also five steam-driven serrvices on Saturdays and 12 on Sundays.
The first departure from Chamby is at 1000 hours and the last leaves Blonay at 1815
arriving back at Chamby at 1830 hours.
*Tariff*: Blonay to Chamby costs an adult CHF 7 for a single journey and CHF 14 for
a return. The single journey, including a visit to the museum, costs CHF 13 and a
return CHF 16. Children between 6 and 16 years travel at half price and under 6
years of age go free. A day roamer ticket costs an adult CHF 25 (2006).
*Comments*: Said to have the largest collection of historic railway locomotives and
carriages in Switzerland. It also has a café and a shop selling souvenirs.

On 22nd October, 2006 the coal-driven steam locomotive G2 2/2 No. 105 built in 1918 by MBG, Karlsruhe is seen heading for the depot and museum at Blonay. *Author*

Standing here at Blonay-Chamby station is the 1903-built BCe 4/4 No. 111 awaiting passengers for the first service of the day on 22nd October, 2006. In the left background one can see the attractive château at Blonay. *Author*

## 18  Transports publics du Chablais [TPC]

*Locations*: Aigle and Bex, 17 km and 25 km respectively south of Montreux.
*Canton*: Vaud (VD).
*Michelin map reference*: E7 and F7.
*Routes and Distances*: a) Aigle-Leysin - 6.2 km (*see entry 12*); b) Aigle-Ollon-Monthey-Champéry - 23.1 km (*see entry 13*); c) Aigle-Sépey-Diablerets - 22.3 km (*see entry 14*); and, d) Bex-Villars-Bretaye - 17 km (*see entry 15*).
*Journey times*: a) 28 minutes; b) 62 minutes; c) 48 minutes; and, d) 58 minutes.
*Gauge*: All routes operate on the narrow (metre) gauge.
*Traction*: Electric-powered a) 1,500V DC with the Abt rack/cogwheel system, b) 850V DC with the Strub rack/cogwheel system, c) 1,500V DC by adhesion only, and, d) 650V DC with the Abt rack/cogwheel system.
*Rolling stock*: See the individual railway entries.
*Near here*: The medieval Château d'Aigle sitting in the heart of the local vineyards retains a wine museum which is well worth visiting.
*Contact details*: Transports publics du Chablais, rue de la Gare 38, CH-1860 Aigle. Telephone: 024 468 03 30 Fax: 024 468 03 31. E-mail: info@tpc.ch
*Website*: www.tpc.ch (fr en)
*Operating dates and tariffs*: See individual railway entries.
*History*: Railways arrived in the Chablais region of the cantons of Vaud and Valais with the opening of the Lausanne-Simplon railway in 1857. The town of Aigle was on this route and it quickly became a focal point for developing other railways to reach the communities in the mountains. The Aigle-Leysin route was one of the first to be built. In the late 19th century Leysin with its excellent climate became a health resort particularly for the treatment of tuberculosis sufferers. It is interesting to note that the journey from Aigle to Leysin, which nowadays takes 28 minutes by train, in those days took between three and five hours by stagecoach. Discussions to build the railway line began in 1880s leading to formal approval being granted at the end of 1898. No time was wasted in constructing the line and so it was on 5th November, 1900 that services began to and from Aigle and Feyday (Leysin). Over the following 15 years Leysin saw significant development. In 1912, negotiations began which led to the opening of an extension of the line to the Grand Hotel de Leysin, the connection becoming active in 1915. The line turned out to be very successful not least for the revenues it earned from the transport of freight. However, with economic depression in the 1930s there came a down turn which led to the service to Grand Hotel terminating in 1932 and two years later the hotel itself was closed. After World War II, the fortunes of the line improved with Leysin becoming a major tourist destination with the introduction of ski-lifts, the Bernese aerial tramway, a sports centre and so on. However the Aigle-Leysin line was not the first to operate. In January 1898, a concession had been granted to the Bex authorities to build its line in three stages. The construction of the first part proceeded at breakneck speed as evidenced by the opening of the Bex-Bevieux section in September of that same year. The year 1900 saw the opening of the Bevieux-Gryon section and a year later the connection between Gryon and Villars. But that was not the end of the line. In 1905 the Federal authorities agreed to the extension to Chesières. Again construction advanced quickly and the first train from Bex to Chesières ran on 12th August, 1906 and the final section to the Col de Bretaye opened in December 1913. Aigle also became the departure point for another railway in the early 19th century. In 1897 the authorities approved the building of a railway line between Aigle-Ollon-Villars.

However, there was much argument about which route should be adopted. Eventually, in 1900, a concession was granted to build and operate a railway between Aigle and Monthey via Ollon but progress was slow compared to its companion railways for it was not until April 1907 that the line saw its first trains. The line was further extended from Monthey to the township of Champéry in early 1908. At the time there was always the idea that the line would have a spur from the village of Illiez to Morgins but, because of poor profitability forecasts and the impending world war, this section was never built. The final section of the route followed more than 80 years later when a kilometre of track was opened from Champéry town to the Champéry-Planachaux lift thus providing another link from the valley floor to the mountains. The last railway in this area to first run its trains was the ASD built from Aigle to Les Diablerets via Le Sépey. It was not until 1905 that the Federal authorities granted the necessary approvals but ground was not broken and construction begun until 1911. There were serious civil engineering challenges to the building of this line including that of building the Vanel viaduct. This structure first required the building of an aerial tramway to transport men and building materials and scaffolding across the Ormonts valley. This same scaffolding was later used to build the Les Planches viaduct on the same line. The railway from Vers l'Eglise to Les Diablerets was opened on 6th July, 1914 with a permit from the Federal authorities following the next day permitting services to be run from Aigle to Les Diablerets. The railway suffered a major setback in 1940 when its depot was destroyed by fire. As a result of this three electric-powered rail cars and four passenger carriages were lost. There was serious talk of abandoning the railway at that time. Fortunately, positive decisions were made to recover as much as they could from the fire and lease rolling stock from other railway companies to keep operating. Ideas were mooted in Bern in 1985 for the Federal authorities to cease the funding for all privately run railways; ASD was likely to be a casualty. Fortunately, there was a re-think and subsequently a concession was granted until the year 2035. Attempts were made in 1996 by the Vaud canton and local communities to get the Federal Government to revoke this concession due to spiralling costs of running the railway. Again good fortune followed for Bern recognised the importance of this railway and granted it status and funding as a public transport carrier. The four railways now all operate efficiently and effectively and provide an important service to local citizens and tourists alike. Investment has continued, the latest project being to construct a new departure station at Aigle, alongside the SBB main line station. This is expected to be fully operational in 2008.

*Comments*: TPC also provides extensive bus services in the area.


### 19  Train du Chocolat - Schokoladezug - Chocolate Train

*Locations*: Montreux and Gruyères, the latter is a 60 km drive east from Lausanne.
*Cantons*: Vaud (VD) and Fribourg (FR).
*Michelin map reference*: E6 and F6.
*Operated by*: GoldenPass Services.
*Nearest main line station*: Montreux.
*Route*: Montreux to Gruyères and by road to Broc, a total distance on the railway route of 44 km.
*Journey time*: Allow a full day.
*Gauge*: Narrow (metre) by adhesion only.

The most popular 'Chocolate Train' which would be better named the 'Cheese and Chocolate Train', is seen here with two of its ex-Compagnie Internationale de Wagons Lits et des Grands Express Européens (CIWL) carriages at Gruyères on 18th October, 2006.
*Author*

*Traction:* Electric-powered (900V DC).
*Rolling stock:* 1914-built ex-CIWL *Belle Époque* coaches (Compagnie Internationale de Wagons Lits & des Grands Express Européens) Nos. Ars 101 and As 102 and modern GoldenPass *panoramique* coaches. The locomotives used to haul these carriages are normally of the GDe 4/4 or Ge 4/4 classes.
*Near to here:* Gruyères cheese factory and the Cailler Nestlé chocolate factory at Broc.
*Places to see:* Gruyères Castle.
*Contact details:* Rail Center GoldenPass, rue de la Gare, CH-1820 Montreux. Telephone: 0900 245 245 or 0840 245 245. E-mail: www.mob.ch
*Website:* mob@mob.ch
*Operating dates:* The Chocolate Train runs every Monday, Wednesday and Thursday from June to October. The train leaves Montreux central station at 0935 hours and arrives back at 1752 hours
*Tariff:* An adult ticket costs CHF 85.40 and for a child, CHF 55.20. Reductions are available for those carrying Swiss cards or Swiss passes. The price includes the return trip in 1st class accommodation, coffee and croissant served on leaving Montreux, admission to the Gruyères cheese factory and admission to Gruyères Castle. At the Cailler Nestlé factory in Broc there is a film presentation, a mini-tour, complimentary chocolate tasting and discount prices to be found in the factory shop.
*Comments:* SBB standard gauge refrigerated wagons move chocolate products out of the Broc factory on metre gauge track using special conversion bogies.

## 20  Train Touristique du Pays des Fées
## also known as Association RVT-Historique

*Location*: Travers, 22 km west of Neuchâtel.
*Canton*: Neuchâtel (NE).
*Michelin map reference*: E5.
*Nearest main line stations*: Travers and Neuchâtel.
*Routes*: a) Neuchâtel (Gorges de l'Areuse) to Buttes via Travers and Fleurier and, b) Travers to Les Verriers to Pontarlier (on the border with France). The distance for a) is 34.9 km and, for b) 30.9 km.
*Journey times*: Fleurier to Neuchâtel - 55 minutes and Neuchâtel to Les Verrières - 2 hours.
*Gauge*: Standard.
*Traction*: Electric-powered (15,000V 16.7Hz).
*Rolling stock*:  Electric-powered rail car ABDe 2/4 named *L'Etincelante* (en: 'Sparkling') formerly an ABFe 2/4. This is one of the two rail cars that was introduced to the Travers and Fleurier/St Sulpice line when it was electrified between 1944 and 1945. The other rail car, also an ABDe 2/4, was named *Flamboyante* (en: 'Shining'). Both rail cars were retired from commercial operations in December 2004. The Association also maintains a 1967-built electro-diesel shunter Tem II, formerly CFF 292.
*Near to here*: Vallée du Joux (*see entry 22*), Compagnie du Train à Vapeur de la Vallée de Joux (CTVJ) (*see entry 23*) and Vapeur Val-de-Travers (VVT) (*see entry 35*).
*Contact details*: Association RVT-Historique, rue de la Gare 19, CH-2105 Travers. Telephone: 032 863 24 07 Fax: 032 863 21 55. E-mail: info@rvt-historique.ch
*Website*: www.rvt-historique.ch (de fr en es)
*Operating dates*: In 2007, the rail car will run on the following Saturdays: 12th & 26th May, 9th & 23rd June, 7th & 21st July, 11th & 25th August, 8th & 22nd September and 13th October. Departures will be at 0845 from Fleurier arriving at Neuchâtel at 0940 and returning from Neuchâtel at 1000 and arriving back at 1103 hours. Services will also run on the route Neuchâtel to Les Verrières on Saturdays: 12th May, 7th July, 11th August and 13th October. Departures from Neuchâtel will be at 1000 arriving at Travers at 1045 and at Les Verrières at 1200 hours. The rail car returns from Les Verrières at 1445 and arrives at Travers 1505 (NB: this links with the VVT steam train for St Sulpice which departs at 1515 hours) and reaches Neuchâtel at 1540 hours. Finally, the rail car leaves Neuchâtel at 1605 and will arrive back at Travers at 1703 hours.
*Tariff*: An adult single fare for Fleurier to Travers is CHF 10 (return CHF 15), for Fleurier to Neuchâtel CHF 20 (return CHF 35), for Neuchâtel to Travers CHF 15 (return CHF 25), Neuchâtel to Les Verrières CHF 25 (return CHF 40) and for Travers to Pontarlier or Les Verrières CHF 15 (return CHF 25). Children under 6 years travel free and each child aged between 6 and 16 years travels free with one adult (2007).
*Comments*: It is possible to charter the train for special events at a reasonable price. For example to charter the rail car for a special journey from Buttes to Travers to Noiraigue and return would cost CHF 600 (or €400).

## 21 Transports Publics Fribourgeois [TPF]
## formerly Chemins de Fer Fribourgeois [GFM]

BDe 4/4 No. 122 of the Transports Publics Fribourgeois (TPF) awaiting departure from Montbuvon station on 1st February, 2007. Montbuvon is where TPF services meet those of the GoldenPass/Montreux-Oberland-Bahn (MOB).                *Author*

**Location:** Gruyères, 20 km north-east of Vevey-Montreux.
*Canton:* Fribourg (FR).
*Michelin map reference:* F5.
*Nearest main line station:* Palézieux on the SBB's Bern-Lausanne line.
*Routes:* Palézieux - Châtel-St-Denis - Bulle - Gruyères-Montbuvon and the Bulle-Broc routes, the narrow gauge network totalling 48.2 km. The standard gauge railway operates the Bulle-Romont and Fribourg-Murten-Ins routes with a total length of 50 km.
*Gauge:* Narrow (metre) but also standard gauge for the Bulle-Romont and Fribourg-Murten-Ins routes. All lines operate by adhesion with the maximum gradient on the narrow gauge lines of 5.5 per cent and on the standard gauge lines of 5 per cent.
*Traction:* Electric-powered - on the narrow gauge 900V DC is utilised and on the standard gauge line, 15,000V 16.7Hz.
*Rolling stock:* Locomotives: GDe 4/4 101-102 (narrow gauge) and Ae 417 191-192 (standard gauge). Electric-powered rail cars engaged on narrow gauge services: BDe 4/4 Nos. 121-124 & 141-142 and Be 4/4 Nos. 131 & 151-152; and on standard gauge: ABDe 4/4 Nos. 161-164 & 167, Abe 4/4 No. 166 and RABDe 4/4 Nos. 171-173 & 181-182. Non-powered rail cars on narrow gauge: Bt Nos. 221-226, 251-252, & 253-256 and BDt Nos. 271-273. Standard gauge trailers: Bt 50 36 20-24 Nos. 371-8, 373-4 & 381-822, BT 50 36 29-33 Nos. 374-4 and ABt 50 36 39-33 Nos. 372-5. Historic material safeguarded in narrow gauge: Be 4/4 No. 116, B2 Nos. 237 & 232, Bp No. 235, Brs Nos. 245 & 247. B 343 in standard gauge is also preserved.
*Near to here:* This railway meets the MOB/GoldenPass services (*see entry 4*) at Montbovon.

*Contact details*: Transports Publics Fribourgeois, rue des Pilettes 3, Case postale 1536 CH-1701. Telephone: 026 351 02 00  Fax: 026 351 02 90. E-mail: tpf@tpf.ch
*Website*: www.tpf.ch (fr de)
*Operating dates and tariff*: Daily frequent services throughout the year. Local fare structure applies. Consult local timetables, visit TPF's website or go to www.sbb.ch/en
*History*: The Palézieux-Montbovon line was established at the beginning of the 20th century (1901 to 1904) and the Bulle to Broc line began operating services from 1912. From the outset, both lines were run by the 'Chemins de fer électriques de la Gruyère (CEG)', which later amalgamated with the standard gauge railways to become the Gruyere-Fribourg-Morat railway (GFM) in 1942.
*Comments*: TPF offers a nostalgic Train-Rétro service. It operates on most Friday and Saturday evenings and Sunday lunch times throughout the year. The evening services depart from Bulle at 1830 and arrive at Montbovon at 1904 leaving there at 2130 to return to Bulle by 2204 hours. The Sunday service leaves Bulle at 1145, reaches Montbovon by 1224 and departs from there at 1452 arriving back at Bulle at 1523 hours. Passengers travel in the 1926-built historic carriage *Molejon* on the 'La Gruyère' train which also has a 1932-built bar saloon 'La Grevire' all hauled by a 1922-built electric rail car. The cost for an adult is CHF 40, for young people (13-20 years) CHF 36 and accompanied children under 13 years CHF 13. The fare includes the trip on the train, a fondue followed by meringues with double Gruyère cream (definitely not for those on a diet!).

'Broc Fabrique' is the station, more really a halt, alongside the Cailler Nestlé factory in the small village of Broc. Here is BDe 4/4 No. 124 led by non-powered rail car Bt 225 on 18th October, 2006.  Although the gauge here is only a metre wide, SBB standard gauge freight wagons reach here by means of special conversion bogies.                                    *Author*

## 22 Vallée de Joux formerly Pont-Brassus [PBr]

Travys SA operate this regular service between Le Brassus and Le Pont as well a pleasure boat service on the lake using *Caprice II* which can be seen in the foreground moored close to Le Pont.                                                                                    *Author*

*Location*:  Le Pont and Le Brassus, the latter is 51 km south-west of Yverdon-les-Bains.
*Canton:*  Vaud (VD).
*Michelin map reference*:  D5.
*Operated by*:  Travys SA.
*Nearest main line stations*:  Le Pont, Le Brassus or Vallorbe.
*Route*:  Le Pont to Le Brassus, a distance of 14 km.
*Journey time*:  22 minutes.
*Gauge*:  Standard and by adhesion only on a maximum gradient of 2.3 per cent.
*Traction*:  Electric-powered (15,000V 16.7Hz).
*Rolling stock*:  Electric-powered rail cars: RBDe 568 Nos. 384-385 and ABDe 536 No. 616-6.
*Near to here*:  Musée de Fer et Chemin de Fer located at Vallorbe (*see entry 39*). Nyon-St-Cergue-Morez railway at La Cure (*see entry 29*). Chemin de fer Touristique de Pontarlier-Vallorbe [CFTPV] also known as Coni'fer is just over the border at Les Hôpitaux-Vieux in France (*see page 78 of the author's* **The Essential Guide to French Heritage and Tourist Railways** *published by Oakwood Press for more information about this attractive railway*). For a photograph of Coni'fer's Tigerli see page 84.
*Places to see*:  The beautiful valley set in the Grande Chaîne du Risoud with the lakes of Le Joux (8 sq. km), the Brenet (3 sq. km) and the Ter which is much smaller in area when compared to the other two.
*Contact details*:  Travys SA, quai de la Thiele 32 CP 387, CH-1401 Yverdon-les-Bains. Telephone: 024 424 10 70 Fax : 024 424 10 80. E-mail: info@travys.ch

*Website*: www.travys.ch (fr)
*Operating dates*: Daily with hourly services; for times and frequency consult local timetables or www.sbb.ch/en/index
*Tariff*: An adult 2nd class single ticket is CHF 7.20 (2006).
*History*: This line was inaugurated on 21st August, 1899.
*Comments*: Travys SA also operates boat services on the lake utilising their motor vessel *Caprice II*. This line is also used by Compagnie du Train à Vapeur de la Vallée de Joux (*see next entry*) for steam excursions.

### 23  Compagnie du Train à Vapeur de la Vallée de Joux [CTVJ]

Steam locomotive E 3/3 No. 8523 was built in 1915 by SLM at Winterthur. It is seen here leaving its depot at Le Pont for the afternoon excursion on 9th July, 2006.        *Author*

*Location*: Le Pont near Vallorbe, about 5 km from the French border.
*Canton*: Vaud (VD).
*Michelin map reference*: D5.
*Operated by*: Travys SA.
*Nearest main line station*: Vallorbe.
*Route*: Le Pont via Le Lieu, Esserts-de-Rive, Le Rocheray, Le Sentier to Le Brassus at an average altitude of 1,030 m over a total distance of 14 km.
*Journey time*: about 46 minutes each way.
*Gauge*: Standard by adhesion only on a maximum gradient of 2.3 per cent.
*Traction*: Steam & diesel locotracteur.
*Rolling stock*: Steam locomotives: E 3/3 No. 8494 and E 3/3 No. 8523; locotracteur: TM1 No. 102, Db 10378 (Brun rouille); carriages: Abi 4420 (red) in the process of renovation, B4i 7373 (green ex-BLS), B4i 7717 (brown); and, goods wagons: 18290 (Bordeaux red) and D3 18227 (midnight blue).

*Near to here & places to see*:  See previous entry for Vallée de Joux, formerly Pont-Brassus.
*Contact details*:  Travys SA, quai de la Thiele 32 CP 387, CH-1401 Yverdon-les-Bains. Telephone: 024 424 10 70 Fax: 024 424 10 80. The President of CTVJ is Monsieur Georges Guex, Champ-Rond 38, CH-1010 Lausanne. Telephone: 021 653 20 80 or 079 341 34 61. E-mail: vapeurctvj@citycable.ch or info@travys.ch
*Website*:  www.ctvj.ch & www.travys.ch (fr)
*Operating dates*:  The 2007 programme of steam-hauled excursions follows the pattern of previous years: Journée Vapeur trains will operate on 24th June, 8th July, 22nd July, 5th August, 19th August, 2nd September, 16th September and 7th October, departing Le Pont at 1358 and arriving at Le Brassus at 1444 hours. The train departs Le Brassus at 1537 and arrives back at Le Pont at 1620 hours. The Train Fondue operates on 23rd June, 1st September and 6th October departing Le Pont at 1936 and arriving back by 2215 hours. Prior reservations for the Train Fondue are essential by telephoning 021 653 20 80 or 079 341 34 61.
*Tariff*:  A return journey on the Journée Vapeur service costs an adult CHF 18 and a child CHF 8. For a single ticket an adult is charged CHF 12 and a child CHF 5. There are reductions for groups of 10 or more on prior request. The Train Fondue costs an adult CHF 40 and a child CHF 30 (2007).
*History*:  The line, used for these steam excursions, was first opened in 1899 and ran steam-driven locomotives until the autumn of 1938 when the line was electrified. Steam traction returned to this route in February 1985 and has been operated successfully on a regular basis ever since.
*Comments*:  This heritage railway service is run all by volunteers and is well worth visiting and supporting. The quality and condition of the rolling stock is superb.


### 24  Chemins de Fer du Jura [CJ]

*Location*:  La Chaux-du-Fonds, 20 km north of Neuchâtel.
*Canton*:  Jura (JU).
*Michelin map reference*:  E4.
*Nearest main line stations*:  La Chaux-de-Fonds, Glovelier and Tavannes.
*Routes*:  La Chaux-de-Fonds to Le Noirmont; from Le Noirmont trains either continue on to Saigneléger and Glovelier, or to Tavannes: all are on standard gauge track. Another route offered by this railway is to and from Porrentruy and Bonfol on narrow gauge but does not connect with the standard gauge services. The distances involved are: 74 km on standard gauge and 11 km on narrow gauge (metre) track. There are a total of 25 bridges and eight tunnels on these routes.
*Journey time*:  La Chaux-de-Fonds to Glovelier takes 1 hour 42 minutes.
*Gauge*:  Standard by adhesion only operating on a maximum gradient of 5 per cent and narrow (metre) also by adhesion only operating on a maximum gradient of 2.8 per cent.
*Traction*:  Electric-powered - standard gauge (15,000V 16.7Hz) and narrow gauge (1,500V DC).
*Rolling stock*:  Locomotives in narrow gauge: De 4/4 I Nos. 401-402 & De 4/4 II No. 411 and in standard gauge: De 587 Nos. 111-6. Electric-powered rail cars utilised on narrow gauge: ABDe 4/4 I 603, BDe 4/4 621, BDe 4/4 I 607-608, BDe 4/4 II 611-614, ABe 2/6 631-634, Abe 4/4 641 (ex-RhB) & ABef 4/4 642 (ex-RhB) and on standard gauge: BDe 577 101-102.  Non-powered rail cars on the narrow gauge: Bt Nos. 701-706, ABt Nos. 711-714 & BDt Nos. 721-722 and on standard gauge: Bt 50 36 29-03

A Chemin de Fer du Jura train powered from the rear by  BDe 4/4 II No. 614 approaching la Ferrière on 21st October, 2006.                                                    *Author*

Nos. 921-8. Historic material includes: BCe 2/4 No. 70 and C 7. The latter is used regularly for historic/nostalgic excursions.
*Near to here*: La Traction (*see entry 34*).
*Places to see*: Watch Valley - the home of many Swiss watch companies, e.g. Tissot is located at La Locle close to La Chaux-de-Fonds.
*Contact details*: Chemins de Fer du Jura, rue Général-Voirol 1, CH - 2710 Tavannes. Telephone: 032 482 64 50 or 032 422 15 45 Fax: 032 482 64 79. E-mail: information@les-cj.ch
*Websites*:  www.les-cj.ch  (de fr) or www.cj-transports.ch  (de fr)
*Operating dates*: Services daily throughout the year.
*Tariff*: An adult 2nd class single ticket from La Chaux-de-Fonds to Glovelier costs CHF 31 (2006).
*History*: The narrow gauge network which operates today in the Jura canton is a result of a merger of several different railway companies. The first line to be constructed in this area, in 1884, was the Tavannes-Tramelan line. Eight years later saw the line from La Chaux-de-Fonds to Saignelégier added and, in 1904, the standard gauge route from Saignelégier to Glovelier. The final section came in 1913 when the Tramelan-Le Noirmont route opened. All of these railway companies, some operating steam locomotion and others electric-powered traction, merged in 1944 to form Chemins de Fer du Jura. In 1953, in order to bring about standardisation to the network, the amalgamated company converted the Saignelégier-Glovelier to standard gauge line from metre gauge. Since that time, electric-powered trains have operated throughout the entire standard gauge network. Narrow gauge, however, is still retained on the Porrentruy-Bonfol route which is independent of the rest of the network having no direct connection to the rest of the Chemins de Fer du Jura services.
*Comments*: The railway company also operates bus services in the area.

## 25  Lausanne-Echallens-Bercher Bahn [LEB]

1910-built G 3/3 No. 8 *Echallens* standing at Echallens station on 17th October, 2006.

*Author*

*Location:*  Lausanne, 63 km north-east of Geneva.
*Canton:*  Vaud (VD).
*Michelin map reference:*  D6.
*Nearest main line station:*  Lausanne.
*Route:*  Lausanne-Echallens-Bercher, a distance of 23 km.
*Journey time:*  39 minutes.
*Gauge:*  Narrow (metre) by adhesion only with a  maximum gradient on the line of 4 per cent.
*Traction:*  Electric-powered (1,500V DC) and preserved steam.
*Rolling stock:*  Electric-powered rail cars: Be 4/4 Nos. 26-27 and Be 4/8 Nos. 31-36. Non-powered rail cars: Bt Nos. 51-52. Historic material preserved includes a 1910-built G 3/3 No. 8 steam locomotive named *Echallens*, a 1935-built electric-powered BDe 4/4 No. 21 *Ropraz* and a 1947-built Are 4/4 No. 25 *Gros de Vaud*; carriages B2 10, 11 & 12 and Z2 5 baggage car complete the rolling stock.
*Contact details:*  Chemin de fer Lausanne-Echallens-Bercher, place de la Gare 9, CH-1040 Echallens. Telephone:  021 886 20 00 Fax: 021 886 20 19. E-mail: admin.leb@leb.ch
*Website:*  www.leb.ch (fr)
*Operating dates:*  Daily with 29 services each way every half-hour from 0530 to 1830 hours.
*Tariff:*  An adult 2nd class single for Lausanne to Echallens to Bercher costs CHF 9 and for 1st class CHF 15. Children (6-16 years) travel at half the adult fare (2007).

1947-built Are 4/4 No. 25 *Gros de Vaud* standing at Echallens station with modern Be 4/4s in the background.                                                                 *Author*

*Heritage services*: Steam excursions are organized on Sundays from the first week in August to the end of the third week in September. Trains depart Echallens at 1028, 1200, 1400 & 1528 hours travelling to and from Cheseaux and Bercher. The last train of the day arrives back at Echallens at 1650 hours. An adult ticket costs CHF 14 and for a child CHF 7 (2006). Information about these heritage services can be obtained from Gare d'Echallens by telephoning 021 886 20 15.

*History*: The line, the first in Switzerland to employ the metre gauge, was built in 1872, the first section constructed being between Montétan and Jouxtens. On the 1st January, 1913, 'la Compagnie du chemin de fer Lausanne-Echallens-Bercher' was founded.

### 26  Chemin de fer Martigny-Orsières [MO]
### also referred to as the St Bernard Express

*Location*: Martigny, 42 km south of Montreux.
*Canton*: Valais (VS).
*Michelin map reference*: F7.
*Operated by*: Transports de Martigny et Régions [TMR].
*Nearest main line station*: Martigny.
*Route*: Martigny to Orsières, a distance of 26 km.
*Journey time*: Martigny to Sembrancher  takes 16 minutes and to Orsières 26 minutes.
*Gauge*: Standard, by adhesion only with the maximum gradient on this line of 3.7 per cent.
*Traction*: Electric-powered (15,000V 16.7Hz).

*Rolling stock*: Electric-powered rail cars: RABe 527 Nos. 511-513, ABDe 4/4 Nos. 6-8 and ABDe 4/4 No. 9. Non-powered rail cars: Bt Nos. 31-33.

*Near to here*: Swiss Vapeur Park (*see entry 44*) and Trains Touristique d'Emosson (*see entry 42*).

*Places to see*: The Gianadda Foundation, the Roman amphitheatre and the Bâtiaz Tower at Martigny. The Grand-Saint-Bernard Hospice.

*Contact details*: TMR SA, rue de la Poste 3, Case postale 727, CH-1920 Martigny. Telephone: 027 721 68 40 Fax: 027 721 68 59. E-mail: pascal.may@tmrsa.ch

*Website*: www.tmrsa.ch (fr de it en)

*Operating dates*: Daily frequent services, consult the SBB timetable service on www.sbb.ch/en

*Tariff*: An adult 2nd class single ticket costs CHF 9.80 (2006).

*History*: The project to build this railway has a long history. In 1846, one year before the Zürich-Baden line was opened, a proposal was made to build the line to connect, via a tunnel, to Aosta in Italy. A contract was signed in 1851 and work commenced five years later, simultaneously in Italy and in Switzerland. However, on the Swiss side of the construction the difficulties were soon realised of building a 2,231 m-long tunnel at an altitude of 2,307 m. The conclusion was that the project, at that time, was unrealistic and was abandoned. In 1906, the Swiss Federal authorities in Bern authorized the construction of a narrow gauge railway between Martigny and Orsières. The decision was made to construct in standard gauge and therefore make it compatible with the main line passing through Martigny. It was at this time that an English company bought the water rights of the River Dranse, their intention being to build an aluminium factory at Orsières. As a consequence, the company agreed to finance the construction costs of the railway line and work began in July 1907. It was on 27th August, 1910 that the township of Martigny celebrated the opening of a the line to Orsières in the Entremont valley. Ironically, after the railway had opened the aluminium factory project was abandoned. This was because the Valais canton authorities were afraid that Martigny would become more important than Sion, the then, as now, capital. In 1953, following the construction of the Mauvoisin dam the Martigny-Orsières railway increased the length of its network with an 18 kilometre extension connecting Sembrancher to Le Châble.

*Comments*: The train leaves Martigny in the Rhône plain and heads for Sembrancher, where one train service travels to Orsières, the terminus. From there, buses take passengers to various destinations, e.g. the Champex lake, Val Ferret and the Grand-Saint-Bernard Hospice. The other train service heads for Le Châble, in the Bagnes valley, where, at an altitude of 1,500 m, the well-known ski-station of Verbier is located. The Martigny-Chatelard international route to and from Martigny and St Gervais-les-Bains in France (*see entry 8*) also runs from here.

## 27  Transports publics du Littoral Neuchâtelois [TN]

*Location*: Neuchâtel, 48 km west of Bern.

*Canton*: Neuchâtel (NE).

*Michelin map reference*: E5.

*Routes*: Boudry to Neuchâtel (route 5) a distance of 9 km.

*Traction*: Electric-powered.

*Rolling stock*: Six electric-powered rail cars: Be 4/4 Nos. 501-506 and four non-powered rail cars: Bt Nos. 551-554 all painted in their distinctive yellow and green livery.

TRN's standard gauge RABe 527 No. 322 *Nina* leaving Travers for Neuchâtel. *Author*

TRN's narrow gauge BDe 4/4 No. 7 about to leave Les Ponts de Martel for La Chaud de Fonds. *Author*

*Contact details:* Transports publics du Littoral Neuchâtelois, quai Philippe-Godet 5, Case postale 3156, CH-2001 Neuchâtel. Telephone: 032 720 06 00 Fax: 032 724 51 34. E-mail: via the Contact page of the website.

*Website:* www.tnneuchatel.ch (fr)

*Operating dates:* Every day with services every 20 minutes in both directions from about 0550 to 2345 with later services on Saturday evenings.

*Tariff:* An adult single ticket is CHF 2.50 and for a child (6-16 years) CHF 1.70 (2007).

*History:* Transports publics du Littoral Neuchâtelois was founded as a company in 1894 but one of the funiculars had been opened earlier in 1890 and steam traction had been running on the Neuchatel-Boudry/Cortaillod route as early as 1892; this line was converted to electric power in 1902.

*Comments:* In addition to rail services, TN operates four trolleybus routes, eight bus routes and three funiculars in the area of Neuchâtel. TN has a strong supportive relationship with Association Neuchâteloise des Amis du Tramway (ANAT) (*see entry 41*).

## 28  Transports Régionaux Neuchâtelois [TRN]

*Location:* La Chaux de Fonds, 20 km north-west of Neuchâtel.

*Canton:* Neuchâtel (NE).

*Michelin map reference:* E4.

*Routes:* Three main rail services are operated by TRN with distances of 14 km on standard gauge and 20 km narrow gauge lines. Val de Travers rail services run on standard gauge between Neuchâtel and Butts via Travers. Montagnes Neuchâteloises operate narrow gauge trains from La Locle to Les Brenets and from La Chaud de Fonds to Les Ponts de Martel.

*Journey times:* Neuchâtel to Butts - 43 minutes; La Locle to Les Brenets - 7 minutes; and, from La Chaud de Fonds to Les Ponts de Martel - 23  minutes.

*Gauge:* Standard operating on a maximum gradient of 1.7 per cent and narrow (metre) operating on a maximum gradient of 4 per cent.

*Traction:* Electric-powered - standard gauge (15,000V 16.7Hz) and narrow gauge (1,500V DC).

*Rolling stock:* Locomotives: standard gauge Be 417 Nos. 301-9. Electric-powered rail cars: RABe 527 Nos. 321-322, ABDe 537 Nos. 311-312 & 313-9 and RBDe 567 Nos. 315-7 & 316-317. Narrow gauge electric-powered rail cars: BDe 4/4 Nos. 2-5 & 6-8.

*Near to here:* Chemins de fer du Jura (*see entry 24*) and Travys SA-operated routes (*see entry 36*).

*Places to see:* The beautiful Lac des Brennets alongside the Swiss-Franco border is a short 10 minute walk from the TRN station.

*Contact details:* Transports Régionaux Neuchâtelois, Allée des Défricheurs 3, CP 1429, 2300 La Chaux de Fonds. Telephone: 032 924 24 24  Fax: 032 924 24 09. E-mail: info@trn.ch

*Website:* www.trn.ch (fr)

*Operating dates:* Daily with frequent services on all routes between 0600 and 2300 hours.

*Tariff:* Not published - enquire locally.

*History:* The former independent railway company Chemins de Fer des Montagnes Neuchâteloises is now part of TRN.  Rail services began on standard gauge in 1883 and on narrow gauge in 1889.

*Comments:* An 030 steam locomotive, built in 1890, ran train services on this line to Les Brenets for 60 years. It was one of three of this type constructed, the other two being *Le Doubs* and *Les Brenets*. *Les Brenets* has not survived but *Le Doubs* can be found at Chemin de fer-Musée Blonay-Chamby (*see entry 17*). *Le Pere Frederic* is now located as a static exhibit (behind glass) within the precincts of Les Brenets station.

### 29  Nyon-St-Cergue-Morez (NStCM)

A Be 4/4 No. 201 and Bt trailer climbing to the station at La Cure on the Swiss/Franco border. Not far from here in France is the town of Morez where the SNCF-TER service 'Les Hirondelles' can be seen spiralling its way up the mountain side.          *Author*

*Location:* Nyon, on Lake Geneva 26 km north-east of Geneva.
*Canton:* Vaud (VD).
*Michelin map reference:* C6.
*Operated by:* Transports publics de la région Nyonnaise SA (TPN).
*Nearest main line station:* Nyon on the edge of Lac Léman.
*Route:* Nyon to La Cure on the border with France via Bassins and St-Cergue, a total distance of 27 km.
*Journey time:* 50 minutes.
*Gauge:* Narrow (metre) adhesion only on a maximum gradient of 6 per cent.
*Traction:* Electric-powered (1,500V DC).
*Rolling stock:* Electric-powered rail cars: Be 4/4 Nos. 201-205, BDe 4/4 Nos. 211, & 221 & 223 and non-powered rail cars: Bt Nos. 301-305 & Bt 331 (ex-Chemins de Fer du Jura).
*Near to here:* Le Pont and Le Brassus for Vallée de Joux service (*see entry 22*) and Compagnie du Train à Vapeur de la Vallée de Joux (*see entry 23*) both operated by Travys SA (*see entry 36*).

*Places to see*: Situated 20 km from Nyon and 40 km from Geneva is EspaceDôle which offers superb skiing in winter and great walking in summer.

*Contact details*: Transports publics de la région Nyonnaise SA, rue de la Gare 45, CH-1260 Nyon. Telephone : 022 994 28 40 Fax: 022 994 28 41. E-mail: nstcm@tprnov.ch or Gare de St-Cergue, CH-1264 St-Cergue. Telephone: 022 360 12 13 Fax: 022 360 26 93. E-mail: gare.st-cergue@tprnov.ch

*Website*: www.tprnov.ch (fr) The website includes a short video with commentary in French describing the route.

*Operating dates*: Daily throughout the year with 17 services to and from Nyon and La Cure. The first train from Nyon is at 0529 and the last at 1915 hours. The first from La Cure is at 0628 and the last at 2017 hours. There are other services operating the shorter journey between Nyon and St-Cergue.

*Tariff*: Local fare structure applies - enquire locally. A daily Rail Dôle Pass is offered in winter which allows for transport on the train to and from La Cure for one passenger with skis, transport on the bus service from La Cure to Cuvaloup and Les Dappes and return. The pass costs CHF 52 for journeys commencing at Nyon and CHF 36 from St-Cergue. As many journeys both by train and bus can be taken during the day as required (2007).

*History*: The idea of building this line was proposed by a French man in the late 19th century, his thoughts at that time being that it should be constructed with either 80 cm or 60 cm gauge track. Unfortunately, the project did not attract local interest and was abandoned in 1900. It was not until some 12 years later that approval was given to build a metre gauge railway from Nyon to the French border. Construction began immediately but the advent of World War I slowed progress. However, this did not stop development of a railway on the other side of the border - the President of the French Republic in 1913 had signed an agreement to build a railway line between Morez (in France) and the Swiss border at La Cure. In July 1916, in spite of the war, the section between Nyon and St-Cergue was opened to traffic followed by the section from St-Cergue to La Cure a year later. However, the final section from La Cure to Morez was not opened until March 1921. Between 1921 and 1958 this railway was jointly run by two companies, one Swiss - la Compagnie du Chemin de fer Nyon-St-Cergue-Morez and the other French - Chemins de fer électriques du Jura (CFEJ). Unfortunately in 1958, the section in France was closed and replaced by a bus service. In 1963, NStCM presented a proposal for financial aid for the renovation of the railway's infrastructure and rolling stock. Although not an unreasonable request given the importance of the route and its historic rolling stock no decision was reached. There followed eight commissions over the next 20 years to consider the requests and the future of the railway. At last, a decision was made in 1982 to keep the railway but funds for replacement/improvement were limited and progress was slow. Happily, more recently, matters have improved significantly, perhaps best evidenced by funds being made available in 2002 to build a new underground station at Nyon; the station was opened for train services in July 2004.

*Comments*: A popular route both in summer and winter for its attractive scenery and access to good walking and skiing. A number of promenades are recommended by the company: a) Le Sentier des Toblerones (a distance of 17 km taking about 4 hour 20 minutes but not difficult); b) La Givrine-La Dôle (1677 m)-La Barillette - St-Cergue (a distance of 14.3 km in 4 hours 30 minutes with significant hill climbing) and, c) St-Cergue - Ruines d'Oujon - Arzier (a distance of 6.75 km in 1 hour 45 minutes with a medium degree of hill climbing). Winter skiing can be enjoyed from this railway especially at EspaceDôle near St-Cergue.

## 30  Orbe-Chavornay-Bahn [OB]

Standing at Orbe station is the Travys-operated Orbe-Chavornay service here using Be
557 No. 614.                                                                    *Author*

*Location*: Orbe, 48 km south-west of Neuchâtel.
*Canton*: Vaud (VD).
*Michelin map reference*: D5.
*Operated by*: Travys SA.
*Nearest main line stations*: Chavornay and Yverdon-les Bains.
*Route*: Orbe-Chavornay, a total distance of 5 km.
*Journey time*: 9 minutes.
*Gauge*: Standard - adhesion only with maximum gradient of 2.5 per cent.
*Traction*: Electric-powered (750V DC).
*Rolling stock*: Electric-powered rail cars: Be 557 Nos. 614-5. Historic stock preserved
includes a BDe 4/4 No. 13 and a De 2/2 No. 32.
*Near to here*: Musée de Fer et Chemin de fer at Vallorbe (*see entry 39*) and Yverdon-
les-Bains-Ste Croix railway (*see entry 37*) operated by Travys SA.
*Contact details*: Chemin de fer Orbe-Chavornay c/o Travys SA, quai de la Thièle
32 CP 387, CH-1401 Yverdon-les-Bains. Telephone: 024 424 10 70 Fax: 024 424 10 80.
E-mail: info@travys.ch
*Website*: www.travys.ch (fr)
*Operating dates*: Daily throughout the year with 31 services each way between
Orbe and Chavornay.  From Chavornay there are connecting services, also operated
by Travys SA, to the very attractive town of Yverdon-les-Bains.
*Tariff*: Local fare structure applies.
*History*: It was in April 1894 that the first trains circulated between Orbe and
Chavornay, a connection previously provided by a (horse) bus service. Up until New
Year's Eve in 1992 the railway  was a department of the local manufacturing company
- la societé des Usines de l'Orbe (UO), thereafter the railway became independent. In
June 2003, Travys SA took over the responsibility for the running of the service.

## 31 Chemin de fer des Pléiades

Here, near to Blonay station, Beh 2/4 No. 72 *Astro Pléiades* helped by the Strub rack/cogwheel system begins its ascent to Les Pléiades.               *Author*

*Location*: Vevey, 19 km east of Lausanne.
*Canton*: Vaud (VD).
*Michelin map reference*: E6.
*Nearest railway station*: Blonay accessed from Montreux by the Chemin de fer Legère de Rivière (*see next entry*).
*Operated by*: GoldenPass Services as part of Montreux-Vevey Riviera [MVR].
*Route*: Blonay-Les Pléiades, a distance of 8 km.
*Journey time*: Blonay up to Les Pléiades takes 20 minutes and down, 24 minutes.
*Gauge*: Narrow (metre) operating rack/cogwheel on the Strub design negotiating a maximum gradient of 20 per cent.
*Traction*: Electric-powered (900V DC).
*Rolling stock*: Powered rail car Beh 2/4 No. 72 and named 'Astro Pléiades'.
*Places to see*: The views from the summit of Lake Geneva, the Alpine peaks to the east and the Mont Blanc range to the south are truly outstanding. From Les Pléiades there are nine recommended walks varying in degrees of difficulty and in time from 20 minutes to 2 hours 30 minutes. A brochure describing the routes is available from Blonay station. A more detailed Guide de Parcours can also be purchased at Blonay station.
*Contact details*: Rail Center GoldenPass, Case postale 1426, rue de la Gare, CH-1820 Montreux 1. Telephone: 0900 245 245 or 0840 245 245. E-mail: mob@mob.ch Website: www.mob.ch (fr en)
*Operating dates*: Daily throughout the year with services in both directions running every hour. The first service leaves Blonay at 0638 and the last at 1858 hours. The first journey down from Les Pléiades is at 0700 and the last at 1933 hours.
*Tariff*: An adult single ticket costs CHF 12.40 and a return CHF 19.40 and for a child the single fare is CHF 6.20 and a return CHF 19.40 (2006).

*History*:  The Chemin de fer Electriques Veveysans (CEV) was formed in 1902 by the amalgamation of two railway companies - one providing services from Vevey to Blonay and the other from Blonay to Les Pléiades. In 1990, CEV became part of the Montreux-Oberland-Bahn (MOB) and now as Transports Montreux-Vevey Riviera [MVR] (*see next entry*) is part of the GoldenPass group of rail services.

*Comments*:  This railway also offers, from May to October, at the summit of Les Pléiades an exposition - Astro Pléiades - comprising four open air exhibits on the themes of:  a) Our earthly observatory; b) The solar system; c) To the nearby stars; and, d) Our galaxy and the local cluster.

**32  Chemin de fer Legère de Rivière**
**sometimes referred to as Transports Montreux-Vevey-Riviera [MVR] and**
**formerly known as Chemins de Fer Électriques Veveysans [CEV]**

On the south-facing slopes above Lake Geneva vines grow in abundance; here Be 2/6 No. 7003 negotiates its way down to Vevey and Montreux from Blonay in October 2006.
*Author*

*Location*:  Vevey, 19 km east of Lausanne.
*Canton*:  Vaud (VD).
*Michelin map reference*:  E6.
*Operated by*:  GoldenPass Services (MOB).
*Nearest main line station*:  Vevey.
*Route*:  Vevey to Blonay, a distance of 10 km.
*Journey time*:  14 minutes.
*Gauge*:  Narrow (metre) by a combination of adhesion and rack/cogwheel operating on the Strub system for the maximum gradient of 20 per cent.
*Traction*:  Electric-powered (900V DC).
*Rolling stock*:  Powered rail cars: Be 2/6 Nos. 7001-7004, Beh 2/8 No. 71 and BDeh 2/4 Nos. 73-74 & 75 and non-powered rail cars are: Bt Nos. 221, 222 & 223.  Powered rail cars BDe 4/4 Nos. 103 & 105 are safeguarded as historic exhibits.

*Near to here*: Connects to Chemin de fer des Pléiades at Blonay (*see previous entry*) and the Chemin de Fer-Musée Blonay-Chamby (*see entry 17*).
*Places to see*: The château at Blonay from where there is a superb view of Lake Geneva (Lac Léman).
*Contact details*: Rail Center GoldenPass, Case postale 1426, rue de la Gare, CH-1820 Montreux 1. Telephone: 0900 245 245 or 0840 245 245 E-mail: mob@mob.ch
*Website*: www.mob.ch (fr en)
*Operating dates*: Throughout the year with services at half-hourly intervals commencing at 0639 from Vevey and 0602 hours from Blonay. The last service from Vevey leaves at 0041 hours and from Blonay at 0002 hours.
*Tariff*: An adult single all the way from Vevey to Les Pléiades costs CHF 16.20 and a return CHF 32.40 (2007).
*History*: The Chemin de fer Electriques Veveysans (CEV) was formed in 1902 by the amalgamation of two railway companies one providing services from Vevey to Blonay and the other from Blonay to Les Pléiades. In 1990, CEV became part of the Montreux-Oberland-Bahn (MOB) and is now part of the GoldenPass group of rail services.

## 33  Montreux Glion Rochers-de-Naye [MGN]
**formerly known as Chemin de fer Montreux-Territet-Glion-Naye [MTGN]**

The Abt rack/cogwheel system is utilised here on 800 mm gauge track for Bhe 4/8 No. 302 *en route* to Montreux.                                                    *Author*

*Location*: Montreux, 27 km south-east of Lausanne.
*Canton*: Vaud (VD).
*Michelin map reference*: E6.
*Operated by*: GoldenPass Services.
*Nearest main line station*: Montreux.

**Route:** Montreux station via Glion to the summit of Rochers-de-Naye (alt. 2,045 m) a total distance of 10 km.
**Journey time:** 55 minutes.
**Gauge:** Narrow (800 mm) operating entirely by a rack/cogwheel system of the Abt design for the maximum gradient of 22 per cent on this line.
**Traction:** Electric-powered (850V DC).
**Rolling stock:** Electric-powered rail cars: Beh 2/4 Nos. 201-208 and Bhe 4/8 Nos. 301-304. Historic items of interest retained are B16, B17,B2, B2 GN, B2 MG and B5.
**Places to see:** Near to the Rochers-de-Naye terminus is a special park for marmots with seven species drawn from all over the world and five species of marmots from Russia and North America. All the marmots are visible in huge parks which allow visitors to see the animals in their dens. There is also a learning centre which, by way of multi-media facilities, tells the visitor all he or she would want to know about the 14 species of marmots living in the world. Entrance to the park is free. Chemin de Fer-Musée Blonay-Chamby is not far away (*see entry 17*). Château de Chillon is close to Montreux in the direction of Villeveuve. The château, which was built in the 11th century for the Dukes of Savoy, was immortalised in 1816 by Lord Byron in his poem 'The Prisoner of Chillon'.
**Contact details:** Rail Center GoldenPass, rue de la Gare, CH-1820 Montreux 1. Telephone: 0900 245 245 or 0840 245 245. E-mail: mob@mob.ch
**Website:** www.mob.ch (fr en)
**Operating dates:** All the year round but reduced services in the winter. The first direct service to Rochers-de-Naye leaves Montreux at 0846 and operates every hour until the last departure at 1846 hours. The first departure from Rochers-de-Naye for Montreux is at 0946 and hourly until the last departure at 1946 hours. There are other services on this line to and from Montreux and Caux which has become a popular residential area for the peoples of Montreux. Special journeys for groups can be arranged.
**Tariff:** From 1st July to 30th September an adult return ticket from Montreux to Rochers-de-Naye is CHF 55 and for a child CHF 36. In the low season (the rest of the year) the fares are CHF 49 and CHF 36 respectively (2006). Discounts for groups are available.
**History:** The original line from Glion to Rochers-de-Naye was opened in September 1892 and the section from Montreux to Glion followed in April 1909. The latter was always electric-powered but the original line used steam traction until mid-1938 when electricification was introduced. However, since 1992 steam traction has returned to the line following the acquisition of a then newly-built locomotive by SLM at Winterthur. Steam services occasionally operate in Spring and Autumn but only to and from Caux and Rochers-de-Naye.
**Comments:** The peak of Montreux's mountain backdrop - Rochers-de-Naye - rises to 2,045 m. On a clear day from the summit one can see the Eiger, the Mönch, the Jungfrau and the Mont Blanc range. In June 2006, this company introduced a novel form of camping facility which is available to the general public for hire. It is in a genuine Mongolian Yurt (or Ger as it is sometimes referred to) of which there are eight available. Each yurt can sleep up to eight persons and being heated in the traditional Mongolian manner ( wood-burning stove) allows it to be used all the year round. The hire of the yurt for the each night period from 1645 to 1100 hours the next morning is CHF 240 irrespective of the number of occupants. The take-up of this leisure facility has been surprising especially for overnight stays in the winter months.

## 34 La Traction

La Traction's Mallet E 164 visited the Baie de Somme steam festival in April 2006. Here it is standing at Noyelles-sur-Mer. *Author*

*Location*: Pre-Petitjean near Montfaucon in the Franches-Montagnes, 40 km west of Basle.
*Canton*: Jura (JU).
*Michelin map reference*: E4.
*Nearest main line stations*: SBB at La Chaux-de-Fonds and Chemins de fer du Jura at Glovelier and Tavannes.
*Routes*: La Traction runs about 30 public and private trains each year. It is also possible to charter a train for marriages, anniversaries, company promotions and other such-like events. The trains are made up of superbly restored historic carriages. It is also possible to have hot and/or cold meals on board the train.
*Gauge*: Narrow (metre) by adhesion only.
*Traction*: Steam and electric/diesel.
*Rolling stock*: A Mallet steam locomotive built by Henschel & Sohn, a combined electric/diesel locomotive in the course of restoration and numerous historic carriages and goods wagons.
*Near to here*: Le Locle and La Chaux-de-Fonds, world famous as the home of Swiss watches, hence the local description 'Watch Valley'. Chemins de fer du Jura (*see entry 24*) is not far away.
*Places to see*: The local railway company Chemins de Fer du Jura crosses the beautiful unspoilt landscape of Jura, the altitude of the track varying between 500 m to over 1,000 m. Horse breeding is a speciality in the area.

*Contact details*: La Traction, Chemins de fer du Jura, Service de promotion, CH-2350 Saignelégier, Telephone: 032 952 42 90 Fax: 032 952 42 93. E-mail: promotion@les-cj.ch

*Website*: www.la-traction.ch (fr de en)

*Operating dates*: Steam excursions on various days throughout the year. Consult the annual programme published on the website. The provisional programme for 2007 indicates that the Mallet will run on 13th May, 3rd June, 10th June, 16th June, 25th July (a staged attack on the train), 1st, 7th, 8th & 25th August and 15th & 16th September. Some of these outings are for private charters but visitors are welcomed to view.

*Comments*: La Traction runs two steam locomotives that were bought in Portugal and restored in Germany, one in 1993 and the other in 1999. They are among the biggest metre-gauge steam locomotives actually running in Europe. The enthusiasts at La Traction have also taken their Mallet to other locations in Europe. For example, in April 2006 it visited France for the Chemin de fer de la Baie de Somme (CFBS) steam festival as the photograph on page 79 depicts.

## 35  Vapeur Val-de-Travers [VVT]

Polish-built TKt 48 188 seen here on 9th July, 2006 departing Gouvet station close to Travers in the canton of Neuchâtel.                    *Author*

*Location*: St Sulpice, 40 km drive north of Yverdon-les-Bains.

*Canton*: Neuchâtel (NE).

*Michelin map reference*: D5.

*Route*: St Sulpice to a) Travers; and, b) Neuchâtel travelling over distances of: a) 12 km; and, b) 35.6 km.

*Journey times*: a) 23 minutes; and, b) 1 hour 23 minutes.

*Gauge*: Standard, by adhesion only.
*Traction*: Steam.
*Rolling stock*: In operational order are a 1956-built TKt No. 48 188 ex-Poland, 1942-built E3/3 No. 16388 ex-Austria, 1911-built E3/3 No. 8511 ex-Switzerland, and E2/2 No. 2 also ex-Switzerland. In the course of restoration: 1943-built German-Austrian No. 52 221 and a 1952-built TKp 16 ex-Poland. On display are a magnificent 1951-built 241 P 30 'Mountain' ex-France, a 1935-built 01.22 Tabacloc ex-Bulgaria, an 1890-built E3/3 No. 855 ex-Switzerland, a 1925-built E2/2 No. 20593 also ex-Switzerland and a 1951-built E2/2 No. 2951 ex-Belgium.
*Near to here*: Yverdon-les-Bains to Ste Croix (*see entry 37*), Orbe to Chavornay (*see entry 30*), Vallée de Joux services (*see entry 22*), preserved steam of the Compagnie du Train à Vapeur de la Vallée de Joux (*see entry 23*) and Train Touristique du Pays des Fées also known as Association RVT-Historique is linked closely with this railway (*see entry 20*).
*Contact details*:   Vapeur Val-de-Travers, Case Postale 21, CH-2123 St Sulpice. Telephone: 032 861 34 98. E-mail: info@vvt.ch
*Website*: www.vvt.ch (fr de en)
*Operating dates*: Various weekends throughout the spring, summer and autumn. The depot is open from 1330 hours on days when trains are operating. The timetables of the VVT steam trains are listed in the official Swiss timetable ('Kursbuch') at entry 221.1. Departures and arrivals of the steam trains are adjusted to the train timings of the local railway company - RVT. In 2007 steam trains are running on 12th & 13th May, 9th & 10th June, 7th & 8th July, 11th & 12th August, 8th & 9th September and 13th & 14th October.
*Tariff*: For the journey from St Sulpice to Travers, an adult return is CHF 15 and for a child under 16 years CHF 10. Entry to the depot costs CHF 7 for adults and CHF 5 for children under 16 years. However, entry is free if in possession of a train ticket for that day (2006).
*Comments*: VVT have very friendly and helpful volunteer staff. The Vice-President speaks excellent English. Special excursions are run during the year. VVT is an extremely efficiently run railway and well worth a visit.


## 36  Travys SA

*Location*:  Yverdon-les-Bains, 37 km north of Lausanne.
*Canton*:  Vaud (VD).
*Michelin map reference*:  D5.
*Nearest main line station*:  Yverdon-les-Bains.
*Routes*:  Travys operates services Yverdon-les-Bains to Ste Croix (*see next entry*), Orbe to Chavornay (*see entry 30*), Vallée de Joux services (*see entry 22*) and preserved steam in the form of the Compagnie du Train à Vapeur de la Vallée de Joux (*see entry 23*). Travys SA also operates comprehensive bus services in the area.
*Gauge*:  Mixed according to location/route. The narrow metre gauge metre lines of which there are 24 km have a maximum gradient of 4.4 per cent. The standard gauge has 13 km of lines with a maximum gradient of 2.3 per cent.  Both gauges operate by adhesion only.
*Traction*:  Electric-powered (15,000V 16.7Hz) on both the narrow and standard gauge lines.

Approaching the attractive town of Yverdon-les-Bains at the southern end of Lake Neuchâtel is Be 4/4 No. 2 on 20th October, 2006. *Author*

*Rolling stock*: Locomotive: a gaily-painted Ge 4/4 Krokodil. Electric-powered rail cars operating on narrow gauge: Be 4/4 Nos. 1-2 & 4-5 and Be 2/6 Nos. 2001-2002. Operating on standard gauge: ABDe 536 Nos. 616-6 (ex-Thurbo/MThB) and RBDe 568 Nos. 384-385. Non-powered rail cars operating on narrow gauge: Bt Nos. 51-52 and BDt Nos. 53-54; and, operating on standard gauge: Bt 50 34 29-34 Nos. 984-985. *Contact details*: Travys SA, quai de la Thiele 32 CP 387, CH-1401 Yverdon-les-Bains. Telephone: 024 424 10 70 Fax : 024 424 10 80. E-mail: info@travys.ch
*Website*: www.travys.ch (fr)
*Operating dates and tariff*: Services are operated throughout the year on all routes. Consult local timetables or visit the website and take advantage of the excellent interactive timetable or, alternatively, visit www.sbb.ch/en
*History*: The railway began running services on narrow gauge in 1893 and on standard gauge in 1899.
*Comments*: Travys SA also operate a special restaurant carriage (la voiture-restaurant-bar) on the Yverdon-les-Bains to Ste Croix route. This historic superbly renovated carriage named *La Traverse* is available for charter to groups but at least 10 days' notice must be given. On the website there is an interesting section - La Coin du Fan - which records the history of the 'Gyro bus' which celebrated its 50th anniversary in 2003.

## 37 Yverdon-Ste Croix

There can be little doubt that this is a 'Krokodil' seen here at Yverdon-les-Bains station on 20th October, 2006.                                                                                          *Author*

*Location*: Yverdon-les-Bains, southern end of Lake Neuchâtel 36 km north of Lausanne.
*Canton*: Vaud (VD).
*Michelin map reference*: D5.
*Operated by*: Travys SA.
*Nearest main line station*: Yverdon-les-Bains.
*Route*: Yverdon-les-Bains to Ste Croix, a total distance of 21 km.
*Journey time*: 36 minutes.
*Gauge*: Standard by adhesion only.
*Traction*: Electric-powered (15,000V 16.7Hz).
*Rolling stock*: See Travys SA listings in previous entry.
*Near to here*: Transports publics du Littoral Neuchâtelois (*see entry 27*).
*Places to see*: The train travels along the dramatic Gorges of the Coratanne. Ste Croix has two museums and is the world's centre for the recording of the history of the music box and automata.
*Contact details*: Travys SA, quai de la Thiele 32 CP 387, CH-1401 Yverdon-les-Bains. Telephone: 024 424 10 70 Fax : 024 424 10 80. E-mail: info@travys.ch
*Website*: www.travys.ch (fr)
*Operating dates*: Daily services every hour in each direction from 0612 hours to midnight.
*Tariff*: An adult single fare is CHF 9.80 (2007).
*Comments*: Yverdon-les-Bains, with its massive Château d'Yverdon built by Peter II of Savoy in the 13th century, is a delightful town close to Lake Neuchâtel.

A view from Vallorbe's bridge overlooking the river towards the museum which can be seen to the left behind the large metal wheel. *Author*

Coni'fer's Tigerli No. 5 seen here at the highest point on the journey from Chapelle-Mijoux to Les Hopitaux-Vieux on the 9th July, 2006. *Author*

## Museums

### 38 Musée Communal d'Estavayer-le-Lac [SBB Historic]

*Location*: Estavayer-le-Lac, on the southern shore of Lake Neuchâtel, 54 km west south-west of Bern.
*Canton*: Fribourg (FR).
*Michelin map reference*: E5.
*Nearest main line station*: Estavayer-le-Lac.
*Exhibits*: A huge and extensive collection of railway lamps is on display. The museum is also dedicated to the story of frogs!
*Near to here*: Biel-Taulfelen-Ins railway (*see entry 50*).
*Contact details*: Musée Communal, rue du Musée 13, CH-1470 Estavayer-le-Lac. Telephone: 026 663 24 48. E-mail: info@museedesgrenouilles.ch or info@froeschemuseum.ch
*Website*: www.estavayer-le-lac.ch (fr)
*Opening dates*: March to June and September to October open on Tuesdays to Sundays from 1000 to 1200 & 1400 to 1700 hours. In July and August the museum is also open on Mondays for the similar hours. From November to February the museum is open on Saturdays and Sundays from 1400 to 1700 hours.
*Tariff*: An adult is charged CHF 5 and a child CHF 3. There are discounts for groups (2007).
*Comments*: This museum is part of SBB's Heritage Foundation - SBB Historic (*see entry 2*).


### 39 Musée de Fer et Chemin de Fer

*Location*: Vallorbe, 27 km west of Yverdon-les-Bains.
*Canton*: Vaud (VD).
*Michelin map reference*: D5.
*Exhibits*: Various artefacts reflecting the history of the local iron industry and railway. There is a working forge in the museum with expert blacksmiths on hand. There is a model, HO scale, of Vallorbe station *circa* 1908 before the construction of the Mont d'Or tunnel and a 35 minute multimedia show depicting the history of the Paris-Milan line. There is also a model railway display. Allow at least an hour for a worthwhile visit.
*Near to here*: Vallée de Joux services (*see entries 22 and 23*). Just over the border into France and 11 km north at Les Hôpitaux-Vieux is Chemin de Touristique de Pontarlier-Vallorbe also known as Coni'fer which operates steam excursions.
*Places to see*: A beautifully constructed multi-arched stone-constructed viaduct stands at Vallorbe. The viaduct carries TGV trains on the Paris to Milan route. Paris is a 3 hours 15 minutes journey by rail from Vallorbe.
*Contact details*: Musée du Fer et du Chemin de Fer, c/o Office de Tourisme, Grandes Forges de Vallorbe 11, CH-1337 Vallorbe. Telephone: 021 843 25 83 Fax: 021 843 22 62. E-mail: contact@vallorbe.ch and musee.du.fer@bluemail.ch
*Website*: www.vallorbe.ch (fr) and www.vallorbetourisme.ch (fr)
*Opening dates*: Every day from Palm Sunday (*Rameaux*) to 1st November (*Toussaint*) from 0930 to 1200 and 1330 to 1800 hours. Special arrangements can be made to have access out of season.

*Comments*: Vallorbe is a small Jura town on the banks of the River Orbe which owes its existence to iron working. The first factory was opened there in the last quarter of the 13th century due to the necessary resources being ready to hand. The strong river flow activated the waterwheels, wood was in plentiful supply for building and the production of charcoal and most importantly, iron ore was nearby at Mont Orzières. By 1670 Vallorbe was operating three high-furnaces, many refining fires where the iron was cast and about 30 forges. However, by the end of the 17th century the high-furnaces were closing due to the supplies of iron ore being exhausted and coal stripping had ruined the local forest. As a consequence, the local inhabitants had to buy in their supplies of iron and began to specialise by becoming nail makers, farriers, locksmiths and armourers. These activities continued successfully until about the mid-19th century. Since then the manufacturing of tools, chains and files has continued helped by the demand from the local watch industry. The museum, which opened in 1980, is located in a heritage protected site. The buildings are owned by the local town council and also house the tourist office. Metal working has gone on here on this site since 1495. On both sides of the nearby canal fed by the River Orbe's waters, are four waterwheels, formerly of the Grandes Forges and Forge Estoppey which still today operate the working machinery in the museum.

<h3 style="text-align:center">Related Interest</h3>

### 40  Association du Tram 70undefined

*Location*: Geneva.
*Canton*: Geneva (GE).
*Michelin map reference*: C7.
*Nearest main line station*: Geneva.
*Rolling stock*: The beautifully restored Tram No. 70 in its distinctive blue and white livery.
*Contact details*: Association du Tram 70undefined, CH-1211 Geneva 2. Telephone: 07 200 35 20. E-mail: info@tram-bleu.ch
*Website*: www.tram-bleu.ch  (fr)
*History*: Tram No. 70 is one of a series of trams built at the beginning of the 20th century by Herbrand in Cologne and AEG in Berlin. It was saved from the scrap heap in 1997 and restored to its present condition by the Association between 1998 and 2000.
*Comments*: This tram is now fully operational undertaking occasional tours on the tramlines of Geneva alongside its modern counterparts. The tram is available for hire for special events, tours around Geneva's tram network and for general publicity/advertising. Tram 70 features in the book *Les Tramways Genevois* published by Editions Mythraz (see www.mythraz.com ) at the cost of CHF 49.

### 41  Association Neuchâteloise des Amis du Tramway [ANAT]

*Location*: Boudry, 11 km south-west of Neuchâtel.
*Canton*: Neuchâtel (NE).
*Michelin map reference*: E5.
*Nearest main line station:* Boudry.

*Route*: Boudry to Neuchâtel (place Pury) via Areuse, Colombier, Auvernier, Serrières, a total distance of 9 km.
*Journey time*: 35 minutes to Neuchâtel and 29 minutes back to Boudry.
*Tram stock*: 1921-built tram Be 2/2 No. 73 and trailer B 112 active on the route Boudry-Neuchâtel. Kept at the old SBB depot at Le Locle is a 1947-built tram Be 4/4 No. 83 & 1902-built tram Be 2/4 No. 45 and trailers B2i No. 1 & B2 No. 143.
*Near to here*: La Traction (*see entry 34*).
*Places to see*: Lake Neuchâtel, Lac des Brenets near to Le Locle (Watch Valley) and La Chaux-de-Fonds for the Swiss Jura.
*Contact details*: Association Neuchâteloise des Amis du Tramway (ANAT), Case postale 1668, CH-2001 Neuchâtel. E-mail: info@anat.ch
*Website*: www.anat.ch (fr de en)
*Operating dates*: Usually runs on five Sundays during the year. The 2007 dates are 8th April, 13th May, 10th June, 9th September and 7th October with four journeys in each direction, departing Boudry at 1311, 1431, 1551 & 1711 hours and departing place Pury at 1351, 1511, 1631 and 1751 hours.
*Tariff*: Free, but donations are always much appreciated.
*Comments*: The Association was founded in 1976 just as the last urban trams of Neuchâtel were being replaced by modern trolleybuses. The principal objective of the Association is to preserve, restore and where possible to run the old trams and similar transportation of the Neuchâtel area. The local transport company for public transportation in the area of Neuchâtel area, Transports publics du Littoral Neuchâtelois (TN) (*see entry 27*), has been particularly helpful to the Association. For example, for the celebration of the centenary of TN in 1994, the company completely renovated Tram 73 and Trailer 114.


## 42 Trains Touristiques d'Emosson [TTE]

*Location*: Le Châtelard, is situated 23 km west of Martigny via the Forclaz Pass and 19 km north-east of Chamonix via the Montets Pass.
*Canton*: Valais (VS).
*Michelin map reference*: E7.
*Nearest main line station*: Le Châtelard on the Mont Blanc Express (Chemin de fer Martigny-Chatelard) (*see entry 8*). The journey takes 42 minutes.
*Gauge*: Narrow (600 mm) by adhesion only.
*Traction*: Steam- and electric-powered.
*Rolling stock*: A Decauville-type steam locomotive.
*Near to here*: The railways running from Aigle and Bex (*see entries 12, 13, 14 & 15*) and the Swiss Vapeur Park at Le Bouveret (*see entry 44*).
*Places to see*: Mont Blanc - what more can be said?
*Contact details*: Parc d'Attractions du Châtelard VS SA, Gare du Funiculaire, CH-1925 Le Châtelard. Telephone: 027 769 11 11 Hotline: 078 893 42 27 Fax: 027 769 11 15. E-mail: info@emosson-trains.ch
*Website*: www.emosson-trains.ch (fr de it en nl jp es)
*Comments*: Le Châtelard offers three interesting rail attractions - a two-carriage funicular built in 1920 and negotiating a maximum incline of 87 per cent making it the steepest in the world, a small scenic train operating on 600 mm gauge and mini-funicular offering excellent views of the Mont Blanc range in the heart of the Swiss/French Alps.

**43 Geneva Tram Museum - Association Genevoise du Musée des Tramways [AGMT]**

*Location*: Geneva.
*Canton*: Geneva (GE).
*Michelin map reference*: C7.
*Route*: Carouge to Gare Eaux-Vives, a distance of 3.2 km.
*Journey time*: The round trip takes 1 hour 22 minutes.
*Preserved material*: Powered trams: a 1901-built (rebuilt 1936) Be 4/4 No. 67, a 1920-built Be 2/2 No. 125, and a 1952-built Be 4/4 No. 729. Tram trailer carriages: a 1951-built B No. 308, a 1919-built Bi No. 363 and an 1890-built rotary snow clearer (*racleuse à neige*) No. X 603.
*Near to here*: Nyon-St-Cergue-Morez line (*see entry 29*).
*Places to see*: The Old Town of Geneva and the Cathédrale St Pierre.
*Contact details*: Association Genevoise du Musée des Tramways, Case postale 5465, CH- 1211 Geneva 11. E-mail: info@agmt.ch
*Website*: www.agmt.ch
*Operating dates*: Usually the third Sunday in the months of May to September inclusive leaving Carouge (rotunde) in Geneva at 0940, 1110, 1240, 1410, 1540 and 1710 hours. There may also be services on the first Sunday in November.
*Tariff*: An adult fare for the round trip is CHF 6 and for a child (6-16 years) CHF 4. A day ticket can be purchased costing an adult CHF 10 and a child CHF 6 (2006).
*History*: AGMT was founded in January 1973 by a small group of enthusiasts whose objective was to safeguard Be 4/4 No. 67.
*Comments*: AGMT have regular meetings and there is always something happening in every month of the year. Private individuals and organisations can hire the trams and trailers for special occasions. AGMT also catalogues the history of Geneva's tram services with over 9,900 documents including photographs and videos in their archives. Much of this material is available on their website and copies can be downloaded. A bulletin *La Platforme* is regularly published.


**44 Swiss Vapeur Park**

*Location*: Le Bouveret near Villeneuve, 18 km driving distance south-west of Montreux.
*Canton*: Valais (VS).
*Michelin map reference*: E6.
*Nearest main line station*: Le Bouveret. It is also possible to sail over Lac Léman (Lake Geneva) to Le Bouveret from Vevey with the maritime company Bateaux GGN, an adult return fare costing CHF 30 comparing favourably with the return train fare from Vevey of CHF 28.40 (2006).
*Distance*: The track laid totals 1.5 km.
*Gauge*: 7¼ inch.
*Rolling stock*: Most of the numerous locomotives are 1:4 scale. Six locomotives are propelled by steam and six others have built-in gas engines with hydrostatic transmission.
*Near to here*: The townships of Aigle and Bex, the departure points for four mountain railways operated by Transports Publics du Chablais (*see entry 18*).
*Places to see*: Also near to here are the interesting Mines de Sel de Bex (open March to October). Starting on a  former miners' train the visitor is taken to a maze of passages, shafts, stairways and caverns over a surprising 50 km underground - see www.mines.ch  (fr de it en)

*Contact details*: Telephone: 024 481 44 10. E-mail: info@swissvapeur.ch
*Website*: www.swissvapeur.ch (fr de en)
*Operating dates*: From mid-March to mid-October on most days from 1330 to 1800 hours
and from mid-May to mid-September with extended hours from 1000 to 1800 hours.
*Tariff*: Adults are admitted for CHF 14 and children CHF 12 (2007).
*Comments*: The Swiss Vapeur Park is said to be Europe's most beautiful miniature
railway. It features an intricate passenger-carrying miniature railway which takes you past
many of Switzerland's famous beauty spots, albeit at ⅕th of their original size. The route is
set in 17,000 square metres of beautiful parkland. As well as travelling on the train, the
visitor can also view the delightful scenery from the many footpaths throughout the park.


**Discontinued Railway**


**45  Train Touristique Le Rive Bleu Express**

*Location*: Le Bouveret near Villeneuve, 18 km driving distance south-west of Montreux.
*Canton*: Valais (VS)
*Nearest main line station*: Le Bouveret.
*Route*: Le Bouveret-St Gingolph-Evian, a distance of 17 km. The route was
sometimes known as 'Ligne de Tonkin'.
*Gauge*: Narrow (800 mm) and when operating by adhesion only.
*Traction*: Steam.
*Rolling stock*: Steam locomotive E 3/3 No. 2 named *Hansil* was built by SLM at
Winterthur in 1893 (build No. 795). Capable of a maximum speed of 35 km/h it was
used for hauling tourist trains on this line until 1998. It is now to be found in Zürich
(*see entry 80*).
*Contact details*: Association chablaisienne du chemin de fer touristique Rive-Bleue
Express, Case Postale 62 - CH 1897 Le Bouveret. E-mail: ot.bouveret@bluewin.ch
*History*: The railway line traces its history back to 1857 when it was part of the Chemin
de fer d'Italie, a connection between France, Switzerland and Italy. This line carried
passengers and goods traffic until 1938 when the French national railway (SNCF) was
formed and took over responsibility for the railway. However, not long after a quick
decision was made to declare the carriage of passengers as unprofitable and the service
was halted. Goods traffic continued using steam locomotives until 1954 and then electric-
powered traction until the service was finally withdrawn in May 1988. The Train
Touristique had begun running in 1986 and continued after the closure of the main
railway. It enjoyed a relatively successful 10 years but with the departure of the regular
railway and its routine maintenance programme, not least for the track, the condition of
the railway began to deteriorate. As with preserved railways the world over, the issue
became one of financing a track maintenance programme. Sadly, this proved too difficult
and the Rive Bleu Express eventually closed its tourist services down in December 1998.
It was ironic that 1998 had been its best year for the carriage of passengers, a record 6,765.
Initially *Hansli* was put on static display under cover near to the Aquaparc du Bouveret
but was sold on in December 2004 to Zürcher Museums Bahn (*see entry 80*). The
locomotive is still preserved there (2007).
*Comments*: There is a group of enthusiasts with some official backing hoping to
resurrect the railway one day. A website is maintained to keep supporters informed
but unfortunately there have been no updates since April 2005.

# Mittelland, Bernese Oberland and Valais Region (including Bern)

This region is situated left of centre in Switzerland and has international boundaries with France and Italy. It has three cantons: Solothurn (SO), Bern (BE) and Valais (VS). Its principal cities and towns are Bern, Sion and Zermatt. It has 20 railways, two museums and three places for items of related interest. The world-famous Glacier Express leaves Zermatt in this region for St Moritz in Eastern Switzerland (*see entry 3*). German is the principal language spoken.

### Railways

### 46  Aare Seeland mobil AG

*Location*:  Langenthal, 52 km north-east of Bern.
*Canton*:  Vaud (VD).
*Michelin map reference*:  H4.
*Nearest main line station*:  Langenthal.
*Routes*:  Biel-Taufelen-Ins (*see entry 50*); Langenthal-Oensingen (referred to as the Oberaargau). The distance travelled on the BTI route is 21 km and on the Oberaargau route, 22 km.
*Gauge*:  Narrow (metre) by adhesion only for a maximum gradient on the BTI of 4.8 per cent and the Oberaargau of 6.5 per cent.
*Traction*:  Electric-powered on the Biel-Taulfelen-Ins route - 1,300V DC and on the Oberaargau route - 1,200V DC.
*Rolling stock*:  Locomotives: De 4/4 No. 121, Ge 4/4 No. 126 and De 4/4 No. 321. Electric-powered rail cars: Be 4/4 Nos. 101-102, 107, 1103-1104, 301-304 (BTI) & 521, Xe 2/2 No. 508 (BTI), Bme 4/4 Nos. 523-525 (BTI) and Be 2/6 Nos. 558 & 501-507 (BTI). Non-powered rail cars: Bt Nos. 1152-1153, 151, 154, 351-354 & 552 (BTI). Historic vehicles kept: Be 4/4 No. 108, BRe 4/4 No. 116, Br Nos. 161-162 (Seeland) and BRe 4/4 No. 516 (Ankerstube).
*Near to here*:  Regionalverkehr Mittelland at Burgdorf (*see entry 61*) and Verein Historische Eisenbahn Emmental (*see entry 69*).
*Places to see*:  The famous Swiss Langenthal porcelain can be seen at Bleienbachstrasse 22 in the town where there is an outlet store.
*Contact details*:  Aare Seeland mobil AG, Grubenstrasse 12, 4900 Langenthal. Telephone: 062 919 19 11 Fax: 062 919 19 12. E-Mail: info@asmobil.ch
*Website*:  www.aare-seeland-mobil.ch (de)
*Operating dates*:  Daily frequent services, for the timetable consult Aare Seeland's website or go to www.sbb.ch/en where routes and fares can be found.
*Tariff*:  Local fare structure applies which can also be found online.
*History*:  The origins of Aare Seeland mobil go back to 1907, when the Langenthal-Jura Railway (LJB) ran the Oberaargau rail services between Langenthal and Oensingen. BTI began operations in 1916. Over the following years other transport companies merged until when, in 1999, the present company was formed by the merger of four smaller public transport companies in the region. The Ligerz-Tessenberg funicular was added in 2003. After some work this resumed passenger services in 2004 under a new title 'vinifuni'; it has already proved to be a most popular attraction.

*Comments*:  Aare Seeland mobil operates regional passenger services by train and bus in the Oberaargau and Seeland regions with connection to the national and international transport network at Langenthal, Solothurn, Herzogenbuchsee, Biel and Ins. Aare Seeland mobil also provides freight services outside the major commercial centres. There are plans to extend the Biel-Taufelen-Ins railway line from Biel station to Bözingenfeld in 2007.

## 47  Ballenberg-Dampfbahn [BDB]

The UK-based Railway Touring Company chartered the 1926 SLM-built No. 1068 and period carriages for their 'Snow Ice and Steam in Switzerland and Italy' tour. Here the train is seen approaching Grindelwald station from Zweilütschinen on 2nd February, 2007.                                                    *Caroline Jones*

*Location*:  Interlaken, 22 km south-east of Thun.
*Canton*:  Bern (BE).
*Michelin map reference*:  H6.
*Nearest main line stations*:  Interlaken Ost and Giswil.
*Route*:  A popular excursion for this railway is Interlaken Ost via Meiringen to Giswil, a distance of 45 km on what is the main Brünig line.
*Journey time*:  On average 3 hours 48 minutes including stops.
*Gauge*:  Narrow (metre) by adhesion and rack/cogwheel (Riggenbach design) for the Brünig section.
*Traction*:  Steam.
*Rolling stock*:  Cogwheel steam locomotives: No. 1068 built by SLM Winterthur in 1926 (Works No. 3134) and No. 208 also built by SLM but in 1913 (Works No. 2403). Both are coal-fired and have been restored to 'better than new'. They are both actively involved in fulfilling the occasional excursions as well as frequent charters. In the excellent well-equipped spotlessly clean Ballenberg-Dampfbahn workshops steam locomotive C 5/6 (4-cylinder compound) No. 2969 is in the course of restoration.
*Near to here*:  Brünig line (*see entry 84*) and the Bernese Oberland Bahn (*see next entry*).

1926 SLM-built No. 1068 approaching Brünig station having climbed the 12 per cent gradient from Meiringen using the Riggenbach rack system. This photograph was taken on 3rd February, 2007 when the train was chartered by the Railway Touring Company for their 'Snow Ice and Steam in Switzerland and Italy' tour. *Caroline Jones*

1926 SLM-built No. 1068 steam locomotive leaving Wilderswil station for Grindelwald on 2nd February, 2007. Having just arrived is the Bernese Oberland Bahn's ABeh 4/4 No. 312. *Author*

*Places to see*: The north face of the Eiger.
*Contact details*: Ballenberg Dampfbahn, CH-3855 Brienz. Telephone: 033 971 35 87.
E-mail: info@dampfbahnen.ch (de)
*Website*: www.dampfbahnen.ch
*Operating dates*: Steam traction runs on various Sundays during the year. In 2007, the dates on which trains will run will be 15th July, 5th August, 19th August and 2nd & 16th September. The train leaves Interlaken Ost at 0920 and arrives Giswil at 1309 hours. For the return, it departs Giswil at 1445 and arrives back at Interlaken Ost station at 1832 hours.
*Tariff*: Interlaken to Giswill costs an Adult CHF 35 for a single and CHF 48 for a return journey (2007).
*Comments*: The workshops are often open during the week in the daytime whilst maintenance of the rolling stock and restoration of the C 5/6 is being undertaken.

## 48  Bernese Oberland Bahn [BOB]

With the Wetterhorn mountain (3,701 m) in the background one of Bernese Oberland Bahn's ABeh 4/4s with ABt trailers heads for Grindelwald from Zweilütschinen on 9th October, 2006.                                                                     *Author*

*Location*: Interlaken, 22 km south-east of Thun.
*Canton*: Bern (BE).
*Michelin map reference*: H6.
*Nearest main line station*: Interlaken Ost.
*Routes*: Interlaken to: a) Grindelwald; or b) Lauterbrunnen. A combined train leaves Interlaken Ost and travels to Zweilütschinen where it divides with one half going to Grindelwald and the other to Lauterbrunnen. The distances covered for the routes

are: a) 20 km; and b) 19 km. There are a total of 24 bridges and two tunnels on Bernese-Oberland-Bahn's routes.

*Journey times*:  a) 34 minutes; and, b) 20 minutes.

*Gauge*:  Narrow (metre) by adhesion and on a section of 4.6 km by the Riggenbach rack/cogwheel system for the maximum gradient of 12 per cent.

*Traction*:  Electric-powered (1,500V DC).

*Rolling stock*:  Locomotives: He 3/3 Nos. 24 & 29. Electric-powered rail cars: BDeh 4/4 Nos. 302-303, BDe 4/4 Nos. 321-322 and ABeh 4/4 Nos. 304-308, 310 & 311-313. Non-powered rail cars: Abt Nos. 411-415 and BDt Nos. 401-403. Historic vehicles which are preserved are passenger carriage BC4 No. 203 and baggage car D3 No. 515.

*Near to here*:  Meiringen-Innnertkirchen Bahn (*see entry 60*) and Jungfraubahnen services (*see entries 55, 56 & 63*).

*Places to see*:  The valley taking the traveller to Jungfraujoch, the Mönch, the Eiger, the Schilithorn, etc.

*Contact details*:  Jungfraubahnen Hoheweg 37, CH-3800 Interlaken. Telephone: 033 828 72 33 Fax: 033 828 72 60. E-mail: info@jungfrau.ch

*Website*:  Via the parent site www.jungfraubahn.ch (de fr en)

*Operating dates*:  All year with a half-hourly service with five train compositions. At present (2006) compositions must be changed at each terminus to allow the electric railcar to be at the front.

*Tariff*:  An adult 2nd class single fare to Grindelwald is CHF 9.80 and to Lauterbrunnen CHF 6.50 (2007).

*History*:  The railway began operations in 1890 and was electrified in 1914. In 1999, a 2.5 km section of dual track was laid between Zweilütschinen and Wilderswil to reduce delays by allowing trains to pass.

*Comments*:  The centre of Bernese-Oberland-Bahn's operations is at Zweilütschinen where the depot headquarters and the main workshops are located.

An ABeh 4/4 operated by Bernese Oberland Bahn approaching Grindelwald on 2nd February, 2007.                                                                              *Author*

### 49  Regionalverkehr Bern-Solothurn [RBS]

*Location*: Bern, the capital of Switzerland.
*Canton*: Bern (BE).
*Michelin map reference*: G4 and G5.
*Nearest main line station*: Bern.
*Route*: Bern-Solothurn, a distance of 55 km, seven kilometres of which has a third rail for SBB freight use.
*Journey time*: Between 37 and 49 minutes.
*Gauge*: Narrow (metre) by adhesion only for a maximum gradient on this line of 4.5 per cent.
*Traction*: Electric-powered (1,250V DC) except for line G which is 600V DC.
*Rolling stock*: Locomotives: De 4/4 Nos. 101-102 & 103, Ge 4/4 Nos. 111-112 and Gem 4/4 No. 121. Electric-powered rail cars: Be 4/12 Nos. 41-61, Be 4/8 Nos. 81-89 and Abe 4/12 Nos. 62-72. Non-powered rail cars: Bt Nos. 211 & 213. Historic items safeguarded: Bre 4/4 No. 1, CFe 4/4 No. 11, Bt Nos. 222-223, BDe 4/4 No. 6, C 4 No. 61 and C 78.
*Contact details*: Regionalverkehr Bern-Solothurn RBS, Metrohaus, Postfach 119, CH-3048 Worblaufen. Telephone: 031 925 55 55 Fax: 031 925 55 66. E-Mail info@rbs.ch
*Website*: www.rbs.ch
*Operating dates*: Daily with very frequent services - consult local timetables or visit www.sbb.ch/en
*History*: Between 1898 and 1916 four railway lines were constructed to provide an interurban line between Bern and Solothurn and tramways for the northern and eastern suburbs of Bern.


### 50  Biel-Taufelen-Ins [BTI]

*Location*: Biel, 47 km north-west of Bern.
*Canton*: Bern (BE).
*Michelin map reference*: F4.
*Operated by*: Aare Seeland mobil AG.
*Nearest main line station*: Biel.
*Route*: Biel to Ins, a total distance of 21 km.
*Journey time*: 34 minutes.
*Gauge*: Narrow (metre) by adhesion only for a maximum gradient of 4.8 per cent.
*Traction*: Electric-powered (1,300V DC).
*Rolling stock*: Electric-powered rail cars: Be 4/4 301-304 & 521, Xe 2/2 No. 508, Bme 4/4 Nos. 523-525 and Be 2/6 Nos. 558 & 501-507. Non-powered rail cars: Bt 351-354 and Bt 552. Historic vehicles kept by the parent company are: Be 4/4 108, BRe 4/4 116, Br 161, 162 (Seeland) and BRe 4/4 516 (Ankerstube).
*Near to here*: The Museum of Historic Railway Lamps at Estaveyer-le-Lac (sponsored by SBB Historic) (*see entry 38*).
*Places to see*: The route runs alongside the attractive southern coast of Lake Neuchâtel.
*Contact details*: Aare Seeland mobil AG, Grubenstrasse 12, 4900 Langenthal. Telephone: 062 919 19 11 Fax: 062 919 19 12. E-Mail: info@asmobil.ch
*Website*: www.aare-seeland-mobil.ch

A Stadler-built Be 2/6 bearing No. 5021 leaving Biel for Taulfelen on 14th October, 2006.
*Author*

*Operating dates*: Daily services every half-hour.
*Tariff*: An adult 2nd class single is CHF 10.40 (2007).
*Comments*: This line is to be extended in 2007 from Biel to Bözingenfeld.

### 51  Brienz Rothorn Steam Railway (Brienz Rothorn Bahn) [BRB]

*Location*: Brienz, 15 km east of Interlaken at the eastern end of the Brienz lake.
*Canton*: Bern (BE).
*Michelin map reference*: I5
*Nearest main line station*: Brienz.
*Route*: Brienz to Rothorn, a total distance of 7.6 km and rising in altitude by 1,678 metres. There are six tunnels and two galleries on the route.
*Journey time*: 52 minutes.
*Gauge*: Narrow (800 mm) utilising the double lamella rack/cogwheel system designed by Roman Abt for the gradients of up to 25 per cent.
*Traction*: Steam and diesel.
*Rolling stock*: Three coal-fired steam engines (Nos. 1, 2 & 5) built 1891/2, two coal-fired steam engines (Nos. 6 & 7) built in 1933 and 1936, four oil-fired steam engines (Nos. 12, 14, 15 & 16) and, finally, three diesel-hydrostatic engines (Nos. 9, 10 & 11) built between 1975 and 1987.

*Near to here*: Brünig Bahn (*see entry 84*) and the Meiringen-Innertkirchen Bahn (*see entry 60*).

*Places to see*: Brienz is the centre of wood-carving and also undertakes violin making. There are schools here addressing these crafts which can be visited, the latter by prior appointment.

*Contact details*: Brienz Rothorn Bahn, Postfach, CH-3855 Brienz. Telephone: 033 952 22 22 Fax: 033 952 22 13. Railway reservations: Telephone: 033 952 22 22 Fax: 033 952 22 10. Information automatically delivered on telephone 033 952 22 20. The Office secretary's telephone is: 033 952 22 11. Rothorn Kulm Mountain Hotel's telephone is: 033 951 12 21 Fax: 033 951 12 51. Restaurant Rothorn Brienz telephone is: 033 951 11 15 Fax: 033 951 11 02. E-mail: info@brienz-rothorn-bahn.ch and for the hotel: hotel-rothorn@brienz-rothorn-bahn.ch

*Website*: www.brienz-rothorn-bahn.ch (de fr en)

*Operating dates*: Daily, from 17th May to 28th October (extensive servicing is undertaken by the engine drivers in the winter months). Trains leaves Brienz at 0833, 0933, 1005, 1040, 1140, 1240, 1340, 1440, and 1540 hours; there are extra services at 0733 and 1620 in high season

*Tariff*: An adult single ticket for the full journey from Brienz to Rothorn is CHF 46 and for a return CHF 72. Children travel at half price (2007).

*History*: This line has the distinction of being Switzerland's oldest cog railway having been first opened in 1892. With the opening of the nearby Brünig Bahn (*see entry 84*) the idea of a constructing a mountain railway to the summit of the Brienzer Rothorn became a reality. Work began in 1890 and was completed at breakneck speed two years later. The two designers, engineer Lindner and building contractor Bertschinger, were helped by the railway engineer Roman Abt, who equipped the

SLM-built oil-fired steam locomotive No. 12 aided by the Abt rack/cogwheel system pushing its carriages up the incline towards Rothorn Kulm also known as the 'Queen of the Mountains' on 10th October, 2006. *Author*

line with his then newly-developed double lamella rack/cogwheel system. The railway quickly achieved success carrying over 11,000 passengers in its first season. However, there were dark clouds on the horizon as the company got into financial difficulties. Competition with the Schynige Platte Bahn, which had opened in 1895 and the Jungfraubahn three years later, took customers away. The financial problems were further compounded with the outbreak of World War I in 1914. As a consequence, a decision was taken to close the line from the beginning of August 1914. It remained closed for 16 years. In 1931, ironically at the high point in the Depression, a new company was formed to resurrect the railway and its services. It was successful. In the 1940s and 1950s many railways embarked upon programmes of electrification. However, Brienz-Rothorn Bahn decided on a different course of action, i.e. to retain its steam-driven operations. In this it was helped by the Furka Cogwheel Steam Railway, the only railway company at that time with regular steam operations in Switzerland. However, because of the age and condition of the original steam locomotives, it was necessary for Brienz-Rothorn Bahn to purchase four diesel locomotives of the type Hm 2/2 in order to preserve their ageing rolling stock. Nonetheless, steam returned in a novel format, when, in 1992, the Swiss locomotive manufacturer - SLM at Winterthur - built three brand new locomotives for the railway. Brienz-Rothorn Bahn was not the only railway company to see the commercial benefits of steam. Newly constructed locomotives were also supplied to the Montreux-Glion-Rochers-de-Naye railway (*see entry 33*) and to two railways in Austria - the Hochschneeberg and the Schafberg near Krems an der Donau. The locomotives are oil-fired which allows for one-man-operation bringing obvious economies to the company's tourist operations.

Brienz Rothorn's steam locomotive No. 12 leaves Brienz for the summit on 10th October, 2006.                                                                                        *Author*

*Comments*: At the summit there is the Rothurn Kulm hotel. There is excellent walking on the mountain with many way-marked routes which are listed in a pamphlet available from the ticket office at Brienz. There is a 'Friends of the Brienz-Rothorn Steam Railway Association' which raises funds to ensure preservation of the rolling stock and improve facilities; for example, a coal-loading system has recently been installed.


## 52  Verein Dampfbahn Bern

*Location*: Bern, the capital of Switzerland.
*Canton*: Bern (BE).
*Michelin map reference*: H8.
*Nearest main line station*: Bern.
*Route*: Various excursions throughout Switzerland.
*Gauge*: Standard.
*Traction*: Steam and diesel. Deploys locomotives from Burgdorf (RM) (*see entry 61*), Laupen (STB) (*see entry 64*), St Sulpice (VVT) (*see entry 35*) and Spietz (BLS) (*see entry 57*). Dampfbahn Bern has strong cooperative links with Sensetalbahn AG (STB) (*see entry 64*) the former BLS Lötschbergbahn AG, in Bern (E-mail charter@bls.ch) and Regionalverkehr Mittelland at Burgdorf (E–mail: kundencenter.burgdorf@rm-rail.ch). The latter two companies are now (2006) amalgamated as BLS AG (*see entry 57*).
*Rolling stock*: Based at BLS's depot at Spiez is steam locomotive Ed 3/3 No. 3 ex-GTB; based at RM's depot at Burgdorf are steam locomotives Eb 3/5 No. 5810 ex-SBB (in restoration), Ec 4/5 No. 11 ex-SMB, Ed 4/5 No. 8 ex-EB, Ed 3/4 No. 51 ex-BSB (in restoration) and diesel locomotive Breuer Type V No. 3039 ex-Von Roll; based at VVT's St Sulpice depot is steam locomotive E 3/3 No. 855 ex-JS; and based at STB's Laupen depot are steam locomotives E 3/3 No. 1 *Lise* ex-Gaswerk Stadt Bern and E 3/3 No. 853 ex-JS and diesel locomotive Tm 75 ex-BLS No. 235 075. There are also six passenger carriages, three bar carriages, a postal car, a service carriage and a special carriage 'Club Salon Bleu', all being of declared historic interest.
*Contact details*: Verein Dampfbahn Bern, Postfach 5841, CH-3001 Bern. Telephone: 031 302 39 68. E-mail: reisedienst@dbb.ch
*Website*: www.dbb.ch (de)
*Operating dates*: Runs excursions on a number of Sundays each year.
*Comments*: Follow the website to learn when and where excursions are taking place and with what traction/rolling stock.


## 53  Furka Cogwheel Steam Railway (Dampfbahn Furka Berstrecke) [DFB]

*Location*: Realp, 8 km south-west of Andermatt.
*Canton*: Valais (VS).
*Michelin map reference*: J6.
*Nearest main line station*: Realp.
*Route*: From Realp, near to the entrance of the Furka base tunnel, to Gletsch over the Furka pass, a distance of 13 km. There 11 bridges on the route, including the famous Steffenbach bridge constructed in 1925 and re-built in 1988, and five tunnels one being the long summit tunnel.

No. 9 *Gletschhorn* (repatriated from Vietnam) of the Dampfbahn Furka Berstrecke (DFB) about to descend the incline into the village of Gletsch on 30th September, 2006, the penultimate day for the summer season's services.    *Caroline Jones*

**Journey time:** 1 hour 40 minutes from Realp to Gletsch and five minutes longer in the opposite direction.
**Gauge:** Narrow (metre) operating on the rack/cogwheel system of the Abt design for the maximum gradient of 11 per cent.
**Traction:** Steam.
**Rolling stock:** Steam locomotives: a 1902-built HG 2/3 No. 6 *Weisshorn*, a 1913-built HG 3 /4 No. 1 *Furkahorn*, a HG 3/4 No. 2 and a HG 3/4 No. 9 *Gletschhorn*. All the locomotives were constructed by Switzerland's premier engine builder at the time, SLM at Winterthur.
**Near to here:** The Glacier Express (*see entry 3*) passes nearby and through the Furka base tunnel. Also worth seeing is the rack/cogwheel railway operated by the Matterhorn Gotthard Bahn (MGB) running between Göschenen and Andermatt up (or down) the beautiful Schöllenen valley (*see entry 59*).
**Places to see:** Set in outstandingly beautiful but wild scenery, the railway line climbs from a height of 1,538 m at Realp to the top of the Furka Pass at 2,160 m and then descends to Gletsch passing the Rhône Glacier on the way.
**Contact details:** Dampfbahn Furka-Bergstrecke AG, Reisedienst, Postfach 141, CH-6490 Andermatt. Telephone: 084 800 01 44 Fax: 055 619 30 39. E-mail: reisedienst@fu-be.ch (information and reservations).
**Website:** www.furka-bergstrecke.ch (de fr en)
**Operating dates:** Late June to early October on Fridays, Saturdays and Sundays and daily from mid-July to mid-August. Trains depart Realp at 1040 and Gletsch at 1400 hours. Extra services are run in July and August at weekends.
**Tariff:** An adult 2nd class single ticket from Realp to Gletsch is CHF 58 and a return CHF 93. A 1st class single is CHF 96 and a return CHF 154. Children aged 6-16 years travel free if accompanied by one fare-paying parent or grandparent. If unaccompanied, a child pays half the adult fare. Euros are also accepted in payment (2006).

*History*:  The line was originally built between 1911 and 1925 by the Brig-Furka-Disentis railway company (BFD) and later developed by its successor the Furka-Oberalp Railway (FO). The railway used to run only in the summer months due to the harsh winter conditions in the pass. The line was finally closed to traffic in the early 1980s as soon as the 15.3 km long Furka base tunnel was opened in 1982 allowing all year round operations to run between Realp and Oberwald. The Furka-Oberalp Railway planned to remove the old line but fortunately some railway enthusiasts managed to save it from demolition. In 1983, 'Verein Furka-Bergstrecke' (VFB) was founded to restore the former track. Later the Furka Cogwheel Steam Railway was created to re-establish steam operations. The first success came in 1988 when steam locomotive HG 2/3 6 *Weisshorn* was restored to operational order having earlier been reduced to being kept as a static exhibit. In 1990, Verein Furka-Bergstrecke managed to rescue and repatriate some of the original Brig-Furka-Disentis steam engines which had been found to be deteriorating rapidly in Vietnam. These engines, built in 1911, had been sold off in 1941 and moved out to Vietnam. The engines HG 3/4 No. 1 *Furkahorn* and No. 2 were restored by railway workshops in Meiningen, Germany. In 1992, came the re-opening of the first part of the line from Realp to Tiefenbach and some traffic was introduced to it later the same year. In 1993, the line was extended to Furka station. In 1996, the reconstruction of the Furka tunnel was completed making it possible eventually, after much track renewal, to re-open services, but as before, only in the summer months between Realp and Gletsch. It is hoped that one day the line will be re-opened from Gletsch to Oberwald at the other end of the Furka base tunnel which will extend the line by a further 6 km.

*Comments*:  The route from Realp over the Furka Pass to Gletsch passing the receding Rhône Glacier is perhaps one of the most interesting, indeed often most exciting lines in the whole of the Alps.

## 54  Gornergratbahn [GGB]
### formerly known as Gornergrat-Monte-Rosa-Bahnen

*Location*:  Zermatt, south-east of Sion by road 80 km.
*Canton*:  Valais (VS).
*Michelin map reference*:  H8.
*Nearest main line station*:  Zermatt. (NB: automobile traffic is not allowed to travel into Zermatt. The last point to which one can drive is Täsch and thereafter the traveller is obliged to take the modern MGB shuttle train.)
*Route*:  Zermatt to Gornergrat, a total distance of 9.34 km. There are five bridges and five tunnels on the route. There are intermediate stations at Riffelalp, Riffelberg and Rotenboden. The Gornergrat station is opposite the MGB station in Zermatt. It is possible to alight at any station and walk down all or part of the way, or for that matter, up!
*Journey time*:  40 minutes.
*Gauge*:  Narrow (metre) utilising a rack/cogwheel system of the Abt design for the maximum gradient of 20 per cent.
*Traction*:  Electric-powered - three phase (725V 50Hz).
*Rolling stock*:  Locomotives: He 2/2 Nos. 3001-3002. Electric-powered rail cars: Bhe 2/4 Nos. 3011-3022, Bhe 4/8 Nos. 3041-3044, & 3051-3054 and Bhe 4/4 Nos. 3061-3062. Non-powered rail cars: Bt Nos. 3071-3072. Historic stock which is retained: X

Bhe 4/4 No. 3062 awaiting departure at Gornergrat station on 12th October, 2007. The station stands at 3,089 m and as can be seen here one can enjoy a magnificent view of the Matterhorn.       *Author*

Riffelberg station (alt. 2,582 m) on the Gornergratbahn with Bhe 4/8 No. 3051 passing
through in October 2006.                                                    *Author*

3092 Spurpflug, X 3099 Montagewagen, X 3912 Kranwagen and X rot e 3931 & 3932.
It is worth noting that the acquisition of the Bhe 4/4's about 1993 had the effect of
quadrupling the speed of the trains that had originally made the journey. In 1898,
the speed was 7.2 km/h, in 1965 14 km/h and today 28 km/h.

*Near to here*: Matterhorn Gotthard Bahn services (*see entry 59*).

*Places to see*: The Matterhorn and other 4,000 m high mountains - Monte Rosa,
Dom, Weißhorn, Dent Blanche and, of course, the Gornergrat itself.

*Contact details*: Gornergrat Bahn, Nordstrasse 20, CH-3900 Brig. Tel: 027 921 41 11
Fax: 027 921 41 19. E-mail info@gornergrat.ch

*Website*: www.gornergrat.ch (de fr en)

*Operating dates*: Daily with summer departures up from Zermatt at 0710, 0800,
0912, 1000, 1112, 1200, 1312, 1400, 1512  1600, 1712 & 1800 hours and down from
Gornergrat at 0755, 0907, 0955, 1107, 1155, 1307, 1355, 1507, 1619, 1707, 1755 & 1843
hours (2007). As one might expect, given this is a ski resort, there are more services
operating in winter.

*Tariff*: For the complete journey an adult single ticket is CHF 36 and a return CHF
72. Children (6-16 years) travel at half price and under 6-year-olds travel free (2007).

*History*: In the early 1890s the building of this railway was delayed owing to
opposition from the local politicians who thought the local economy and, in
particular, the employment of mountain guides and porters would be adversely
affected. Notwithstanding, the railway was eventually built and services began in
1898. It was the first electric-powered mountain railway to be constructed in the
whole of Switzerland. The 9.3 km-long railway used, then as now, three-phase
current and, like the Brig-Visp-Zermatt (BVZ) railway, was built purely as a tourist

The station at Kleine Scheidegg with the Jungfraubahn's BDhe 4/8 No. 216 about to depart for the terminus at Jungfraujoch which stands at 3,454 m. on 11th October, 2006.

*Author*

service for operation only in the summer months. With the increasing popularity of winter sports, it extended its operations to the winter season. In order to achieve this, avalanche protection had to be installed, especially for the upper sections of the line. When the Gornergratbahn first started operations they ran with what were referred to as 'rowan-trains' i.e. half the first coach of the train's composition was supported by a banking locomotive. After the end of World War II hostilities, faster lightweight rail cars were acquired; however, there are still three of the old locomotives available for use as goods and service trains. The line runs from Zermatt on a gradient of 20 per cent passing through the stations of Riffelalp, Riffelberg and Rotenboden before reaching the Gornergrat mountain station at an altitude of 3,089 m. During the trip there is a continuing view of the Matterhorn in all its splendour (*see back cover*). From Gornergrat station there is a 360° view of a number of mountains in excess of 4,000 m high, e.g. Monte Rosa, Dom, Weißhorn and Dent Blanche. The prime role of the Gornergratbahn in the winter months is to provide easy access to this excellent skiing region. In fact, so popular did the route become that the railway has found it necessary to lay parallel tracks to facilitate passing trains and thereby increase the number of services to cope with demand. The route now between Riffelalp and Riffelboden and Riffelberg and Rotenboden-Gornergrat is mainly twin-tracked. The railway's depot is located near to Zermatt station, the tracks of the depot being in a cavern under the Sunegga mountain.
*Comments*:  The railway was re-named Gornergratbahn in 1998, its centenary year.


### 55 Jungfraubahn [JB]

*Location*:  Interlaken, 68 km south-west of Luzern.
*Canton*:  Bern (BE).
*Michelin map reference*:  H6.
*Nearest main line station*:  Interlaken Ost.
*Route*:  Kleine Scheidegg to the Jungfraujoch, a distance of 11.8 km of which 9.3 km is operational. There are six stations/halts and two tunnels on the route.
*Journey time*:  52 minutes.
*Gauge*:  Narrow (metre) operating on the Strub rack/cogwheel system to travel a maximum gradient of 25 per cent.
*Traction*:  Electric-powered (1125V 50Hz, 3-phase).
*Rolling stock*:  Locomotives: He 2/2 Nos. 8-9 & 10-11. Electric-powered rail cars: BDhe 2/4 Nos. 201-210 and BDhe 4/8 Nos. 211-214 & 215-218. Non-powered rail cars: Bt Nos. 25-34. There is also a rotary snow plough. Historic vehicles safeguarded are: locomotives He 2/2 Nos. 6 & 11 and carriages: B2 Nos. 13 & 17.
*Near to here*:  Wengernalpbahn (*see entry 65*), Brünig Bahn (*see entry 84*) and the Brienz-Rothorn Bahn (*see entry 51*).
*Places to see*:  The mountain terminus at the Jungfraujoch, at an altitude of 3,454 m, houses two underground station halls making it Europe's highest altitude railway station. The line has a 7 km tunnel through the Eiger and the Mönch. There are two intermediate stations blasted out of the rock, one at Eigerwand and the other at Eismeer; both have panoramic windows affording breath-taking Alpine views which are not to be missed.
*Contact details*:  Jungfraubahnen, Harderstrasse 14, CH-3800 Interlaken. Telephone: 033 828 72 33 Fax: 033 828 72 60. E-mail: info@jungfrau.ch or jb@jungfrau.ch
*Website*:  www.jungfraubahn.ch (de en) or www.jungfrau.ch (de en)

A Jungfraubahn maintenance team led by superb teak-constructed traction approaches Kleine Scheidegg station on 11th October, 2006. *Author*

*Operating dates*: All year trains are operating from 0745 to 1845 hours at about half-hour intervals, services varying according to the time of year.
*Tariff*: An adult single fare is CHF 65 and for a return CHF 107. Early birds can buy a 'Good Morning' return ticket for CHF 83 (2007).
*History*: The railway was opened in stages beginning in 1898. Because of financial difficulties during the construction of the great tunnel, it took the constructors seven years to build the final section from Eismeer to Jungfraujoch. Consequently, it was only in 1912 that the Jungfraujoch was eventually reached and rail services first began. Unlike the Wengeralpbahn, which was built using 800 mm gauge, the railway constructors chose metre gauge which they installed with the then newly-designed Strub rack/cogwheel system. Initially, the Jungfraubahn operated on a three-phase electricity supply with a line voltage of 500V 40Hz but this was later changed to what is today's supply, 1,125V 50Hz.
*Comments*: The Jungfrau Railway connects the Kleine Scheidegg station of the Wengernalpbahn with the Jungfraujoch station, the highest in Europe. The line first runs from Kleine Scheidegg to the Eiger Glacier station which also has the record as the highest railway workshop in Switzerland. Thereafter it travels through a long tunnel under the Eiger and the Mönch, then past the Eigerwand and Eismeer stations to reach its destination at the Jungfraujoch. A few of the old locomotive-hauled trains are still kept in reserve today and are occasionally used to meet heavy demand. Incidentally, one the 'rowan-trains' from the early days of the Jungfraubahn's operations and similar to those used on the Gornergratbahn (*see previous entry*), is preserved and is on display in the Transport Museum in Luzern (*see entry 96*). Today, regular traffic is handled by 14 rail cars with matching trailers. Trains leave frequently from Kleine Scheidegg stopping briefly on the ascent at Eigerwand and then at Eismeer so that passengers can absorb the atmosphere and admire the spectacular scenery. The cost of the journey for the train journey some may consider is not cheap but in the author's view it is worth every penny! In winter, special winter sports trains operate every half-hour over the Kleine Scheidegg/Eiger Glacier route.

### 56  Bergbahn Lauterbrunnen-Mürren [BLM]

*Location*: Lauterbrunnen, 9 km south-west of Interlaken.
*Canton*: Bern (BE).
*Michelin map reference*: H6.
*Operated by*: Jungfraubahnen.
*Nearest main line station*: Interlaken Ost.
*Route*: Grütschalp to Mürren, a distance of 4.3 km. with a passing point mid-way.
*Journey time*: 14 minutes.
*Gauge*: Narrow (metre) by adhesion only for a maximum gradient of 5 per cent.
*Traction*: Electric-powered (525V DC).
*Near to here*: Bernese Oberland Bahn (*see entry 48*) and the Wengernalpbahn (*see entry 65*).
*Rolling stock:* Three four-axle rail cars: Be 4/4 Nos. 21-23.
*Places to see*: The car-free town of Mürren from where one can take a cable car to the summit of the Schilithorn (2,970 m) where there is a revolving restaurant.
*Contact details*: Jungfraubahnen, Harderstrasse 14, CH-3800 Interlaken. Telephone: 033 828 72 33 Fax: 033 828 72 60 E-mail: info@jungfrau.ch or jb@jungfrau.ch
*Website*: www.jungfraubahn.ch (de en) or www.jungfrau.ch (de en)

Bergbahn Lauterbrunnen-Mürren's   Be 4/4 No. 23 about one kilometre short of its
destination at Mürren on 11th October, 2006.                                    *Author*

*Operating dates*:   Daily with frequent services every 15 minutes. Consult
Jungfraubahnen timetables for precise timings.
*Tariff*:  An adult single for the Lauterbrunnen-Grütschalp-Murren journey is CHF
9.80 (2007).
*History*:  The railway was first opened to traffic in 1891 with rail cars powered by
electricity from the outset.
*Comments*:  Lauterbrunnen is the terminus of the Bernese Oberland Bahn and also the
arrival/departure point for the Wengernalpbahn Railway and the Bergbahn
(Mountain Railway) Lauterbrunnen-Mürren. The latter service operates in two parts.
Firstly, a funicular travels from Lauterbrunnen up to Grütschalp. (In late 2006, because
of geological problems this access facility was being completely revamped and access
to the railway was only by taking a cable car from Stechelberg further up the valley
directly into Mürren.) The second part of this service is located at Grütschalp where
the metre-gauge adhesion railway is found for the journey to Mürren. As the railway
is independent of the rest of the Jungfraubahnen network, the rail cars are maintained
in a small workshop at Grütschalp. The high-altitude line offers a magnificent view of
the Lauterbrunnen Valley to Wengen with the mountain chain the Eiger, Mönch and
the Jungfrau providing the backdrop. This is a railway not to be missed.

## 57  Lötschbergbahn [BLS AG]

*Location*: Bern, the capital of Switzerland in the north-west part of the country.
*Canton*: Bern (BE).
*Michelin map reference*: H6.
*Nearest main line station*: Bern.
*Routes*: Regional rail passenger services - RegioExpress Berne-Kerzers-Neuchâtel,
RegioExpress Interlaken Ost-Spiez-Zweisimmen (GoldenPass Panoramic),
RegioExpress Berne-Langnau-Lucerne, RegioExpress/Regio Thun-Burgdorf-
Solothurn, Regio Moutier-Solothurn, Regio Langenthal-Wolhusen-Lucerne/
Trubschachen, Regio Payerne-Murten, Regio Kerzers-Lyss-Büren a.a., Regio Spiez-
Reichenbach(-Frutigen), Regio Goppenstein-Brig, Regio Interlaken Ost-Spiez-
Zweisimmen, RegioExpress Spiez-Kandersteg-Brig (starting 2007). S-Bahn
passenger services Bern: Fribourg/Laupen-Berne-Thun, Schwarzenburg-Berne-
Langnau, Biel-Berne-Belp-Thun, Rosshäusern-Berne-Burgdorf-Affoltern-Weier-
Langnau-Wiler, and Berne-Kerzers-Neuchâtel-Murten-Payerne.
*Length of network*: 115 km excluding the 163 km of the recently amalgamated
Regionalverkehr Mittelland AG (*see entry 61*).
*Journey times*: Vary according to routes taken – consult local timetables.
*Gauge*: Standard operating by adhesion only for a maximum gradient of 2.7 per cent.
*Traction*: Electric-powered (15,000V 16.7Hz).
*Rolling stock*: Locomotives: Re 4/4 Nos. 161-189 & 190-195, Re 4/4 II Nos. 420 &
501-506, Re 465 Nos. 001-018 and Re 485 Nos. 001-020. Electric-powered rail cars:
RABe 525 Nos. 001-036 and RBDe 565 Nos. 721-742. Non-powered rail cars: Bt 50 63
20-33 Nos. 950-953, Bt 50 63 29-34 Nos. 990-996 (Bt EW III), ABt 50 63 39-33 Nos. 954-
956, ABt 50 63 39-33 Nos. 971-979, ABt 50 63 39-33 Nos. 982-989, ABt 50 63 39-33 Nos.
992-996, BDt 50 63 82-33 Nos. 939-4 (ex-SBB DZt Nos. 912-4), BDt 50 63 82-33 Nos.
940-941, BDt 50 63 82-33 Nos. 942-945 and BDt 50 63 82-33 Nos. 946-949. Historic
material includes: Ae 6/8 No. 205, Ae 4/4 Nos. 251 & 257-258, Ae 8/8 Nos. 273 &
275, Ed 3/3 No. 3, Ce 4/6 No. 307, Bi 50 63 20-03 No. 052-7 and Be 4/4 No. 761.
*Places to see*: An enjoyable day can be spent in the capital city of Switzerland. It is
possible to visit the Bundeshaus building when Parliament is not sitting. There is an
interesting Museum of Communication in Bern containing, amongst many other
things, one of the world's largest postage stamp collections.
*Contact details*: BLS AG, Genfergasse 11 Postfach, CH-3001 Bern. Telephone: 031
327 27 27 Fax: 031 327 29 10. E-mail: info@bls.ch
*Website*: www.bls.ch (de fr en)
*Operating dates*: Daily frequent services  - consult appropriate local timetables or
go to www.sbb.ch/en
*Tariff*: Local fare structure applies.
*History*: After the Gotthard route commenced operations the net effect was that the
canton of Bern was excluded from the main north-south rail route. Consequently,
the canton decided to create its own rail route, in spite of fierce opposition from the
Federal authorities and as a result the denial of Federal funding. After much local
political debate it was eventually decided that the proposed Lötschberg route would
be selected and to further that choice a company was created - the Bernese Alpine
Railways Company BLS (Bern-Lötschberg-Simplon) in July 1906. One of the most
important major engineering works was the building of the Lötschberg tunnel (*see
next entry*). However, the tunnel was only part of the overall project. What was also
required was the building of the Frutigen-Spiez mountain route, an overall distance

BLS's Bt 50 63 20-33 No. 950, a non-powered rail car, being hauled with other trailers by locomotive Re 4/4 No. 167 seen here at Interlaken Ost station on 13th October, 2006. To the left is BLS's Tea 245 022-9 built by Stadler in 1993.    *Author*

A BLS-Regio service leaving Spiez for Zweisimmen on 13th October, 2006.    *Author*

of 58 km. Work began in October 1906 taking almost seven years to complete for this truly was civil engineering on a massive scale. In all 22 bridges, 33 tunnels and three avalanche galleries were constructed. The railway was officially opened to traffic on 19th June, 1913. Also in 1913, BLS took over the Lake Thun railway (TSB), the consequence being that BLS became the operating company for the Bern-Neuchâtel (BN) railway (43 km), the Gürbetal-Berne-Schwarzenburg (GBS) railway (52 km) and the Spiez-Erlenbach (SEZ) railway (35 km). It also became the proprietor of the shipping company operating on Lakes Brienz and Thun. In 1915, BLS opened the Grenchenberg line between Moutier and Lengnau with its 8.5 km tunnel bringing Lötschberg that much closer to France. Unfortunately (for BLS that is) the importance of this route was diminished when, after the hostilities of World War I had ended, the region of Alsace and Lorraine was returned to France. The consequence of this was it allowed rail traffic to be routed more efficiently and effectively via Basle/St Louis. However, all was not lost for BLS for over the following decades freight traffic increased significantly between Germany and Italy using the Lötschberg-Simplon route. In 1976, Switzerland's Federal council approved a loan of CHF 620 million to upgrade the line to double track. Construction work began in 1977 and was finally completed in 1992. In 1997 BLS merged with the jointly-operated BN, GBS and SEZ railways to form BLS Lötschbergbahn AG. In 2001, an agreement on task sharing was struck between SBB and BLS which was implemented towards the end of 2004. BLS took over the running of SBB's S-Bahn lines and at the same time BLS transferred their long-distance railway operations to SBB, the latter now being responsible for rail network management across Switzerland. Also agreed was that on completion of the NEAT-Lötchsberg project in 2007, BLS will take full responsiblity for all train services on the entire Lötchsberg-Simplon route. (NEAT, incidentally stands for Neue Alpentransversale and also referred to as AlpTransit, a term which perhaps better explains its purpose.) The NEAT project allows for the building of a two-tube base tunnel which will connect Frutigen with the Rhône valley. For financial reasons the project has had to be downsized. At first only one tube will be operational with the other remaining as a shell and the overall length has been reduced from 41 km to 34.6. Nonetheless, this project will bring greater efficiency to operations with trains being able to travel through the tunnel at speeds of between 160 and 200 km/h! It is anticipated, at the time of writing, that the new tunnel will be inaugurated on 15th June, 2007. Full traffic will commence early December 2007 once a new timetable has been implemented. In June 2006, Regionalverkehr Mittelland AG merged with BLS Lötschbergbahn AG to become BLS AG, the outcome being that the new company is now the second biggest (after SBB) operating rail traffic on standard gauge track in the whole of Switzerland. In essence it means that BLS AG covers regional traffic between Lake Neuchâtel and Lake Luzern and between the Jura mountains and the Simplon Massif.

*Comments:* BLS AG, in addition to looking after the former Regionalverkehr Mittelland AG, also oversees the Sensetlbahn's railway operations (*see entry 64*) as well as operating local bus services and boat services for tourists on the lakes Thun and Brienz.

## 58  Lötschberg Tunnel Railway

Automobile-carrying carriages belonging to BLS Autoverla, loaded and about to leave Goppenstein for Kandersteg on 12th October, 2006.                    *Author*

*Location*:  Kandersteg, 37 km south of Thun.
*Cantons*:  Bern (BE) and Valais (VS).
*Michelin map reference*:  H6.
*Operated by*:  BLS AG.
*Nearest main line stations*:  Kandersteg and Brig 30 km south-east.
*Routes*:  a) Kandersteg to Goppenstein, a total distance of 15 km, the tunnel being 14.6 km in length. In winter, when the Goppenstein to Gampel road is closed by adverse weather conditions, the auto train continues beyond Goppenstein to Hohtenn.  BLS also operate, b) the auto train service Kandersteg to and from Iselle in Italy.
*Journey times*:  a) 15 minutes, and, b) 2 hours 20 minutes.
*Gauge*:  Standard operating by adhesion only on a maximum gradient of 2.7 per cent.
*Traction*:  Electric-powered (15,000V 16.7Hz).
*Rolling stock*:  BLS AG Autoverlad operate with eight different types of Sdt 50 63 98-03 vehicle-carrying trailers some being open and others enclosed by roofs. Locomotive types used are listed in the previous entry.
*Places to see*:  The beautiful parish church in the village of Kandersteg.
*Contact details*:  BLS AG, Autoverlad, Genfergasse 11, CH-3001 Bern. Telephone: 031 327 27 27 Fax: 031 327 28 10.  E-mail: autoverlad@bls.ch
*Website*:  www.bls.ch/autoverlad
*Operating dates*:  Daily services to and from Kandersteg and Goppenstein every 30 minutes and at weekends and throughout July and October every 15 to 20 minutes. There is no need to make a reservation. There are significantly fewer services on the

Kandersteg-Iselle service and therefore advanced reservation is strongly recommended.
*Tariff*: Route a) travelling on Mondays to Thursdays a car with up to nine passengers costs CHF 20 and Fridays to Sundays CHF 25, and for route b) CHF 90. Prices are for single journeys (2007).
*History*: The building of the Lötchsberg tunnel was key to the establishment of the Bern-Lötchsberg-Simplon railway route. Construction work on the tunnel began in late 1906 and although initially the Swiss Federal authorities had been fiercely against the project, in 1907 they ordered BLS to enlarge the tunnel to double track. In July 1908 during drilling work under the Gastern valley, large volumes of water and sedimentary rock collapsed into the tunnel gallery. In all 25 Italian miners were killed. As a direct consequence, all construction work was stopped for about six months. The rubble-filled gallery was sealed and a new route was designed to avoid the disaster scene. This meant that three curves had to be constructed effectively lengthening the tunnel by almost a kilometre from its original plan. The mountain was finally tunnelled through on 31st March, 1911. After the construction of the tunnel access ramps and other parts of the route were completed, the line was officially opened to traffic on 19th June, 1913.
*Comments*: This important route allows easy access from say Interlaken at the foot of the Eiger to Zermatt at the foot of the Matterhorn. Automobiles are moved quickly, frequently and efficiently. The cost of the transfer is very reasonable especially when compared with, for example, a journey under the English Channel/La Manche.

### 59  Matterhorn Gotthard Bahn [MGB]

**Location:** Brig, 54 km east of Sion.
*Canton*: Valais (VS).
*Michelin map reference*: H7.
*Routes*: a) Disentis to Brig; b) Andermatt to Göschenen; c) Brig to Zermatt via Visp; d) Car transport between Realp and Oberwald through the Furka base tunnel; and, e) a shuttle service to and from Täsch and Zermatt (a traffic-free environment). MGB also operates with Rhätische Bahn (RhB) (*see entry 101*) the Glacier Express (*see entry 3*).
*Distances*: Overall, the MGB network amounts to 144 km.
*Journey times*: a) 3 hours 52 minutes; b) 15 minutes; c) 1 hour 26 minutes; d) 15 minutes; and, e) 12 minutes.
*Gauge*: Narrow (metre) using both adhesion and rack/cog-wheel. The rack/cogwheel sections operate on the Abt system for the maximum gradient being 17.9 per cent on a section of track which was previously operated by the Schöllenebahn company.
*Traction*: Electric-powered (11,000V 16.7Hz).
*Rolling stock*: The mainstay of the MGB network is the HGe 4/4 II (an example is pictured on page 114), a design which was originally produced for the Brünig railway. Electric-powered locomotives: HGe 4/4 II Nos. 1-5 (ex-BVZ), HGe 4/4 No. 16 (ex-BVZ), Deh 4/4 Nos. 21-24 (ex BVZ). Electric-powered rail cars: BDeh 2/4 Nos. 41-42 & 44-45, BDeh 6/6 Nos. 2031-2032, ABDeh 8/8 class Nos. 2041-2043 and BDSeh 4/8 Nos. 2051-2052. Other traction includes: Gm 3/3 71-72, Tm 2/2 Nos. 73, 74 & 2922, and Xmh 1/2 2962. MGB also preserves steam locomotive HG 2/3 No. 7 and three 'Crocodile' HGe 4/4s Nos. 11, 12 & 15.
*Near to here*: Furka Cogwheel railway (*see entry 53*).

The viaduct at Göschenen with a Deh 4 / 4 pushing its train up towards Andermatt via the Schöllenen valley on 30th September, 2006.

An Andermatt-bound train from Realp hauled by an HGe II locomotive on 30th
September, 2006.                                                        *Author*

*Places to see*: Throughout the network, there are 126 bridges, 8 galleries and 25
tunnels including the Furka base tunnel (length 15,381 m) opened in 1982. The
network connects a total of 47 stations, has its highest bridge - the Mühlebach (45 m)
on the Stalden'Saas-Kalpetran line and the longest - the Grengiois (173 m) on the
Grengiois-Fiesch line. The car-free resort of Zermatt is a place to visit at any time of
the year.
*Contact details*: Matterhorn Gotthard Bahn (MGB), Nordstrasse 20, CH-3900 Brig
Telephone: 027 927 77 77 Fax: 027 927 77 79. E-mail: info@mgbahn.ch
*Website*: www.mgbahn.ch (de fr en)
*Operating dates*: Daily throughout the year with frequent services on all routes.
*Tariff*: Examples of adult 2nd class single fares on the above described routes are: a)
CHF 45; b) CHF 7.20; c) CHF 33; d) A single journey for a car, driver and passengers
is CHF 25 in summer and CHF 30 in winter (October to April ); and, e) CHF 7.80 (2006).
*History*: The Matterhorn Gotthard Bahn was formed on 1st January, 2003 as a result
of a merger of the former Brig-Visp-Zermatt-Bahn (BVZ) and Furka-Oberalp-Bahn
(FO). The history of the two combining railways goes back to the late 19th and early
20th centuries. From the 1860s the mountains near Zermatt had increasingly gained
an attraction to climbers and explorers. The Matterhorn, with its surrounding
mountains, was the huge draw, the more so after Edward Whymper had made the
first successful attempt to conquer it in 1865. Even though his success had been
marred by a tragic accident on the descent, this did not deter the thousands who
wanted to access the area and enjoy Alpine challenges. Tourism had arrived in
Zermatt and there was money to be made. In 1886 two banks, one in Basel and the
other in Lausanne, made application to build a rack railway using the system
designed by Roman Abt. The town of Visp was selected as the starting point and the
first section to Stalden was opened in March 1890. Another section followed in
August of the same year to St Niklaus and eventually Zermatt was reached in July
of the following year. Thus the VZ railway was established but expansion to travel

A car being loaded on to a car-transporter carriage of the MGB Furka base tunnel service heading ultimately for Oberwald.                          *Author*

A shuttle train for transporting foot passengers from Täsch to the car-free resort of Zermatt.
                                                                                  *Author*

further to the east by connecting with what was then the Furkabahn Brig Furka Disentis (BFD) was not possible until the section from Brig to Visp had been opened in 1930. This final connection led directly to the establishment of the Glacier Express service (*see entry 3*). By this time, the then re-named BVZ route had been electrified ((11,000V, 16.7Hz) throughout its 43.9 km length and the 'Crocodile' HGe 4/4 I locomotives had also been introduced. The Furka Oberalp Bahn (FO) began life as the BFD in May 1910. In 1915, after some delay, the Brig to Gletsch route was opened to traffic. However, further development of the line to Andermatt and Disentis was delayed by the combined problems of the difficult challenges presented in building the Furka Scheiteltunnel and also the unhelpful impact of World War I. Both issues led to a financial crisis and the company went bankrupt in 1923. Happily, in 1924, the rescue of the project began with the formation of a group under the leadership of the VZ. In the group were representatives from the three local cantons as well as two neighbouring railways - the Schöllenebahn and the Rhätische Bahn. No time was wasted and so it was, in October 1925, just before the onset of the winter snows, that the first train could run over the entire route from Brig to Disentis. The traction at this time was steam-driven and it was not until the early 1940s that the line was electrified with the financial aid of the Swiss Federation and the muscle of the Swiss military. Electrification, however, did not overcome the suspension of the services in the winter. These were regularly so severe that the overhead power lines had to be dismantled every autumn and re-assembled in the following spring. It was some 40 years after the electrification of the line that the summer service became a year-round operation. This happened in 1982 when the Furka base tunnel was opened. The tunnel has a length of 15.381 km which, at that time, made it the longest narrow-gauge railway tunnel in the world. Incidentally, it held this record until 1999 when the Rhätische Bahn opened the Vereina tunnel with its length of 19.042 km. In 1961, with financial help from the Swiss Government the Schoellenenbahn merged with the FO and then in 2003 the FO merged with the BVZ and the Matterhorn Gotthard Bahn was born. Investment in the railway has continued. For example, there is now a huge new covered car park in the village of Täsch, the furthermost point on the road to Zermatt where one can drive a road vehicle, and where one can take an MGB shuttle rail service into the resort.

## 60 Meiringen-Innertkirchen-Bahn [MIB]

*Location*: Meiringen, 29 km east of Interlaken.
*Canton*: Bern (BE).
*Michelin map reference*: I5.
*Nearest main line station*: Meiringen connecting to Brünig Bahn and other die Zentralbahn services. The nearest SBB stations are at Luzern and Interlaken.
Route: Meiringen-Innertkirchen, a distance of 5 km.
*Journey time*: 11 minutes.
*Gauge*: Narrow (metre) adhesion only for the maximum gradient on this line of 2 per cent.
*Traction*: Electric-powered (1,200V DC).
*Rolling stock*: Powered rail cars: Be 4/4 Nos. 8 & 9.
*Near to here*: The Brünig Bahn (*see entry 84*) can be joined at Meiringen.
*Places to see*: There are two tunnels on the route one of which is the 1,502 m long Kirchentunnel which by-passes the Aare gorge. Meiringen is located near

Meiringen-Innertkirchen-Bahn's Be 4/4 No. 8 has left Innertkirchen station and is travelling the valley alongside the River Aare and heading for Meiringen via the dramatic Aare Gorge on 3rd February, 2007.    *Caroline Jones*

Stadler AG-built two Be 4/4's for the Meiringen-Innertkirchen-Bahn, No. 8 is seen here at Meiringen on 10th October, 2006.    *Author*

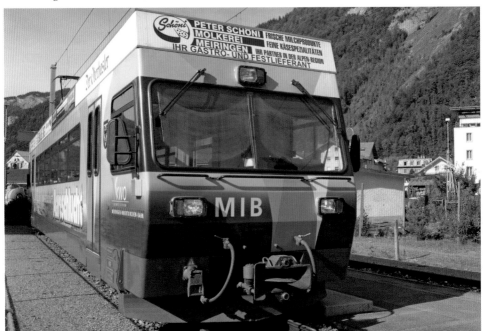

Reichenbachfälle - the waterfalls at which Arthur Conan Doyle set the story of 'the struggle to the death' between Sherlock Holmes and Professor Moriarty. There is a Sherlock Holmes Museum in the basement of the church in Meiringen (open May to September every afternoon except on Monday). A funicular built in 1899 named the Reichenbachfällbahn takes visitors to the 'scene of the murder'. The funicular is open from mid-May to the first week in October. Meiringen, as one might guess from its name, is the home of the meringue. There is a delightful patisserie/café du thé on the main street of the town where one can buy and consume this local delicacy.

*Contact details*: Meiringen-Innertkirchen-Bahn, KWO-MIB, Grimselstrasse, CH-3862 Innertkirchen. Telephone 033 982 26 26 Fax: 033 982 20 05. E-mail: welcome@grimselwelt.ch

*Website*: www.grimselwelt.ch/bahnen/meiringen-innertkirchen-bahn (de)

*Operating dates*: The current timetable identifies up to 25 trains per day in each direction commencing about 0600 and concluding about 1900 hours at half-hourly intervals . The goods traffic is conveyed on demand and consists usually of former SBB Brünig Bahn wagons delivering spare parts for the power stations.

*Tariff*: An adult single ticket is CHF 3.20 and a return CHF 6.40 and for a child (6-16 years) CHF 2.20 and a return CHF 3.20 (2007).

*History*: At the beginning of the 20th century plans were made by the Bernese power stations (BKW) to use water energy for generation of electric power in the Oberhasli and Grimsel passes. A narrow-gauge railway was planned from Meiringen to Guttannen via Innertkirchen by the company Kraftwerke Oberhasli (KWO) which had been formed in 1923. KWO eventually built the narrow gauge railway from Meiringen to Innertkirchen in 1926 for transporting building materials and construction workers. Because of the small population of the valley and also for economic reasons the construction of the part Innertkirchen-Guttannen was abandoned. Instead a system of funiculars was installed for carrying building materials up to the construction sites of the dams and power stations. During the building of the first power plant the Mallet steam engines G 2/2+2/3 No. 23 *Maloja* and No. 24 *Chiavenna*, from the Rhätische Bahn, handled the goods traffic. At the beginning of rail services there was very little in the way of passenger traffic because formal licensing approval had not been granted. Consequently, the carriage of passengers was limited to construction workers and their families. However, in 1946 the Swiss Federal Government gave the necessary approvals and so the Meiringen-Innertkirchen-Bahn was founded. Passenger services were begun using three battery-powered carriages. The first was a twelve-seater Ta 2/2 No. 3 purchased in 1931 followed by two 22 seater CFa 2/2's - No. 4 was acquired in 1939 and No. 5 delivered in 1946. The concession to operate passenger traffic was renewed in 1976 for a further 50 years and so an opportunity was taken to replace track and purchase fresh, albeit second-hand, rolling stock from Germany. However, it was not until after a full 50 years had elapsed from the first opening of passenger services that MIB acquired its first brand new rail car - the current Be 4/4 No. 8, built by Stadler/ABB. As a reserve the MIB has purchased another Be 4/4 now numbered No. 9.

*Comments*: The last stop of the Meringen-Innerkirchen-Bahn is a short distance from the die Zentralbahn (*see entry 95*) station at Meiringen on the Brünig to Interlaken and Brünig to Luzern routes. There is no direct connection between the MIB and other railways owing to the differing electrical power systems. Kraftwerke Oberhasli (KWO) still owns this private railway.

## 61  Regionalverkehr Mittelland AG [RM]

*Location*: Burgdorf, 22 km north-east of Bern.
*Canton*: Bern (BE).
*Michelin map reference*: G4.
*Operated by*: BLS AG since June 2006.
*Route*: The main routes are: a) Affoltern-Langnau-Burgdorf; b) Solothurn-Burgdorf-Rosshäusern; c) Solothurn-Moutier; d) Burgdorf-Konolfigen-Thun; and, e) Langnau-Wohlusen-Luzern/Langnau. The total distance covered by network is 163 km.
*Journey time*: a) 34 minutes; b) 32 minutes; c) 32 minutes; d) 49 minutes; and, e) 1 hour 24 minutes.
*Gauge*: Standard by adhesion only with a maximum gradient of 2.7 per cent.
*Traction*: Electric-powered (15,000V 16.7Hz).
*Rolling stock*: Locomotives: Be 4/4 Nos. 102 & 171, Re 436 Nos. 111-115, and Re 456 142-143 (on hire from Südostbahn). Electric-powered rail cars: BDe 2/4 No. 240, RABe 526 Nos. 260-265 & 280-286, ABe 526 Nos. 290-2, RBDe 566 Nos. 220-227 & 230-242 and De 586 Nos. 257-8. Non-powered rail cars: Bt 50 38 20-03 Nos. 910-911, Bt 50 38 20-33 Nos. 990-4, ABt 50 38 38-33 Nos. 920-927 and ABt 50 38 39-33 Nos. 930-942. Historic vehicles include: BDi 50 38 83-34 Nos. 722-4, WR 50 38 88-03 Nos. 801-808, SR 50 38 89-29 Nos. 802-5 (Bistro Stübli), SR 50 38 89-34 Nos. 803-6, Bi No. 523 (Sennhütte), Bi No. 524 (Schmucktruckli) and Bi Nos. 527 & 538.
*Near here*: Verein Historische Eisenbahn Emmental at Burgdorf (*see entry 69*).
*Places to see*: The old part of the town of Burgdorf with its arcaded houses, Gothic church and a castle founded in the 7th century by the Zähringers.
*Contact details*:  Regionalverkehr Mittelland AG, Bucherstrasse 1-3, CH-3401 Burgdorf.Telephone: 034 424 50 00. E-mail: info@rm-rail.ch
*Website*: www.regionalverkehr.ch/pv/ (de)
*Operating dates and tariff*: Daily frequent services on all routes from 0600 to 2330 hours. Local fare structure applies. Timings and fares can be obtained online by RM's own website or via www.sbb.ch/en
*History*: The first railway between Biberist and Derendingen - the forerunner of the Emmental Railway - was opened as early as the beginning of April 1864, albeit the trams at that time were literally drawn by horse power. The year 1875 saw the Emmental Railway (EB) open the Burgdorf to Solothurn branch line followed in 1881 with the Burgdorf to Langnau (EB). Then in 1889 came the Langenthal to Huttwil (LHB) in 1895, the Huttwil to Wolhusen (HWB) and in 1899 the Hasle to Rüegsau to Thun (HTB). 1908 saw the entry of the Ramsei to Sumiswald to Huttwil route with a line off to Wasen (RSHB). The final railways to join were in 1908 with the Solothurn to Moutier (SMB) and in 1915 the Huttwil to Eriswil (HEB). In 1899 the Burgdorf to Thun line became the first fully electrified railway line in Europe; its success no doubt contributed to the development of electrification throughout Switzerland and neighbouring countries. Regionalverkehr Mittelland AG, itself an amalgamation of three railway companies in 1979 ( EBT, SMB and VHB), was amalgamated with BLS Lötschbergbahn AG in June 2006 to become BLS AG, making it the second largest (after SBB) railway company in Switzerland operating on standard gauge track.

## 62  Oensingen-Balsthal Bahn [OeBB]

The preserved BDe 4/4 No. 1632 standing at Balsthal station  on 14th October, 2006.

*Author*

*Location*:  Oensingen, 49 km south-west of Bern.
*Canton*:  Solothurn (SO).
*Michelin map reference*:  H4.
*Nearest main line station*:  Oensingen.
*Route*:  Oensingen-Balsthal, a distance of 4 km.
*Journey time*:  9 minutes.
*Gauge*:  Standard by adhesion only.
*Rolling stock*:  OeBB safeguards some important historic railway stock including electric-powered rail cars: RBe 2/4 No. 202 Red Arrow, ABDe 4/8 Nos. 244-25, BDe4/4 No. 250 (ex-RM), BDe 4/4 Nos. 1632, 641 & 651 and De 6/6 No. 15301 (Seetalkrokodil - montage). Non-powered rail cars: ABt No. 991 (ex-RM) & Bt No. 900-6. Also retained are locotracteurs: Ce Nos. 102 & 103, electric locomotive RFe 4/4 No. 601, steam locomotives E 3/3 Nos. 1 and 2 (Chluser Schnäggi), Tm 2/2 Nos. 1 & 24, wagons Gklm 091, 159 & 226 (Magazinwagen), Gbs Nos. 1, 2, 4, 6, & 10, Kohlmagazin - E 11 & 12 and carriages WR 401, 402 & 403, AS 411, 412 & 413.
*Near to here*:  Waldenburgerbahn (*see entry 76*).
*Contact details*:  Oensingen-Balsthal-Bahn, 4710 Balsthal, Telephone: 062 391 31 01 Fax: 062 391 17 30. E-mail: info@oebb.ch
*Website*:  www.oebb.ch (de)
*Operating dates*:  Daily, with regular half-hourly services for commuters from 0530 to 2359 hours. Heritage events, including steam excursions, take place on various days throughout the year.

## 63  Schynige-Platte Bahn

He 2/2 No. 61 leading a Schynige-Platte Bahn train down to Wilderswil on 11th October, 2006.                                                                         *Author*

*Location*:  Wilderswil, 3 km south of Interlaken on the route to Lauterbrunnen.
*Canton*:  Bern (BE).
*Michelin map reference*:  H6.
*Operated by*:  Jungfraubahnen.
*Nearest main line station*:  Interlaken Ost.
*Route*:  Wilderswil to Schynige-Platte, a total distance of just over 7.2 km. Schynige Platte is considered by many as one of the best vantage points in the whole of the region.
*Journey time*:  45 minutes.
*Gauge*:  Narrow (800 mm). Rack/cogwheel was adopted at the outset operating on the Riggenbach-Pauli system for the maximum gradient on the line of 25 per cent.
*Traction*:  Electric-powered (1,500V DC).
*Rolling stock*:  Electric-powered locomotives: He 2/2 Nos. 11-20 & 61-63; and, carriages B Nos. 21, 22, 23 24, 3, 41-52, 6, 7 & 8. Retained as of historic interest is H 2/3 No. 5. Some of this rolling stock is used on the Wengernalpbahn (*see entry 65*) in the winter months to help meet the inevitable heavy seasonal tourist traffic.
*Near to here*:  Bernese Oberland Bahn (*see entry 48*).
*Places to see*:  Schynige-Platte is a 2,000 m high plateau with superb views of the two lakes at Interlaken in their mountain setting. Also here is a botanical garden.
*Contact details*:  Jungfrau Railways, Höheweg 37, CH-3800 Interlaken. Telephone: 033 828 72 33  Fax 033 828 72 60. E-mail: info@jungfrau.ch
*Website*:  The website pages for this railway and others are accessible off the main Jungfraubahnen site: www.jungfraubahn.ch/en (de en)

*Operating dates*:  Third week in May to third week in October (2007) from 0600 to 1900 hours with more services when there are longer daylight hours.
*Tariff*:  An adult single ticket from Interlaken Ost via the Bernese Oberland Bahn to Wilderswil and then on the rack/cogwheel to Schynige-Platte is CHF 36.20 and for a return CHF 60.40 (2007).
*History*:  The Schynige-Platte Bahn was inaugurated on 14th June, 1893 and initially was powered by steam locomotives until the line was electrified in 1914. Many of its carriages and locomotives originally started their careers with the Wengernalpbahn.
*Comments*:  The landscape is varied with fertile forests, Alpine pastures and finally a ringside seat of the Bernese Oberland with the Eiger, Mönch and Jungfrau mountains standing in all their majesty. This is not a scene to be missed, summer or winter. The traveller reaches Wilderswil by way of the Bernese Oberland Bahn from Interlaken Ost.


## 64  Sensetalbahn [STB]

*Location*:  Laupen, 20 km west of Bern.
*Canton*:  Bern (BE).
*Michelin map reference*:  F5.
*Operated by*:  BLS AG.
*Route*:  Laupen to Neuenegg, a distance of 7.1 km.
*Journey time*:  6 minutes.
*Gauge*:  Standard by adhesion only.
*Traction*:  Electric (15,000V 16.7Hz) and preserved steam.
*Rolling stock*:  Modern electric-powered rail car. Preserved steam locomotives: E 3/3 No. 1 *Lise* ex-Gaswerk Stadt Bern and E 3/3 No. 853 ex-Jura-Simplon railway, and a diesel locomotive: Tm 75 (ex BLS) No. 235 075.
*Contact details*:  Sensetalbahn AG, Zwyssigstrasse 45, CH-3007 Bern for bus services and for the rail services, BLS AG Genfergasse 11, CH-3001 Bern.
*Website*:  www.stb-bus.ch (de)
*Operating dates*:  Commuter services operate daily on the short Laupen-Neuenegg route at frequent intervals. For the complete timetable consult the website www.sbb.ch/en
*Comments*:  Sensetalbahn receives mention here not for its short distance rail service which is part of a much larger bus operation in the south-west area of Bern, but rather for the historic steam and diesel traction it safeguards.   Their three locomotives contribute regularly to the programme of special historic excursions organised by Verein Dampfbahn Bern (*see entry 52*).


## 65  Wengernalpbahn [WAB]

*Location*:  Lauterbrunnen, 13 km south of Interlaken.
*Canton*:  Bern (BE).
*Michelin map reference*:  H6.
*Nearest main line station*:  Interlaken Ost.
*Routes*:  a) Lauterbrunnen to/from Kleine Scheidegg; and, b) Kleine Scheidegg to/from Grindelwald. (NB: trains do not travel directly from Lauterbrunnen to Grindelwald.) The total distance of operational track is 19 km. There are 28 bridges totalling 599 metres in length on the route and eight tunnels.

Older Wengernalpbahn traction BDhe 4/4 No. 112 with trailer carriage leaving Grund *en route* to Grindelwald on 9th October, 2006. The Eiger stands majestically in the background. *Author*

Modern Wengenalpbahn traction Bhe 4/8 No. 141 arriving at Kleine Scheidegg from Grindelwald on 9th October, 2006. *Author*

Wengernalpbahn's BDeh 4/8 No. 132 approaching Grund from Grindelwald on 2nd February, 2007. The Eiger provides the background. *Caroline Jones*

*Journey times*: a) 45 minutes; and, b) 34 minutes.

*Gauge*: Narrow (800 mm). The railway operates on the Riggenbach-Pauli rack/cogwheel system (which is in the process of conversion to the lamella system) negotiating a maximum gradient of 25 per cent.

*Traction*: Electric-powered (1,500V DC).

*Rolling stock*: Electric-powered locomotives: He 2/2 Nos. 31-32, 51-54 & 64-65. Electric-powered rail cars: BDhe 4/4 Nos. 101-118 & 119-124, BDeh 4/8 Nos. 131-134 and Bhe 4/8 Nos. 141-144. Non-powered rail cars: BT Nos. 211-216, 221-226, 231, 241-244, 251-253 & 261-278.

*Near to here*: There are connections at both Lauterbrunnen and Grindelwald to Bernese Oberland Railways (*see entry 48*).

*Contact details*: Jungfraubahnen, Höheweg 37, CH-3800 Interlaken. Telephone: 033 828 72 33 Fax 033 828 72 60. E-mail: info@jungfrau.ch

*Website*: The website pages for this railway are off of the main Jungfraubahn site, i.e. www.jungfraubahn.ch (de en)

*Operating dates*: Frequent services daily all the year round.

*Tariff*: An adult single fare for route a) CHF 29; and, b) CHF 31 (2007).

*History*: The line was opened in 1893 and electrified between 1909 and 1910.

*Comments*: Wengernalpbahn is the world's longest continuous cogwheel railway with the most active section being from Lauterbrunnen to Wengen. Wengen is a traffic-free zone so the railway plays a key role in the transportation of goods to the village. In the interests of safety the rail cars are always located at the lower end of the train composition which means that trains do not normally cross Kleine Scheidegg. However, there is a triangular section of track built into the mountainside at Kleine Scheidegg which makes it possible trains to be turned if necessary and used on the other side of the pass. This is a very popular railway especially in winter principally because of the excellent skiing facilities which have been developed. Because of this popularity, the Wengernalpbahn often has to borrow carriages from the nearby Schynige-Platte-Bahn to cope with the demand. The Wengernalpbahn depots are located in Lauterbrunnen and at the Grindelwald Grund station.

### Musem/Library/Archive

### 66  Bahn-Treff [SBB Historic]

One of the superb model displays in the SBB-Historic's Bahn-Treff museum at Interlaken.
*Author*

*Location*:  Interlaken, 68 km south-west of Luzern.
*Canton*:  Bern (BE).
*Michelin map reference*:  H6.
*Nearest main line station*:  Interlaken West.
*Exhibits*:  Superbly designed and constructed model railways mainly in HO scale although there is some LGB G-scale.
*Contact details*:  SBB Historic Bahn-Treff, Rugenparkstrasse 24, CH-3800 Interlaken. Telephone: 033 823 25 55. E-mail: bahn-treff@sbbhistoric.ch
*Website*:  www.bahn-treff.ch (de fr it en)
*Opening dates*:  Open on Sundays from end of April to late October from 1100 to 1700 hours. The museum opens an hour earlier from beginning of July to mid-August.

*Tariff:* Adults are charged CHF 10 and children (under 16 years) CHF 5. A family ticket (2 adults with children) costs CHF 24. There are reductions for pre-booked groups (2006).
*Comments:* In 2006 the highlight of the museum was the story of the building of the Simplon Railway and Tunnel which at that time was celebrating its 100th anniversary. This exhibition is part of SBB's Heritage Foundation - SBB Historic (*see entry 2*).


### 67  Library [SBB Historic]

*Location:* Bern.
*Canton:* Bern (BE).
*Michelin map reference:* H6.
*Nearest main line station:* Bern (the library and headquarters of SBB Historic are next door to the main station).
*Archive:* This is Switzerland's most extensive collection of books and magazines on Swiss transportation science and rail history. The library offers documentation and research advice, internet-access, a reading room with reference books, a periodical room with current magazines and current train timetables (including those for non-Swiss railways), background documentation for speakers which can be let out on loan to SBB employees only. There are two archives which can be accessed by prior appointment. Firstly, the Historical Archives which contains texts and plans on the history of the Swiss Federal Railways. Secondly, the Multimedia Archives comprising a large photo archive, film and video archives as well as a large poster collection. The library and archive holdings are continually being amended and updated as new information comes to hand. A recent innovation has been to bring the Historical Archives, the Photo Archive and the Poster and Art collections on line. On www.sbbarchiv.ch there are over 500,000 records and more than 10,000 images available to be viewed. To assist in searching, the website has an extensive help file and a short introduction under the 'Glossary' section.
*Contact details:*  The Library SBB Historic, Bollwerk 12, CH-3000 Bern 65. Telephone: 05 12 20 25 11 Fax: 05 12 20 40 99. E-mail: info@sbbhistoric.ch
*Website:* www.sbbarchiv.ch (de fr it en)
*Opening dates:*  Monday-Friday 9.00-12.00 and 13.30-17.00 hours, or by appointment. Usually closed for the Christmas and New Year fortnight.
*Tariff:* Free.


### Related Interest


### 68  Dampflok-Freunde Langenthal

*Location:* Langenthal, 46 km north-east of Bern.
*Canton:* Bern (BE).
*Michelin map reference:* H4.
*Preserved material:* A superb steam locomotive SMB 2 built by SLM Winterthur in 1907, one of three of the class Ed 3/4 - during its operational career it completed a staggering 1,104,484 km. Also preserved is an ex-CIWL (Compagnie Internationale

de Wagons Lits & des Grands Express Européens) Speisewagen (dining car) No. 2749, formerly 2773 built in 1925, and Gepäckwagen (baggage car) D2 No. 925 built in 1897.
**Contact details**: Dampflok-Freunde Langenthal, zH Sekretariat, Mugenthalstr 41, CH-4900, Langenthal. E-mail: dfl.langenthal@besonet.ch
**Website**: www.dfl-langenthal.ch
**Comments**: This preserved material occasionally is used for excursions - watch the website for details.

### 69  Verein Historische Eisenbahn Emmental [VHE]

**Location**: Burgdorf, 22 km north-east of Bern.
**Canton**: Bern (BE).
**Michelin map reference**: G4.
**Preserved material**: Steam locomotives: Ed 3/4 No. 11 (in the course of restoration) and 64 518 which is in full operating order. Passenger carriages: ABDi 722 (with luggage compartment), Bi Nos. 527, 528 & 538. Restaurant car No. WR 9963 and goods wagon K3 604.
**Contact details**: Verein Historische Eisenbahn Emmental [VHE] Postfach 1574, CH-3401 Burgdorf. E-mail: is via the Kontakt page of the website.
**Website**: www.historische-eisenbahn-emmental.ch/
**Comments**: Excursions using the preserved steam locomotive No. 64 518 take place throughout the year, details of which are regularly posted on the website.

### 70  Verein Pacific 01 202

**Location**: Mühleberg, 17 km west of Bern.
**Canton**: Bern (BE).
**Michelin map reference**: F5.
**Preserved material**: The beautifully preserved and still active Pacific 01 202 built by Henschel & Sohn in Kassel in 1936. This Pacific spent all of its career on the German Railway network starting out first at Dresden, then after the end of World War II it went to Frankfurt. It concluded its main line career in January 1975 at Hof in Bavaria. This organization also looks after the electric-powered locomotive Ae 6/8 No. 208 built by SLM and SAAS in 1939 and formerly operated by the BLS company.
**Contact details**: Verein Pacific 01 202, Wehrstrasse 14, CH-3203 Mühleberg. Fax: 033 345 78 30. E-mail: info@dampflok.ch   For tickets and reservations contact Anita Fankhauser, Ameisenweg 16, CH-3634 Thierachern in writing or via the e-mail address.
**Website**: www.dampflok.ch (de)
**Comments**: This superb locomotive is still very active making regular excursions in Switzerland. The excellent comprehensive website, well worth visiting for more detailed information, also indicates when the Pacific will be operational.

# Northern Switzerland (including Zürich)

This region, as its name indicates, is located in the north of Switzerland and has an international boundary with Germany. It has four cantons: Basel-Stadt (BS), Basel-Landschaft (BL), Aargau (AG) and Zürich (ZH). Its principacities and towns are Basel and Zürich. It has seven railways/routes, three museums and three items of related interest. German is the principal language spoken in the region.

## Railways

### 71 AAR bahn+bus formerly operating as the Wynental und Suhrental Railway [WSB]

*Location*: Aarau, 46 km west of Zürich.
*Canton*: Aargau (AG).
*Michelin map reference*: I3.
*Routes*: a) Aarau to Menziken; and, b) Schöftland to Aarau (Saturdays only). The total distance travelled on the network is 32 km.
*Journey times*: a) 52 minutes; and, b) 21 minutes.
*Gauge*: Narrow (metre) by adhesion only on a maximum gradient of 4.5 per cent.
*Traction*: Electric-powered (750V DC).
*Rolling stock*: Electric-powered locomotives: De 4/4 Nos. 43-45 & 6. Electric-powered rail cars: Be 4/4 Nos. 15-27, 28-34 & 9-14. Non-powered rail cars: Bt Nos. 71-79 and BDt Nos. 80-85. Historic stock retained: Bse 4/4 No. 116 and B2 Nos. 29 & 30.
*Places to see*: Aarau, the capital of the canton, is an attractive town on the banks of the River Aare, its origins going back to the 13th century. There is museum of the town's history in the 11th century castle located on the highest point - the Schlössli.
*Contact details*: AAR bahn+bus, Bahnhof Aarau Hintere, Bahnhofstrasse 48, 5000 Aarau. Telephone: 062 832 83 83 Fax: 062 832 83 93. E-Mail: aarau@aar.ch
*Website*: www.wsb-bba.ch (de)
*Operating dates*: Route a) operates daily frequent services; and, b) on Saturdays only.
*Tariff*: Check locally.
*History*: This railway ran for many years as the Wynental- und Suhrentalbahn (WSB) which was formed in 1958 from an amalgamation of Aarau-Schöftland-Bahn (AS) formed in 1901 and the Wynental-Bahn (WTB) opened three years later. The Wynental-und Suhrentalbahn railway company combined with local Aarau bus services in 2002 and the new company emerged under its new name as AAR bahn+bus.

### 72 Bremgarten-Dietikon Railway [BD]

*Location*: Bremgarten, about 20 km west of Zürich.
*Canton*: Aargau (AG).
*Michelin map reference*: J3.
*Nearest main line station*: Bremgarten.
*Route*: Bremgarten-Dietikon (Route 17 in Zürich urban railway network) a distance of 19 km.

*Gauge*: Narrow (metre) adhesion only on a maximum gradient of 5.6 per cent.
*Traction*: Electric-powered (1,200V DC).
*Rolling stock*: Electric-powered rail cars: Be 4/8 Nos. 21-25, BDe 8/8 Nos. 1-9 and
BDe 4/4 Nos. 10 and 11. The latter is known as *McDonald's Partyzug* and is liveried
accordingly. Of historic interest is C 2 No. 11 (offener Sommerwagen).
*Contact details*: BDWM Transport AG, Zürcherstrasse 10, CH-5620 Bremgarten.
Telephone: 056 648 42 00 Fax: 056 648 42 09. E-mail: info@bdwm.ch
*Website*: www.bdwm.ch and www.bdbahn.ch (which carries a useful and
interesting photo gallery).
*Operating dates*: Daily with frequent services.
*Tariff*: Local fare structure applies.
*History*: The first section of this railway from Wohlen to Bremgarten West opened in 1876 at
that time on standard gauge tracks. In 1902, this was followed with the Dietikon-Bremgarten
section but this time utilising narrow gauge. The problem of different gauges was overcome
in 1912 when the railway bridge over the River Reuss and a third rail was added to the
standard gauge track thus permitting services between Wohlen and Dietikon. In 1916, the
Wohlen-Meisterschwanden (WM) railway began operations and ran for 81 years before it was
converted to being a bus-only operated service. In 2002, it merged with the Bremgarten-
Dietikon (BD) railway thus creating the present company, BDWM Transport AG.
*Comments*: The railway's travel centre at the Bremgarten is also the tourist
information centre for the beautiful town of Bremgarten (Telephone: 0800 888 800 or
056 648 42 07).


### 73  Dampfbahn-Verein Zürcher Oberland [DVZO]

*Location*: Hinwil, 30 km south-east of Zürich and about the same distance south of
Winterthur.
*Canton*: Zürich (ZH).
*Michelin map reference*: J/K3.
*Nearest main line stations*: Bauma and Hinwil.
*Route*: Bauma to Hinwil, a total distance of 11.2 km.
*Journey time*: 40 minutes.
*Gauge*: Standard by adhesion only on a maximum gradient of 2.92 per cent.
*Traction*: Steam- and electric-powered (15,000V 16.7Hz).
*Rolling stock*: Historic coaches and a fully restored buffet wagon. Steam
locomotives which have been run on these rails in recent times are Ed 3/3 No. 2
*Hinwil*, E 3/3 No. 8518 *Baretswil*, E 3/3 No. 10 and E 3/3 *Muni* belonging to Verein
zur Erhaltung der Dampflok Muni (*see entry 115*). Electric-powered rail cars Be 4/4
No. 15 and Be 3/4 No. 1367 have also operated on the route.
*Contact details*: Dampfbahn-Verein Zürcher Oberland , Postfach CH-8340 Hinwil.
Telephone: 052 386 12 41. E-mail: verena.lutz@dvzo.ch (secretary)
*Website*: www.dvzo.ch (de)
*Operating dates*: Trains will run on the following Sundays in 2007: 6th & 20th May,
3rd & 17th June; 1st & 15th July; 5th & 19th August; 2nd & 16th September, and 7th
& 21st October. Steam services leave Bauma at 0930, 1030, 1230, 1330, 1430 and 1530
hours and leave Hinwil at 1030, 1130 1330 1430 1530 and 1630 hours.
*Tariff*: An adult single ticket from/to Bauma and Hinwil is CHF 16 and for a return
CHF 29 (2007).
*Comments*: An active enthusiasts' railway well worth visiting.

## 74 Schinznacher Baumschulbahn [SchBB]
(Schinznach Tree Nursery Railway)

*Location*: Schinznach-Dorf, 47 km west of Zürich.
*Canton*: Aargau (AG).
*Michelin map reference*: I3.
*Nearest main line station*: Schinznach-Dorf.
*Route*: A narrow gauge railway round the garden nursery with a total distance of 3 km.
*Journey time*: 25 minutes with one intermediate stop.
*Gauge*: Narrow (600 mm), the only one in Switzerland.
*Rolling stock*: More then nine locomotives of various types, including a Garratt formerly of South African Railways.
*Near to here*: Bremgarten-Dietikon railway (*see entry 72*).
*Contact details*: Schinznacher Baumschulbahn, (SchBB) Postfach, CH-5107 Schinznach-Dorf. Telephone: 056 463 62 82 Fax: 056 463 62 00. E-mail: direct from the website.
*Website*: www.schbb.ch (de fr en)
*Operating dates*: Late April to early October on Saturdays and Sundays. Steam trains operate from the end of April until the beginning of October every weekend, except for bank holidays. Trains run on Saturdays from 1255 until 1515 and on Sundays from 1330 until 1700 hours at regular 35 minutes intervals. Diesel-hauled trains also operate during season every Wednesday from 1400 until 1630 hours.
*Tariff*: For steam-hauled journeys an adult is charged CHF 6 and a child (aged 6 to 16) CHF 3. There are reductions for groups of 10 persons or more on request. For diesel-hauled journeys an adult is charged CHF 4 and a child CHF 2 (2006).
*Comments*: Features a spectacular narrow gauge railway round a garden nursery and passing through an area of several thousand species of trees and plants as well as crossing a 30 metre long viaduct on its route.


## 75  Sihltal-Zürich-Uetliberg Bahn [SZU] sometimes referred to as Sihltalbahn

*Location*: Zürich.
*Canton*: Zürich (ZH).
*Michelin map reference*: J3 and K4.
*Nearest main line station*: Zürich.
*Route*: Operates: a) Sihltalbahn S4 route (Sihlwald-Zürich HB); and, b) Uetlibergbahn S10 route (Uetliberg-Zürich HB) both meeting the commuter needs of residents of the Zürich area. The entire network has 29 km of track.
*Journey time*: a) 21 minutes; and, b) 26 minutes.
*Gauge*: Standard by adhesion only on a maximum gradient of 7 per cent.
*Traction*: Electric-powered (15,000V 16.7Hz / 1,200V DC).
*Rolling stock*: Electric-powered locomotives: Re 456 Nos. 542-547. Electric-powered rail cars: Be 556 Nos. 521-528 & 531-532 and BDe 576 Nos. 513-514 & 592, 594 & 596. Non-powered rail cars: Bt 50 45 20-03 Nos. 971-973, Bt 50 45 20-33 Nos. 984-987, Bt 50 45 28-29 Nos. 912-913 and Bt 50 45 29-03 Nos. 992-993 & 995. Historic material safeguarded: Ce 026 502-5 *Häde* and C 41.
*Contact details*: Sihltal-Zürich-Uetliberg Bahn, Manessstrasse 152, CH-8045 Zürich. Telephone: 01 205 45 11 Fax: 01 205 45 10. E-mail: info@szu.ch
*Website*: www.szu.ch (de en)

Waldenburgerbahn's powered rail car BDeh 4/4 II No. 11 at Waldenburg station, 14th October, 2006. *Author*

On the afternoon of 14th October, 2006, Waldenburgerbahn's powered rail car BDeh 4/4 II No. 15 climbs up hill to Waldenburg station passing No. 16 parked at the depot. *Author*

*Operating dates*:   Daily frequent services from 0530 to 0015 hours on the Uetlibergbahn S10 and Sihltalbahn S4 routes. Zimmerbergbus also complements these services.
*Tariff*:  Local fare structure applies.
*History*:  This railway company traces back its origins to 1875.
*Comments*:  The company also operates a cable car service - Felseneggbahn and local bus services - Zimmerbergbus.


## 76  Waldenburgerbahn [WB]

*Location*:  Liestal, 18 km south-east of Basel.
*Canton*:  Basel-Landschaft (BL).
*Michelin map reference*:  H3.
*Nearest main line station*:  Basel.
*Route*:  Waldenburg to Liestal, a total distance of 13.1 km.
*Journey time*:  24 minutes.
*Gauge*:  Narrow (750 mm) by adhesion only negotiating a maximum gradient of 3.5 per cent.
*Traction*:  Electric-powered (1,500V DC) and steam.
*Rolling stock*:  Powered rail cars: BDe 4/4 II Nos. 11-17. Non-powered rail cars: Bt Nos. 111-120. Retained of historical interest: As 24 and a 1902-built steam locomotive 3/3 No. 5 *Gedeon Thommen* from SLM at Winterthur.
*Near to here*:  OeBB railway (*see entry 62*).
*Contact details*:  Waldenburgerbahn AG, Haupstrasse 12, CH-4437 Waldenburg. Telephone: 061 965 94 94 Fax: 061 965 94 99. E-mail: info@waldenburgherbahn.ch
*Website*:  www.waldenburgerbahn.ch
*Operating dates*:  Daily with frequent half-hourly services throughout the year from 0530 to 2330 hours.
*Heritage services*:  Steam excursions are run on a number of Sundays during the year. More information can be obtained via the internet by visiting the website www.waldenburgerbahn.ch/dampfzuege/Index-Dampf.htm or by contacting Frau Silvia Schweizer at Waldenburgerbahn AG at the above address. The dates planned for 2007 are 6th May, 10th June, 29th July, 26th August and 23rd September.
*Tariff*:  Local fare structure applies for routine services. For steam excursion the cost of an adult ticket is CHF 19.50 and for a child (6-16 years) CHF 12 (2007).
*Comments*:  The Waldenburg railway with its 750 mm gauge is one of the narrowest gauge railways in Switzerland. It was built in 1880 to provide the residents of the Waldenburg valley with a connection from Liestal to Basel. In the first 70 years of steam service the railway operated with eight locomotives, all except one being built at the SLM works in Winterthur. In 1953, the line was electrified and three rail cars, BDe 4/4 I's, were acquired. In 1985, these were replaced with BDe 4/4 II rail cars and non-powered rail cars. Today, the Waldenburg Railway is regularly used by local residents, thus ensuring the future success of this line.

Zürich's Hardbrucke station.                                                                                      *Author*

Zürcher Verkehrsverbund coordinates all public transport services in the Zürich area including train, bus, trolleybus and tram services. Depicted here is one of the modern trams at the terminus outside Zürich's main station on 4th February, 2007.                                          *Author*

## 77  Zürcher Verkehrsverbund [ZVV]

*Location*: Zürich.
*Canton*: Zürich (ZH).
*Places to see*: The Aviation Museum, Zürich Zoo, Fondue Feast Uetliberg - a fondue feast can be enjoyed on Zürich's local mountain, a short round trip by boat on Lake Zürich, The Rhine Falls at Schaffhausen, and not far away Rapperswil - the city of roses.
*Contact details*: ZVV-Contact, CH-8040 Zürich. Telephone: 0848 988 988 Fax 0848 988 989. E-mail: contact@zvv.ch
*Website*: www.zvv.ch
*Operating dates and tariff*: A day-pass which is valid in all zones after 0900 hours costs an adult CHF 22 and a child CHF 11.
*Comments*: All public transport companies in the Canton of Zürich are linked together as the Zürcher Verkehrsverbund. It provides a comprehensive route network, frequent services at regular intervals and short waiting times for connections. ZVV operates a one-ticket system priced by zone.

### Museums

## 78  Bahnmuseum Kerzers [BMK]

*Location*: Kerzers, 23 km west of Bern.
*Canton*: Fribourg (FR).
*Michelin map reference*: F5.
*Nearest main line station*: Kerzers.
*Rolling stock*: The magnificent 1921-built Ge 6/6 No. 406 'Crocodile', a Montania Benzel locomotive built by Orenstein & Koppel in 1922, a Motorschienen-Draisine No. 3321 built *circa* 1940, two trams Nos. X112 and 13, a landilok BOB No. 26, various locotracteurs including a Jung, various carriages and wagons and signalling equipment and other railway artefacts.
*Contact details*: Bahnmuseum Kerzers (Rolf und Roger Wymann), Aegertenstrasse 2, CH-3210 Kerzers. Telephone: 031 755 89 04   or 031 755 70 20. E-Mail: rolf.wymann@bahnmuseum-kerzers.ch
*Website*: www.bahnmuseum-kerzers.ch
*Opening dates*: From 1st March to 31st October each year.

## 79  SLM Archive [SBB Historic]

*Location*: Winterthur, 25 km north-east of Zürich.
*Canton*: Zürich (ZH).
*Michelin map reference*: K3.
*Nearest main line station*: Winterthur.
*Archive*: SLM was Switzerland's most famous locomotive constructor and here at Winterthur is this important archive open to the public. Stadler (*see entry 116*) now operates the former SLM works at Winterthur.
*Address*: SLM-Archive, SBB Historic, Zurcherstrasse 41, CH-8400 Winterthur.

*Contact details*: via SBB Historic's headquarters in Bern - Telephone: 05 12 20 25 11 Fax: 05 12 20 40 99 and E-mail: info@sbbhistoric.ch
*Website*: www.sbbhistoric.ch/slm-archiv (de fr it en)
*Opening dates*: A visit can be made by prior arrangement with SBB Historic in Bern.
*Comments*: This archive is part of SBB's Heritage Foundation, SBB Historic (*see entry* 2).

## 80  Zürcher Museums-Bahn

*Location*: Zürich, 122 km north-east of Bern.
*Canton*: Zürich (ZH).
*Michelin map reference*: J3.
*Nearest main line station*: Zürich Wiedikon.
*Routes*: Various embracing Zürich Wiediko, Zürich Leimbach, Sihlbrugg, Saalsporthalle, Langnau and Sihhwald. The total distance is 18.6 km.
*Journey times*: Vary according to journey taken. The journey from Zürich Leimbach to Sihhwald, for example, takes 1 hour 9 minutes.
*Gauge*: Standard by adhesion only.
*Traction*: Steam-, electric- and diesel-powered.
*Rolling stock*: An 1899 SLM-built steam locomotive type E 3/3 *Schnaaggi-Schaaggi* (Works No. 1221), a second steam locomotive E3/3 *Hansli* built by SLM in 1893 (Works No. 795) and formerly on the 'Rive Bleu Express' line (now discontinued). Electric-powered rail cars: a 1924-built FCe 2/4 No. 84 *Nostalino*, a 1938-built BDe 2/4 *Degmuetlich Sihltaler* and a 1925-built De 3/4 *Sihtal Krokodil*. Diesel driven: a 1949 Tm 10 and a 1954 Mm 90. Carriages: an 1893-built WR 251 *Spüswageli*, an 1892-built C22, a 1927-built C68, and a 1929-built C69. Wagons: an 1898-built Sihltal-Bahnpostwagen and an 1891-built SOB Packwagen D403.
*Contact details*: Zürcher Museums-Bahn ZMB, Postfach 2172, 8027 Zürich. Telephone: 0848 962 962 Fax: 01 450 45 73. E-Mail: info@museumsbahn.ch
*Website*: www.museumsbahn.ch (de)
*Operating dates*: Steam excursions on various Sundays. In 2007 the following are planned: 8th, 29th April, 27th May, 24th June, 29th July, 26th August, 30th September, 28th October, 1st and 2nd December. The first departure of the day is at 1110 hours from Sihlwald.
*Tariff*: An adult single ticket is CHF 12 and for child (6-16 years) CHF 6 (2007).

## Related Interest

## 81  Association 241 A 65

*Location*: Burgdorf, 22 km north-east of Bern.
*Canton*: Bern (BE).
*Michelin map reference*: J3.
*Traction*: Steam.
*Preserved rolling stock*: The superbly restored 241 A 65 'Mountain' one of 49 built by Fives-Lille in 1931, a number of carriages and wagons and *Roger* a TM II locotracteur.
*Contact details*: Verein 241.A.65, Vreni Holliger, Seetalstrasse 4, CH-5706 Boniswil. Telephone: 079 689 85 55 Fax: 062 777 58 95. E-mail: vreni.holliger@241a65.ch

*Website*: www.241a65.ch (de)
*Comments*: This 'Mountain' occasionally undertakes excursions on standard gauge track in Switzerland. Follow 'News' on the website to learn more of planned outings. The locomotive is available for charter.


## 82 Eurovapor

*Location*: Zürich.
*Canton*: Zürich (ZH).
*Michelin map reference*: J3.
*Contact details*: Eurovapor addresses for its four Swiss sections are listed below.
*Website*: www.eurovapor.ch
*Comments*: Eurovapor, billing itself as 'Nostalgia on Rails', is one of the largest railway clubs in Europe. It has many members who devote their spare time to restoring and maintaining historic locomotives, carriages and other rolling stock at their two bases, one in Switzerland and the other in Southern Germany. Eurovapor organizes from time to time rail excursions in Switzerland and Germany. It has a number of sections, four based in Switzerland and two in Germany.

a) The Club Zürich section has been operating for more than 25 years. There are monthly meetings, usually every third Friday evening in the month. Talks, slide and film shows on railway topics are given and excursions and club trips are also organized from time to time. Club Zürich can be contacted c/o Hans-Joachim Maier, Buechstuden 39, CH-9056 Gais. The telephone number is 071 793 32 53 and e-mail address hajomaier@bluewin.ch
b) The Betrieb Sulgen section was established in 1984 and operates from the former engine sheds near the Sulgen station in the Thurgau canton. The locomotive No. 23 058 is usually stationed there although it also spends time in the Basel area. Since 1997 the section has undertaken restoration work on a Gotthard steam locomotive C 5/6. If the necessary finance is forthcoming this locomotive may again be under steam in 2007. Since 1998, in conjunction with the Rorschach-Heiden Railway (RHB) (*see entry 109*), this section has operated steam trains over the rack/cogwheel line between Rorschach and Heiden with the steam locomotive No. 3 *Rosa* which was originally built for the industrial railroad of the Rueti machine factory. For these trips the RHB uses historic open summer cars or the two historical carriages, Nos. C10 and BC11, which are on permanent loan to them. The DVZO (*see entry 73*) has loaned to this section the Tigerli E 3/3 steam locomotive which is deployed occasionally for special steam excursions in the Thurtal and Lake Constance area. The Betrieb Sulgen section contact details are c/o Chaletstrasse 26a, CH-8583 Sulgen. Fax: 055 240 6784. The e-mail address is webmaster.sulgen@eurovapor.ch
c) The Historic Railroad Emmental section, which was founded in 1997 by members of the former Emmental and Worblaufen sections and the Vereinigte Dampf-Bahnen of Switzerland. The prime focus of this section is to preserve two steam trains which are maintained and operated by club members on the Regionalverkehr Mittelland rail network (*see entry 61*). Until the spring of 2002 the section used to operate narrow gauge steam trains over the regional network Bern - Solothurn (RBS) but these had to be abandoned owing to heavy regular rail traffic and insufficient paths available. The rolling stock of this section is based at Hutwil

where it is maintained by club members in the former VHB shops. This section can be contacted by e-mail on info@historische-eisenbahn-emmental.ch Their website is www.historische-eisenbahn-emmental.ch

d) Basel-Haltingen Nostalgic Rhine River Express section organises historical express train excursions mostly hauled by steam locomotives. Since 1999, more than 100 special trips have been run successfully in Switzerland, Germany and France. In 1997, in conjunction the Swiss Federal Railways (SBB) this historical express train operated during the 150th anniversary year of Swiss Railroads at events in St Gallen, Lausanne and Delemont. The climax was a trip over the Gotthard pass with steam locomotive No. 141 R 1244 from Basel to Mendriso and return. The contact details for this section are c/o Manfred Bitzer, Gundelingerstrasse 135, CH-4053 Basel. Telephone: 061 363 35 32 and Fax: 061 363 35 34.

e) In Germany at Weil am Rhein is Club 41 073 section, its objective being to refurbish the freight steam locomotive No. 41 073 into operational condition and thereafter to deploy it on steam excursions.

f) Also in Germany is the Club Freiburg section which has about 40 active members who meet regularly for talks, slide/film shows and so on.


## 83  Zürich Tram Museum [TMZ]

*Location*: Zürich, 120 km north-east of Bern.
*Canton*: Zürich (ZH).
*Michelin map reference*: J3.
*Nearest station*: Wartau.
*Exhibits*: : Schweizer Tram ZOS Ce 2/2 No. 1, Zürich-Oerlikon-Seebach Ce 2/2 No. 81, Wetzikon-Meilen-Bahn CFe 4/4 No. 2, Umbauwagen Ce 2/2 Nos. 93 & 57, LSB-Postwagen Z 1, Rollwagen X 101, Rangierwagen Xe 2/2 No. 1905 *Laubfrosch*, Kranwagen Xe 2/2 No. 19, Schneefegewagen Xe 2/2 No. 1935, Vierachsanhänger C4 No. 732, Quersitzanhänger C Nos. 626 & 687, 'eingewanderte' Anhänger C 455, Ce 4/4 No. 1392 *Kurbeli*, Ce 4/4 No. 1530 *Pedaler*, Ce 4/4 No. 321 *Elefant*, Ce 2/2 No. 2 *Schnellläufer*, Ce 2/2 No. 176 *Bertschingerwagen*, LSB Ce 2/2 No. 2 *Lisebethli* and Tram Ce 2/2 102.
*Contact details*: Limmatstrasse 260, CH-8049 Zürich. Telephone: 044 634 38 38. E-mail: info@tram-museum.ch
*Website*: www.tram-museum.ch (de fr en)
*Operating dates*: April to October, first Saturday and last Sunday of the month from 1300 to 1800 hours and also on Wednesdays from 1930 to 2130 hours.
*Tariff*: Free (2007).
*Comments*: Has a shop and a model tramway. Tram rides are also offered.

# Central Switzlerland
# (including Ticino)

This region is situated to the right of centre in Switzerland and has an international boundary with Italy. It has seven cantons: Zug (ZG), Luzern (LU), Schwyz (SZ), Uri (UR), Ticino (TI), Nidwalden (NI) and Obwalden (OW. Its principal cities and towns are Luzern and Lugano. It has 12 railways, one museum and one item of related interest. German, Italian and Romansche are the languages spoken in the region.

**Railways**

**84 Brünig Bahn [formerly operated by SBB and now by die Zentralbahn]**

Locomotive He 4/4 No. 101 967-8 approaching the highest point on railway line over the Brünig Pass on 13th October, 2006. *Author*

*Location*: Luzern, 60 south-west of Zürich.
*Canton*: Luzern (LU).
*Michelin map reference*: I5.
*Operated by*: Die Zentralbahn.
*Nearest main line station*: Luzern.
*Route*: Luzern to Interlaken Ost, a total distance of 73 km.
*Journey time*: Between 1½ and 2½ hours according to which service is taken.

The Brunig Bahn's 12 per cent gradient presents a challenge to traction new and old. Here Ballenberg-Dampfbahn's steam locomotive No. 1068 has no problem on the Riggenbach rack as it approaches the summit of the Brünig Pass on 3rd February, 2007. The locomotive and period carriages were on charter on this journey to Luzern from Interlaken Ost to the UK-based Railway Touring Company as one of their excursions on the 'Snow, Ice and Steam in Switzerland and Italy' tour.

*Author*

On 10th October, 2006, having left Brienz, a GoldenPass service hauled by Zentralbahn locomotive HGe 4/4 No. 101 965-2 is headed for Meiringen before the train tackles the Brünig Pass on its way to Luzern.  *Author*

*Gauge*: Narrow (metre) operating by combined adhesion and rack/cogwheel based on the Riggenbach design to negotiate a maximum gradient of 12 per cent.
*Traction*: Electric-powered (15,000V 16.7Hz).
*Rolling stock*: Locomotives: HGe 101 Nos. 101 961-968 and HGm 4/4 Nos. 104 001-3 specifically built for SBB for use on this railway. Electric-powered rail cars: De 110 Nos. 000-005, Deh 120 Nos. 008 & 011 and ABe 130 Nos. 001-010. Non-powered rail cars: ABt 50 85 37-05 Nos. 901-905. Historic stock retained: Deh 120 012-0, Gb-v 2248, A 50 85 17-05 Nos. 111-8 & 181-1, B 50 85 28-05 Nos. 865-6, AB 50 85 38-05 Nos. 473-7, WR 50 85 88-05 No. 426-4, A 50 85 89-05 Nos. 101-2 and D 50 85 92-05 Nos. 610-7.
*Near to here*: There is a wealth of railways close to the Brünig, for example, the Pilatus, (*see entry 92*), the Meiringen-Innertkirchen Bahn (*see entry 60*), Brienz-Rothorn Bahn (*see entry 51*), the Ballenberg (*see entry 47*) and the Bernese Oberland (*see entry 48*) railways, the latter connecting to others such as the Wengernalpbahn (*see entry 65*) and the Schynige-Platte Bahn (*see entry 63*).
*Places to see*: Ballenburg Open Air Museum near Brienz.
*Contact details*: die Zentralbahn AG, Stanserstrasse 2, Postfach 457, CH-6362 Stansstad. Telephone: 051 228 85 85 Fax: 051 228 85 86. E-mail: kundendienst@zentralbahn.ch
*Website*: www.zentralbahn.ch (de)
*Operating dates*: Daily with very frequent services operating between 0600 and 2359 hours.
*Tariff*: An adult 2nd class single ticket from Luzern to Interlaken Ost is CHF 29 and CHF 58 for a return (2007).
*History*: The railway was built in 1888, when it initially linked Brienz with Alpnachstad. Later, in 1889, it was extended to Luzern and finally, in 1913, the Brienz to Interlaken 'lake line' was opened. From the outset and until 1941-42, steam traction operated on the line before the conversion to AC electric power. In June 2006, die Zentralbahn took over the operating responsibility for this line from SBB.

*Comments*: Up until 2006, the Brünig line between Luzern and Interlaken Ost was the only narrow gauge line operated by the Swiss Federal Railways (SBB). Operating in conjunction with the Montreux-Oberland-Bahn (*see entry 4*) it serves the 'Golden Pass of Switzerland' route. The line runs from Luzern passing Alpnachstad to Giswil where it climbs using the rack/cogwheel section of the line. Between Giswil and Brünig-Hasliberg the line climbs to 1,200 m, then drops down to Meiringen, the mid-point of the railway. From Meiringen to Interlaken it runs along the shores of Lake Brienz. At Interlaken it meets the Bernese Oberland Bahn (*see entry 48*) which offers connection to the 'Top of Europe', the Jungfraujoch and other well-known mountains.

### 85  Forchbahn AG [FB]

*Location*: Forch, 12 km south-east of Zürich.
*Canton*: Zürich (ZH).
*Michelin map reference*: J4.
*Nearest main line station*: Zürich (Selnau).
*Route*: Esslingen to Zürich (Stadelhofen) via Egg, Forch, Zumikon and Zollikerberg, a total distance of 18 km.
*Journey time*: 40 minutes.
*Gauge*: Narrow (metre) by adhesion only for a maximum gradient of 6.8 per cent.
*Traction*: Electric-powered (1,200V DC and 600V DC).
*Rolling stock*: Electric-powered rail cars: a 1948-built BDe 4/4 No. 10, 1976-built Be 8/8 Nos. 21-26, 1994-built Be 4/4 Nos. 51-58 and Be 4/6 Nos. 1, 2 & 3. Forchbahn also preserves the 1912-built 24-seater CFe 2/2 No. 4 *Oldtimer* with non-powered rail car seating 56. *Oldtimer* is available for charter costing alone CHF 800 and with its non-powered rail car CHF 850 (2007).
*Contact details*: Forchbahn, Bahnreisezentrum, Kaltensteinstrasse 32, CH-8127 Forch. Telephone: 043 288 11 11 Fax: 043 288 11 10. E-mail: forch@forchbahn.ch and for the *Oldtimer* specials: Forchbahn, Betriebsleitung, CH-8127 Forch. Telephone: 043 288 11 33 Fax: 043 288 11 30. E-mail: info@forchbahn.ch
*Websites*: www.forchbahn.ch (de) and www.vhf-egg.ch (de) is also worth visiting.
*Operating dates*: Daily services throughout the year.
*Comments*: Whilst this is predominantly a routine commuter railway it qualifies for its heritage/tourist entry with its ownership and occasional use of *Oldtimer*.

### 86  Associazione club de San Gottardo

*Location*: Mendrisio, 20 km south of Lugano on the Italian border.
*Canton*: Ticino (TI).
*Michelin map reference*: K8.
*Nearest main line station*: Mendrisio.
*Route*: Mendrisio to Stabio to Valmorea to Cantello, a distance of 9.5 km.
*Journey time*: Vary according to route but on average 30 minutes.
*Gauge*: Standard.
*Traction*: Steam, electric and diesel.
*Rolling stock*: Steam locomotives: a 1910 SLM-built E 3/3 ex-FFS 8501 (Works No. 2076) (used mainly for excursions on selected dates - *see below*), a 1904 SLM-built E

3/3 ex-FSS No. 8463 (Works No. 1623), a 1922 SLM-built Ce 6/8 II ex-GTB No. 312 (Works No. 2773), a 1920 SLM-built Ce 4/4 (ex-Ce 4/6) (Works No. 2494) and a 1932 SLM-built Ae 4/7 ex FSS No. 10997 (Works No. 3536). Also retained is a Saurer-built Tm II No. 785, a 1945-built DM 3634 draisine (SBB/II) and a 1966-built BDe No. 576. Carriages include AB 2ü 161 (1903), AB 2ü 162 (1882), AB 2ü 166 (1906), B 4ü (19??), FNM-A 4(ü) No. Az130 (1924), FNM-A 4(ü) No. A135, FNM-A 4(ü) No. Az136 and a FNM-A 4(ü) No. Az137.

*Near to here*: Ferrovia Lugano-Ponte Tresa (*see entry 88*).

*Places to see*: The Piazza della Riforma in Lugano's historic centre with its colourful and lively street cafés.

*Contact details*: Club del San Gottardo, Casella Postale 1250, CH-6850 Mendrisio. Telephone: 091 646 57 61. E-mail: info@clubsangottardo.ch

*Website*: www.clubsangottardo.ch (it)

*Operating dates*: From June to October on the first and third Sundays of the month. 2007 dates operating on the Valmorea-Cama route are: 7th, 14th May, 2nd, 16th July, 20th August, 17th September, 1st and 15th October and operating on a local Lugano route only on 11th June and 3rd September.

*Tariff*: For the Valmorea-Mendrisio return journey for an adult is CHF 10 and a child (6-16 year) CHF 5. The charges for the Cantello-Valmorea route are CHF 4 and CHF 2 respectively.

*History*: This association of enthusiasts was founded in 1982 with the prime objective of preserving, restoring and occasionally running vintage rolling stock.

*Comments*: Features rare international heritage railway stock and is well worth visiting. The rolling stock is kept in superb condition.


### 87 Guillaume Tell Express operated by Swiss Federal Railways [SBB CFF FFS]

*Location*: Luzern, 60 km south-west of Zürich.

*Canton*: Luzern (LU).

*Michelin map reference*: L7.

*Nearest main line station*: Luzern.

*Route*: Luzern to Flüelen by boat, usually paddle steamer, and then by train to Locarno and Lugano via Göschenen, Biasca and Bellinzona. The total distance for the railway section is 130 km and for the boat voyage 39 km.

*Journey times*: On the boat from Luzern to Flüelen it takes 3 hours 15 minutes and from Flüelen to Lugano on the train a further 2 hours 30 minutes.

*Gauge*: Standard by adhesion only.

*Traction*: Electric-powered (15,000V 16.7Hz).

*Rolling stock*: SBB regular stock.

*Near to here & places to see*: See comments below.

*Contact details*: Via the internet on www.swisstravelsystem.ch  E-mail: via the Kontakt page on the website.

*Website*: www.wilhelmtellexpress.ch (de fr it en)

*Operating dates*: Daily with two journeys in each direction between 1st May and 21st October. Timings are as follows: Travelling north to south - boats leave Luzern at 0921 or 1125 and arrive at Flüelen at 1208 or 1457 hours. Trains leave Flüelen at 1216 or 1516 and arrive at Lugano (having changed at Bellinzona) at 1446 or 1746 hours. Travelling south to north - trains leave Lugano at 0912 or 1212 and (changing at Bellinzona) arrive Flüelen at 1139 or 1438 hours. Boats leave Flüelen at 1220 or

The pleasure boat MV *Brunnen* is about to complete its three hours 15 minutes crossing from Luzern prior to its passengers disembarking and taking the William Tell Express for Lugano.
*Author*

On 8th October, 2006, MV *Brunnen* has come alongside at Flüelen and passengers are disembarking to take the William Tell Express train, the railway platform being less than 100 metres walk away.
*Author*

1503 and arrive in Luzern at 1512 or 1825 hours. It is possible to arrive and depart at/from Locarno which shortens the rail journey times by 27 minutes.
*Tariff:* An adult ticket for a single combined journey on the boat and 1st class rail travel is CHF 158 or with Swiss Card or Swiss Half Fare Card, CHF 98. Children aged 6-16 years travelling with fare paying parents are charged CHF 38 (2007).
*Comments:* The SBB trains offer first-class restaurant facilities. This outstanding journey takes the travellers on the boat past picturesque villages and historic landmarks such as the Rütli and the Tellsplatte. Rütli is where representatives of the cantons of Schwyz, Uri and Unterwalden first met in 1291 and agreed to forge an alliance for what eventually became the Swiss Federation. From Flüelen it is a very short walk from the quay side to the platform to board an air-conditioned first-class panoramic carriage. The train takes its passengers through the fantastic Reuss Valley. The train follows the world-famous Gotthard line climbing 630 metres via numerous spiral and horseshoe-shape tunnels, galleries and bridges especially near Wassen. Such structures are a testimony to the marvellous feats of the engineers who built this railway. Next comes the 15 km-long Gotthard tunnel at Göschenen which claims to be Europe's most important north/south rail route. Certainly, the considerable amount of rail traffic encountered on the route would support that statement. It is said that 50 international express trains and 100 cargo trains pass through the Gotthard tunnel each day and at peak times there may be as many as 270 trains in a day - on average a train every 5 minutes 20 seconds. Swiss timetabling and route management have to be good! Ten minutes later, after emerging from the tunnel, the travellers arrive in the canton of Ticino. Again there follows more horseshoe-shape tunnels, galleries and bridges between Airolo and Giomico in the Leventina Valley crossing breathtaking cantilevered bridges and charming villages on the way down to Bellinzona, Locarno or Lugano.

## 88 Ferrovia Lugano-Ponte Tresa [FLP]

*Location:* Lugano, 76 km north of Milan.
*Canton:* Ticino (TI).
*Michelin map reference:* K7.
*Nearest main line station:* Lugano.
*Route:* Lugano to Ponte Tresa, a total distance of 12.2 km.
*Journey time:* 21 minutes.
*Gauge:* Narrow (metre) by adhesion only for a maximum gradient of 3 per cent.
*Traction:* Electric-powered (1,200V DC).
*Rolling stock:* Powered rail cars: Be 4/12 Nos. 21-25 and Be 4/8 Nos. 41-42 and locomotive (di lavoro) TM 2/2.
*Near to here:* Associazione club de San Gottardo (*see entry 86*), Ferrovia Mesolcinese (*see entry 90*) and the Centovalli railway (*see entry 9*).
*Places to see:* Locarno, Lake Maggiore and the Centovalli (Valley of a Hundred Valleys).
*Contact details:* Ferrovie Luganesi SA, via Stazione 8, CH-6982 Agno. Telephone: 091 605 13 05 Fax: 091 604 61 05 and also Stazione di Lugano, Telephone: 091 923 23 92 Fax: 091 923 23 93. E-mail: stazione.lugano@ticino.com
*Website:* www.flpsa.ch
*Operating dates:* Daily with frequent services (predominantly every 20 minutes) between 0530 and 2345 hours.

A Zentralbahn train on the plain near Grafenort between Engelberg and Stans on 8th October, 2006. The house in the background on the right dates back to 1586.      *Author*

The Riggenbach rack is clearly shown here as the Zentralbahn train descends one of the steeper sections from Engelberg towards the plain and Stans.      *Author*

*Tariff*: An adult single ticket for Lugano-Ponte Tresa is CHF 6.60 (2007).
*History*: Plans to build this railway go back as far as 1870 but it was not until the beginning of 1910 that the Ferrovie Luganesi was formed and work began on building the railway. The line opened to traffic for the first time on 2nd June, 1912. Originally there were also two other railways operating in the area. They were the Lugano-Cadro-Dino (LCD) railway which opened in 1911 and finally stopped all operations in 1970; the other was the Lugano-Tesserete (LT) railway which was the first to begin operations in 1909 and was eventually closed in 1967.
*Comments*: The departure point for FLP trains is situated opposite to the FSS (SBB) station in Lugano in an underground station. Trains leave the station and run through two tunnels under Lugano emerging into the daylight and passing through Agnuzzo, Bioggio and Agno in a wide loop. After Magliaso trains approach another part of the Lake of Lugano with Ponte Tresa station at the end. Up until June 1996, FLP used to operate a pair of mail cars and also had the distinction of using a post office railcar - a Ze 4/4 No. 4 - the only one in Switzerland!

### 89  Luzern-Stans-Engelberg [LSE]
**formerly an independent railway of the same name**

*Location*:  Luzern, 60 km south-west of Zürich.
*Canton*:  Luzern (U).
*Michelin map reference*: I4.
*Operated by*:  Zentralbahn (ZB).
*Nearest main line station*:  Luzern.
*Route*:  Luzern to Engelberg via Stans, a total distance of 24.8 km.
*Journey time*:  Luzern to and from Engelberg takes 53 minutes.
*Gauge*:  Narrow (metre) operating by both adhesion and rack/cogwheel of the Riggenbach design negotiating a maximum gradient of 24.6 per cent for 7.1 km between Obermatt and Engelberg.
*Traction*:  Electric-powered (15,000V 16.7Hz).
*Rolling stock*:  Locomotives: De 4/4 Nos. 121-122. Electric-powered rail cars: BDeh 4/4 Nos. 1-8. Non-powered rail cars: ABt Nos. 23, 24,25, 26-27, 28-30 & 131-132 and At Nos. 21-2.  die Zentralbahn are currently (2007) investing in new rolling stock and have already taken delivery of 10 'Spatz' rail cars built by the Swiss company Stadler (*see entry 116*), the successor to SLM at Winterthur and other companies.
*Near to here*:  Switzerland's most historic funicular - the Stanserhorn.
*Places to see*:  The Benedictine Monastery at Engelberg which is open to visitors.
*Contact details*:  Zentralbahn AG, Stanserstrasse 2, Postfach 457, CH-6362 Stansstad. Telephone: 051 228 85 85 Fax: 051 228 85 86. E-mail: kundendienst@zentralbahn.ch
*Website*:  www.zentralbahn.ch (de)
*Operating dates*:  Daily throughout the year with regular services from 0530 to 2350 hours. Consult www.sbb.ch in a choice of languages.
*History*:  The railway started out life in 1898 as the Stansstad-Engelberg railway (StEB). The line was electrified with three phase current, which was used by both the 'valley' rail cars on the plain and the 'mountain' locomotives. On the plain, traffic was handled by electric-powered rail cars but for the connection with Engelberg these rail cars had to be pushed up the incline by small HGe 2/2 locomotives. However, owing to the failure or inability to replace the ageing rolling stock coupled

with a loss of traffic, the StEB went into bankruptcy in 1964. That same year, a new company was formed, Luzern-Stans-Engelberg (LSE), and a decision made to renew track and rolling stock. A tunnel was also built which allowed for a connection from Stans to Hergiswil on the shores of Lake Luzern. This then made it possible to connect Stans directly with Luzern by sharing the track with the then SBB-operated Brünig line. This arrangement continued until die Zentralbahn took over the responsibility on 1st January, 2005 for the running of both lines as well the Meiringen to Interlaken line further south of the Brünig pass. A tunnel is currently being constructed on route to Engelberg in order to make for easier working by reducing the maximum gradient to 12.5 per cent. However, the completion of the project is delayed owing to geological/water difficulties on the route close to Engelberg.

**90  Ferrovia Mesolcinese [FM] also known as Misoxerbahn**

Former Rhätische Bahn locomotive, BDe 4/4 No. 491, is now preserved and used occasionally for excursions up the Mesolcina valley to Cama from Castione. Here 491 is parked in its open-air storage at Castione, north of Bellinzona on 29th September, 2006.

*Author*

*Location*:  Castione, 34 km north of Lugano.
*Canton*:  Ticino.
*Michelin map reference*:  L8.
*Route*:  Castione to Cama via Grono, a total distance of 13 km.
*Journey time*:  25 minutes.
*Gauge*:  Narrow (metre) by adhesion only.
*Traction*:  Electric-powered (11,000V 16.7Hz).

*Rolling stock*: Historic electric-powered carriages: two 1933-built ABe 4/4 Nos. 1 and 2 formerly numbered AB 41 and 42, red & white in colour, a 1912-built ABe 4/4 No. 3 FLP, blue & white in colour and a 1958-built BDe 4/4 No. 6 ex-RhB/BM formerly No. 491, red in colour. Non-powered rail cars: 1907-built B 51 and 52 ex-RhB/BM, a 1958-built Bt 29 ex-SZB and an 1889-built D 11, ex-RhB.
*Near to here*: Associazione club de San Gottardo (*see entry 86*) and the Centovalli railway (*see entry 9*).
*Places to see*: The Roman Fortress town of Bellinzona with its three different castles.
*Contact details*: Società Esercizio Ferroviario Turistico (SEFT), Casella Postale 2612, CH-6500 Bellinzona. Telephone: 079 262 39 79. E-mail: none available but there is a spoken InfoService on the telephone number listed above.
*Website*: www.seft-fm.ch (de fr it en nl)
*Operating dates*: Various Sundays from June to August. The timetable can be requested from Ente Turistico Bellinzona, Piazza Nosetto 5, CH-6500 Bellinzona. Telephone: 091 825 21 31, Fax: 091 825 38 17. Special trains can be requested in advance by contacting G. Helbling (*chef de service*), Viale G. Motta, CH-6500 Bellinzona.
*Tariff*: An adult return ticket costs CHF 13 and an adult day card is CHF 18 (2006). There are reduced prices for travellers who hold Swiss cards (*see entry 1 for detail of types and costs*) and for groups of at least 10 persons. Children under 16 years travel free if accompanied by at least one fare-paying adult (2006).
*Comments*: The old Misoxerbahn (BM) opened in 1907 and was taken over by the Rhätische Bahn (RhB) in 1942. In 1972, passenger trains ceased but freight continued to be run to and from Mesocco but after 1978 freight only went as far as Cama. The Società Esercizio Ferroviario Turistico (SEFT) was founded in 1995 to operate the Ferrovia Mesolcinese (FM) by running preserved rolling stock between Castione and Cama. SEFT is the owner of the infrastructure and is an independent private railway company. Castione is easily accessible from Bellinzona or Biasca.


### 91 Ferrovia Monte Generoso [MG]

*Location*: Capolago, 15 km south of Lugano.
*Canton*: Ticino (TI).
*Michelin map reference*: L8.
*Nearest main line station*: Capolago.
*Route*: Capolago to Vetta, a distance of 9 km.
*Journey time*: 36 minutes.
*Gauge*: Narrow (800 mm) operating a rack/cogwheel system based on the Abt design. The maximum gradient negotiated on this line is 22 per cent.
*Traction*: Electric-powered (750V DC).
*Rolling stock*: Locomotive: Hm 2/2 No. 7. Electric-powered rail cars: Bhe 4/8 Nos. 11-14. There are two historic items retained G ?? and B2 ?? (more detail not found).
*Near to here*: Associazione club de San Gottardo (*see entry 86*), Ferrovia Mesolcinese (*see previous entry*).
*Places to see*: Como and its lake just inside Italy.
*Contact details*: Ferrovia Monte Generoso SA, CH-6825 Capolago. Telephone: 091 630 51 11. E-mail: info@montegeneroso.ch
*Website*: www.montegeneroso.ch (it)
*Operating dates*: April to November and from about 8th December to 7th January each year with 11 services each day in each direction with the first journey up about

Ferrovia Monte Generoso's Bhe 4/4 No. 13 leaves its departure point adjacent to the SBB station at Capolago for its 36 minute journey up to Vetta close to the summit of Monte Generoso (alt. 1,701 m) on 1st October, 2006. The trailer being pushed at the front contains pedal cycles, it being a popular activity to ride down from the summit. *Author*

Depicted here on 8th October, 2006 is the departure station at Alpnachstad for the Mount Pilatus railway. This railway enjoys climbing a maximum gradient of 48 per cent hence the design of the carriages built as steps. Here at Alpnachstad the gradient as elsewhere on the route is close to its maximum. *Author*

1000 and the last about 1700 hours. There are extra services about 0900 and after 1900 hours in July and August.

*Tariff:* An adult single ticket is CHF 38 and for a child (6-16 years) CHF 19. A family ticket enjoys a 25 per cent reduction. Group discounts can also apply (2007).

*History:* Railway operations on this line first began in 1890.

*Comments:* The view of the lakes from the summit on a clear day is a sight to behold.


## 92  Pilatus Railway [PB]

*Location:* Alpnachstad, 13 km south of Luzern.

*Canton:* Obwalden (OW).

*Michelin map reference:* I5.

*Nearest main line station:* Alpnachstad on the Brünig line (Luzern-Interlaken Ost).

*Route:* Alpnachstad to Pilatus (Fräkmüntegg station) a distance of 4.6 km.

*Journey time:* 30 minutes each way.

*Gauge:* Narrow (metre) operating entirely on the rack/cogwheel designed by Eduard Locher. The Locher system operates two horizontally revolving cogwheels and is the only one of this type in use in Switzerland. The maximum gradient is 48 per cent, making it the steepest rack/cogwheel railway in the world!

*Near to here:* The Brünig Bahn (*see entry 84*) stops at Alpnachstad. The Swiss Transport Museum at Luzern (*see entry 96*) can easily be visited in the same day.

*Places to see:* Lake Luzern pleasure steamers arrive at the quay at Alpnachstad.

*Contact details:* Pilatus Bahnen, Schlossweg 1, CH-6010 Kriens/Luzern. Telephone: 041 329 11 11 Fax No. 041 329 1 12. E-mail: info@pilatus.ch

*Website:* www.pilatus.ch (de fr en)

*Operating dates:* All the year round except for the first two weeks in November when the line is closed for its annual maintenance programme. Pilatus trains leave Alpnachstad every 40 minutes from 0810 until 1735 hours.

*Tariff:* An adult return ticket is CHF 58 and for children (6-16 years) CHF 29. From May to October the 'Golden Round Trip' is offered which comprises a 1st or 2nd class boat trip from Luzern to Alpnachstad, up to Pilatus Kulm, down to Kriens and back to Luzern. The cost for adult travelling 1st Class on the boat is CHF 92.60 and 2nd class CHF 81.60. Children travel at half the adult fare (2006).

*History:* The railway was opened in 1889 and operated steam traction until 1937, the journey time then being 70 minutes. The delay, compared with today's timings, was brought about by the need to stop and take water at the passing station at Amsigenalp. One of the steam-driven rail cars can be seen on static display in the Swiss Transport Museum not very far away in Luzern (*see entry 96*). In May 1937, with the introduction of electrification to the line, the journey time was reduced to 30 minutes.

*Comments:* Pilatus Kulm (the summit) can be reached from Alpnachstad by the train or from Kriens/Lucerne by a panoramic gondola. The latter takes about 30 minutes to glide up the first section to Fräkmüntegg at the foot of Mount Pilatus. From Fräkmüntegg station, an aerial cableway takes gondola passengers to Pilatus Kulm at 2,132 m altitude where they meet those who travelled there by train. In good weather, the view of the Alps and Central Switzerland's lakeland landscape is absolutely stunning.

One of the Pilatus Bahn's Bhe 1/2s, this one being No, 25 which is departing Alpnachstad on 8th October, 2006 for its 30 minute journey up the mountain. The Locher-designed rack is clearly visible.                                                                                                      *Author*

## 93 Rigi Bahnen [VRB & ARB]

The Rigi Bahn station at the water's edge at Vitznau with the modern Bhe 4/4 No. 21 and the older Bhe 2/4 No. 4 on 8th October, 2006. *Author*

*Locations and Cantons*: Vitznau in Luzern, 39 km driving distance east of Luzern and Arth-Goldau in Schywz, 36 km driving distance east of Luzern.

*Michelin map reference*: J4.

*Nearest main line station*: Brunnen.

*Routes*: a) Vitznau to Rigi Kulm (VRB) a travelling distance of 6.8 km and b) Arth-Goldau to Rigi Kulm (ARB) a distance of 9 km.

*Journey times*: a) 30 minutes; and, b) 37 minutes.

*Gauge*: Standard gauge operating entirely on a rack/cogwheel system of the Riggenbach design to negotiate gradients of 25 per cent on the Vitznau to Rigi Kulm route and 20 per cent on the Arth-Goldau to Rigi Kulm route.

*Traction*: Electric-powered (1,500V DC). There are some steam-driven services operated between July and September.

*Rolling stock*: Locomotives: He 2/2 No. 18 & He 2/3 No. 8. Electric-powered rail cars operating on the Vitznau to Rigi Kulm route: Bhe 2/4 Nos. 1-4, Bhe 4/4 Nos. 21-22, BDhe 4/4 No. 5, BDhe 2/3 No. 6 and BDhe 2/4 No. 7 and non-powered rail cars on this route: Bt Nos. 21-24 & 25. Electric-powered rail cars operating on the Arth-Goldau to Rigi Kulm route: BDhe 2/4 Nos. 11-13 & 14 and BDhe 4/4 No. 15 and non-powered rail cars: Bt 31-32. Vitznau to Rigi Kulm traction is liveried in red and white colour and for Arth-Goldau to Rigi Kulm in blue and white. Historic material preserved includes: BD2 Nos. 1-2, 7, 8, 14, 15, & 16, B2(C) No. 11, B2 Nos. 31,32,33, 34 & 35 and steam locomotives H Nos. 16-17.

*Near to here*: Swiss Transport Museum at Luzern (*see entry 96*).

*Places to see*: Glorious scenery with splendid views of the lakes Zugersee and Vierwaldstättersee. The altitude of Rigi Kulm is 1,800 m.

Rigi Bahn's Bhe2/4 No. 4 making its descent from Rigi Kulm on 8th October, 2006. *Author*

*Contact details*: Mt. Rigi Railways, CH-6354 Vitznau. Telephone: 041 399 87 87 Fax: 041 41 399 87 00 or at Mt. Rigi Railways, CH-6353 Weggis - Telephone: 041 41 390 18 44 Fax: 041 41 390 26 10 or at Mt Rigi Railways, CH-6410 Goldau -Telephone: 041 41 859 08 59 & Fax: 041 41 859 08 00. E-mail: rigi@rigi.ch
*Website*: www.rigi.ch (de en)
*Operating dates*: Daily all year round with frequent half-hourly services on both routes. For more precise timings consult the local timetables; however, there is rarely a long wait. Pleasure steamers on the Vierwaldstättersee regularly dock alongside the station at Vitznau.
*Tariff*: An adult single ticket from either Vitznau or Arth Goldau costs CHF 35 and for a child (6-16 years) CHF 17.50. Day cards can be purchased and offer good value for money at CHF 58 and CHF 29 respectively. There are discounts of up to 20 per cent for groups of 10 persons or more travelling (2006).
*History*: The VRB opened in 1871 and the ARB in 1875.
*Comments*: There is a café and shop are near the summit. There are many walks on the Rigi - known as the Queen of the Mountains - from the summit station. The trains have no difficulty in taking wheelchairs and prams. There is plenty of parking at Vitznau, Goldau and Weggis. The local Tourist Office is Weggis Vitznau Rigi Tourism CH-6356 Rigi Kaltbad. Tel. 041 41 397 11 28 Fax 041 41 397 19 82. E-Mail: info.rigi@wvrt.ch


## 94 Sursee-Triengen-Bahn

*Location*: Sursee, 25 km north-west of Luzern.
*Canton*: Luzern (LU).
*Michelin map reference*: I4.
*Nearest main line station*: Sursee (SBB is co-located with the Sursee-Triengen-Bahn at the town's station).
*Route*: The Sursee to Triengen route totals a distance of 8.9 km.
*Gauge*: Standard and by adhesion only.
*Traction*: Steam and diesel.
*Rolling stock*: Steam locomotives: E 3/3 No. 5 built in 1907 by SLM at Winterthur and used by this railway for the 'Komposition Blau' train and E3/3 No. 8522 built in 1913 also by SLM at Winterthur and used for the 'Komposition Rot' train. There is one diesel locotracteur.
*Near to here*: The Swiss Transport Museum at Luzern should not be missed (*see entry 96*).
*Places to see*: Sempacher See, south of Sursee, is an attractive lake to visit.
*Contact details*: Sursee-Triengen-Bahn, Betriebsleitung, Postfach, CH-6210 Sursee. Telephone: 041 921 40 30 Fax: 041 921 42 84. E-mail: via the website or sursee-triengen-bahn@freesurf.ch
*Website*: www.dampfzug.ch (de)
*Operating dates*: Periodic excursions are made by these locomotives but the railway pays for much of its way by offering charters for special events.
*Tariff*: A chartered train from Sursee to Triengen or Triengen to Sursee costs CHF 800, Sursee to Triengen and back costs CHF 1,000 and Triengen to Sursee and back costs CHF 900 (2007).
*Comments*: Watch the website for details of events. On the website there is a comprehensive history of the preserved locomotives as well as an extensive photo gallery. The locomotives are all in a beautiful condition having been lovingly restored and are well worth seeing. A shop sells books, cards and other souvenirs on site and by mail order.

## 95 Zentralbahn

Zentralbahn's HGe 4/4 No. 101 965-2 for use on part of the Brünig line between Interlaken and Luzern seen here at the Interlaken Ost station on 10th October, 2006.

*Author*

*Location*: Stansstad, 11 km south of Luzern.

*Canton*: Nidwalden (NW).

*Michelin map reference*: J5.

*Routes*: Zentralbahn offers the following routes: a) Giswil to Interlaken; b) Luzern to Giswil; c) Stans to Engelberg; d) Meiringen to Interlaken; e) Hergiswil to Luzern; f) Stans to Luzern; and, g) Sarnen to Luzern. The network totals 98.6 km of which 10.93 km operates on the Riggenbach rack/cogwheel system on the Brünig Bahn and 7.1 km also on the Riggenbach system on the Luzern-Stans-Engelberg route between Obermatt and Engelberg.

*Journey times*: a) 1 hour 14 minutes; b) 44 minutes; c) 37 minutes; d) 36 minutes; e) 14 minutes; f) 22 minutes; and, g) 30 minutes.

*Gauge*: Narrow (metre) adhesion only on all the network except on the Brünig and the Luzern-Stans-Engelberg routes where there is a combination of adhesion with rack/cogwheel operation.

*Traction*: Electric-powered (15,000V 16.7Hz).

*Rolling stock*: On the Luzern-Stans-Engelberg line: locomotives: De 4/4 Nos. 121-122. Electric-powered rail cars: BDeh 4/4 Nos. 1-8. Non-powered rail cars: ABt Nos. 23, 24,25, 26-27, 28-30 & 131-132 and At Nos. 21-2. On the Brünig Bahn: locomotives: HGe 101 Nos. 961-968 and HGm 104 001-3 specifically built for SBB for use on this railway. Electric-powered rail cars: De 110 Nos. 000-005, Deh 120 Nos. 008 & 011 and ABe 130 'Spatz' Nos. 001-010. Non-powered rail cars: ABt 50 85 37-05 Nos. 901-905. Historic stock retained: Deh 120 012-0, Gb-v 2248, A 50 85 17-05 Nos. 111-8 & 181-1, B 50 85 28-05 Nos. 865-6, AB 50 85 38-05 No. 473-7, WR 50 85 88-05 No. 426-4, A 50 85 89-05 No. 101-2 and D 50 85 92-05 Nos. 610-7. Zentralbahn is in the process of renewing much of its material. The current inventory counts 228 items of rolling stock.

*Contact details*: Zentralbahn AG, Stanserstrasse 2, Postfach 457, CH-6362 Stansstad. Telephone: 051 228 85 85 Fax: 051 228 85 86. E-mail: kundendienst@zentralbahn.ch *Website*: www.zentralbahn.ch (de)
*Operating dates and tariff*: Daily local services on all lines. Consult local timetables or select journey and fare online at www.sbb.ch/en The fares for routes identified above are: a) CHF 20.80; b) CHF 11.40; c) CHF 10.40; d) CHF 11.40; e) not known; f) CHF 7.20; and, g) CHF 7.80 (2007).
*Comments*: Die Zentralbahn was formed on the 1st January, 2005 as a result of taking over the responsibility from SBB for the Brünig line (*see entry 84*) and combining with its own LSE services (*see entry 89*). A new and distinctive red and white livery was designed for the new company and this has been applied to most if not all of the earlier rolling stock. The company is responsible for 129 bridges/viaducts, 15 tunnels and 36 stations. The highest point trains reach on the network is 1,001 m (Brünig-Hasliberg) and the lowest, 436 m at Luzern. In July 2005 the company employed 282 people.

## Museums

### 96  Swiss Transport Museum (Verkehrshaus der Schweiz)

This is a wealth of Swiss railway and other transport material to be seen in the superb transport museum at Luzern. Here a 3/3 No. 1063 has been cut away to illustrate how a steam locomotive works.                                                                                         *Author*

*Location*:  Luzern, 53 km south-west of Zürich.
*Canton*:  Luzern (LU).
*Michelin map reference*: I4.

Static displays include the inevitable Swiss rotary snow plough pictured here with 2/2 No. 11 built by SLM Winterthur in 1911. *Author*

'Krokodil' No. 402 on permanent display in the Swiss Transport Museum at Luzern. *Author*

*Nearest station*: Luzern.
*Exhibits*: Said to contain one of the world's great railway collections, the museum certainly is well worth a visit; allow at least half a day to gain maximum benefit.
*Contact details*: Lidostrasse 5, CH-6006 Luzern. Telephone: 041 370 44 44. E-mail: mail@verkehrshaus.ch
*Website*: www.verkehrshaus.org (de fr it en)
*Operating dates*: Daily - March to October from 1000 to 1800 hours and from November to February closing an hour earlier.
*Tariff*: An adult entrance ticket costs CHF 24, for a child (6-16 years) CHF 12 and under six year olds enter free (2007). Hotel guests may be able to obtain vouchers giving a discount on entrance prices.
*Comments*: Also has a restaurant and shop. This museum exhibits part of SBB's Heritage Foundation (SBB Historic) railway rolling stock and other artefacts. A Garden Steam miniature railway runs outside the Railways Exhibtion Hall - children are carried free of charge.The Transport Museum addresses more than just railways - all modes of transport are exhibited including two full-sized aeroplanes. Adjoining the Transport Museum is the IMAX Theatre which can be visited for an extra fee. A number of 40 minute high quality films are shown on a huge screen; the current choices are Bears, Sacred Planet, Vikings, Coral Reef Adventure and the Mystery of the Nile. There is also a marvellous Planetarium.


## Related Interest


### 97  Mikado 1244

*Location*: Turbenthal, 14 km south-east of Winterthur.
*Canton*: Schweiz.
*Michelin map reference*: J3.
*Traction*: Steam and electric.
*Rolling stock*: Steam locomotive 141 R (Mikado) No. 1244 (oil fired) built in 1946 by the Montreal Locomotive works; it is currently being overhauled. Also preserved is electric-powered Ae 4/7 No. 11026 built by ADtranz in 1923, a diesel-powered Scheinen TM II No. 826 and an EW II passenger carriage completely restored from what was a badly damaged state by the club's volunteer members.
*Contact details*: Mikado 1244, Postfach, CH-8488 Turbenthal.
*Website*: www.mikado1244.ch (de en)
*History*: In 1975, as steam operations in France came abruptly to an end the club Mikado 1244 was founded in Zürich by a group of Swiss steam enthusiasts. By way of a connection with SNCF, the club learned of the whereabouts of several American-built Mikados and acting quickly they managed to secure No. 1244 which is now restored to its original condition.
*Comments*: The club Mikado 1244 organizes trips using one of the locomotives with their 1st Class carriage together with additional stock sometimes chartered from the Swiss Federal Railways or elsewhere.

# Eastern Switzerland
# and Graübunden

This region, as its name indicates, is situated in the east of Switzerland and has international boundaries with Germany, Austria, Italy and Lietchenstein. It has seven cantons: Schauffhausen (SH), Thurgau (TH), Appenzell-Ausserhoden (AR), St Gallen (SG), Appenzell-Innerrhoden (AI), Glarus (GL) and Graubünden (GR). Its principal cities and towns are St Gallen and St Moritz. It has 16 railways/routes, no museums, two items of related interest and one project. German, Italian and Romansch are the languages spoken in the region.

## Railways

### 98 Appenzellerbahnen [AB]

A modern non-powered rail car Abt No. 111 awaits departure from Gais station bound for Altstatten on 5th October, 2006. Alongside are two of the finely preserved carriages resplendent in their former SGA green and cream livery. *Author*

**Location:** Appenzell, 80 km east of Zürich.
**Canton:** Appenzell Innerrhoden (AI).
**Michelin map reference:** N4.
**Nearest main line stations:** St Gallen or Gossau.
**Routes:** a) St Gallen-Appenzell; b) Altstatten-Gais; c) Gossau-Appenzell-Wasserauen; and, d) Speicherschwendi-Teufen (bus & rail). Now also part of the Appenzellerbahnen are Trogenerbahn (*see entry 112*), Rheineck-Walzenhauzen (*see entry 108*) and Rorschach-Heiden (*see entry 109*) routes. The total distance covered by the network amounts to 59.8 km.
**Journey times:** Consult local timetables according to route(s) taken. For the routes listed above the timings are: a) 46 minutes; b) 22 minutes; c) 54 minutes; and, d) 43 minutes.

*Gauge*: Narrow (metre) operating by combined adhesion and rack/cogwheel based on the Riggenbach-Klose system and the Strub system for a maximum gradient of 16 per cent.
*Traction*: Electric-powered (1,500V DC).
*Rolling stock*: Locomotive: Ge 4/4 No. 1. Electric-powered rail cars: ABDeh 4/4 Nos. 6-7, BDeh 4/4 Nos. 11-15, BDeh 4/4 Nos. 16-17, BDe 4/4 II Nos. 31-33, BDe 4/4 II Nos. 34-35, Abe 4/4 Nos. 41-42 and BDe 4/4 Nos. 46-47. Non-powered rail cars: Abt Nos. 111-115, 116-117, 121-123, 131-133, 134-135 & 146-147 and Ast No. 181 Rubino (ex-B 82). Of historical interest: steam locomotive G 3/4 No. 14, electric-powered rail cars: BCe 4/4 No. 30, B(Ck) No. 39, BCFm 2/4 No. 56 & BCFeh 4/4 No. 5. Also preserved are a variety of A2 & B2 carriages in the former St Gallen-Gais livery and various other carriages and wagon of various vintages and histories.
*Near to here*: The Frauenfeld-Wil-Bahn (*see entry 100*) and Bodensee-Toggenburg Bahn (*see next entry*).
*Places to see*: The mountains of the Ebenalp and Säntis dominate the landscape.
*Contact details*: Appenzellerbahnen, Bahnhofplatz 10, CH-9101 Herisau. Telephone: 071 354 50 60 Fax: 071 354 50 65. E-mail: info@appenzellerbahnen.ch
*Website*: www.appenzellerbahnen.ch (de) See also an enthusiasts' website: www.ag2.ch (de)
*Operating dates*: Daily frequent services throughout the year, consult local or SBB timetables.
*Tariff*: For the routes listed above the adult single fares are: a) CHF 13.40; b) CHF 6; c) not known; and, d) CHF 9.20 (2007).

### 99  Bodensee-Toggenburg Bahn [BT]

Südostbahn's Nesslau-Neu St Johann station is at the end of the line in the Toggenburg valley. The countryside is outstandingly beautiful; for example, in the background here is the Churfirsten range of mountains all with altitudes in excess of 2,000 m.    *Author*

*Location*: St Gallen, 85 km east of Zürich.
*Canton*: St Gallen (SG).
*Michelin map reference*: M3.

*Operated by*: Südostbahn.
*Nearest main line station*: St Gallen.
*Route*: Romanshorn to Nesslau-Neu St Johann, a distance of 62 km.
*Journey time*: 76 minutes.
*Gauge*: Standard, by adhesion only.
*Traction*: Electric-powered (15,000V 16.7Hz).
*Rolling stock*: See the Südostbahn listings (*see entry 110*). The modern electric-powered rail cars operating on this line sport a distinctive dark green and yellow livery.
*Near to here*: Appenzellerbahnen (*see previous entry*).
*Places to see*: The 'Sitterviadukt' on this railway route is well worth a visit. Built between 1902 and 1904 the viaduct has an overall length of 365 m with a central iron girder span of 120 m crossing the River Sitter 99 m below.
*Contact details*: Südostbahn AG, Bahnhofplatz 1a, CH-9001 St Gallen. Telephone: 071 228 23 23 Fax 071 228 23 33. E-mail: info@sob.ch
*Website*: www.suedostbahn.ch (de) see also www.st.gallen.ch/bahnen/bt/ (de)
*History*: The railway was opened to traffic on 3rd October, 1910 and the route was electrified between 1926 and 1932. It amalgamated with the Südostbahn on 1st January, 2001 (*see entry 110*).
*Comments*: The Bodensee Toggenburg Bahn was a small private railway mainly financed by the canton rather than the Federal government. It operated between Romanshorn on the Bodensee (in English, Lake Constance) via St Gallen, Herisau, Degersheim, Wattwil, and Ebnat-Kappel to Nesslau-Neu St Johann. Südostbahn continues to operate normal services on this line as well as operating the Amor Express programme of steam excursions also on this route.


## 100  Frauenfeld-Wil-Bahn [FW]

*Locations*: Frauenfeld, 16 km north-east of Winterthur and Wil, 30 km west of St Gallen.
*Cantons*: Thurgau (TG) and St Gallen (SG).
*Michelin map reference*: K3.
*Nearest main line stations*: Frauenfeld and Wil.
*Route*: Frauenfeld market place to Wil, a total distance of 17 km.
*Journey time*: 28 minutes.
*Gauge*: Narrow (metre) by adhesion only for a maximum gradient of 4.6 per cent.
*Traction*: Electric-powered (1,200V DC).
*Rolling stock*: Electric-powered rail cars: Be 4/4 Nos. 11-17 & 206. Non-powered rail cars: Bt Nos. 111-114.
*Near to here*: Appenzellerbahnen (*see entry 98*).
*Places to see*: Frauenfeld, located on the banks of the River Murg, is a picturesque town with many half-timbered buildings. Ittingen, 4 km north of the town, is where a former Carthusian monastery can be visited. Wil is also an attractive town as is the Toggenburg valley running south to Neslau. Südostbahn trains (S9 service) run through this valley to a terminus at Nesslau-Neu St Johann. The journey time is 49 minutes.
*Contact details*: Frauenfeld-Wil-Bahn AG, Direktion, Bahnhofplatz 10, CH-9101 Herisau. Telephone: 071 354 50 60 Fax: 071 354 50 65. E-mail: info@fw-bahn.ch
*Website*: www.fw-bahn.ch (de)
*Operating dates*: Daily services operate every half-hour in each direction between 0500 and 2300 hours (2006).

Here at Wil, in the canton of St Gallen, opposite the SBB main line station, is a Be 4/4 with its Bt trailer shouting out their distinctive red and white zebra-like livery on 5th October, 2006.                                                                                                          *Author*

*Tariff:* An adult 2nd class single fare is CHF 9.20 (2007).
*History:* This railway was first opened in 1887 and electrified in 1921.
*Comments:* The red and white livery of this railway is striking, likened by some to zebra stripes. One thing for sure, you cannot miss them!

## 101 Rhätische Bahn [RhB] - The Main Network

*Location:* Chur and various other locations mainly in the canton of Graubünden.
*Canton:* Graubünden (GR).
*Michelin Map grid reference:* M5.
*Nearest main line stations:* Landquart and Chur.
*Routes:* Various - the total RhB network amounts to 396 km.
*Journey times:* Vary according to journey taken. For example, a) Landquart to Klosters - 43 minutes; b) Chur to Davos via Landquart - 1 hour 28 minutes; and, c) Thusis to St Moritz - 1 hour 28 minutes.
*Gauge:* Narrow (metre) by adhesion only on maximum gradients of 7 per cent.
*Traction:* Electric-powered (11,000V 16.7Hz).
*Rolling stock:* Locomotives: Ge 6/6 I Nos. 412, 414 & 415, Ge 4/4 I Nos. 601-610, Ge 4/4 II Nos. 611-633, Ge 4/4 III Nos. 641-652, Gem 4/4 Nos. 801-802 (for the Bernina Express services) and Ge 6/6 II Nos. 701-707. Electric-powered rail cars – Abe 4/4 Nos. 41-46 (for the Bernina) and Abe 4/4 Nos. 47-49, 501, 51-56 & 511-516. Non-powered rail cars: ABt Nos. 1701-1702, Bt No. 1703 (for the Arosa line), ABDt Nos. 1711-1714 & 1715-1716 and BDt Nos. 1721-1723, 1731, 1741-1742 & 1751-1758. Historic stock preserved include steam locomotives: G 3/4 No. 1 & G 4/5 Nos. 107-108. Electric-powered rail cars: Ge 2/4 No. 222, Ge 4/6 No. 353, ABe 4/4 Nos. 30 & 34 (Bernina in their distinctive yellow livery), ABe 4/4 Nos. 31, 32 & 35. Carriages: A2 No. 11092, As Nos. 1141-1142 Salonwagen, 1143-1144 Alpin Classic, 1161, 1171

Crossing the magnificient Wiesen viaduct is an RhB service with a Ge 4/4 I leading the way from Filisur and the Landwasser viaduct and heading for Davos Plaza on 4th October, 2006. *Author*

On 2nd October, 2006, a RhB service from Landquart bound for Davos passes the tiny Grüsch station led by ABe 4/4 No. 512. *Author*

Star(c)kes Stück & C 2012. Sporting their yellow livery: B2 Nos. 2091-2093, 2094-2095, 2096-2099 Aussichtswagen, 2100-2102 Aussichtswagen and B 2111 Aussichtswagen. Other carriages include: WS Nos. 3901 3902 & 3903 Ausstellungswagen, WN Nos. 9800 La Bucunda, 9802 Filisurer Stubli and 9851 N 1513/1520. Also of interest is the rotary snow plough, X rot d 9213.

**Contact details:** Bahnhofstrasse 25, CH-2002 Chur. Telephone: 081 254 91 04. E-mail: contact@rhb.ch

**Website:** www.rhb.ch (de fr it en)

**Operating dates:** All year round - consult local timetables for routes and timings or visit www.sbb.ch/en

**Tariff:** According to journey taken. For example, adult 2nd class single fare from a) Landquart to Klosters - CHF 16.80; b) Chur to Davos via Landquart -CHF 26; and, c)Thusis to St Moritz - CHF 27 (2007).

**Comments:** The Rhätische Bahn (RhB) known in English as the Rhaetian Railway, is divided into a number of sections, i.e. the Main Network, the Bernina line, the Bellinzona-Mesocco line and the Chur-Arosa line. The Rhätische Bahn network owes it existence to the building of the Gotthard line. More than a century ago, the canton of Graubünden had hoped for the construction of a railway line through the Splügen valley. However after much debate a decision was made in favour of the Gotthard route. As a direct consequence the canton decided to build a modern transportation rail network to allow easier access to its 150 valleys; and so it was that a large narrow-gauge system was constructed between 1889 and 1913. It was, however, a private citizen who took the first step toward building the railway. A Dutchman, Jan Willem Holsboer, was the owner of a hotel in Davos, and he thought, with good reason, that a railway would bring a considerably greater number of tourists to the area than the horse-drawn carriages and mail coaches could ever do. Consequently the Landquart-Davos Railway (LD) was founded, and in 1889 a line was opened as far as Klosters, reaching Davos a year later. A planned extension through the Scaletta into the Engadin, the valley of the River Inn, was not built. However, the Davos-Filisur section was opened in 1909, thus ensuring a connection with the Albula Railway and, in turn, the Engadin. RhB's main line operating through the Graubünden is the Albula line, construction beginning at the end of the 19th century. This line connected Chur with St Moritz via Thusis, Filisur and Albula, with one of its best known structures being the Landwasser viaduct near Filisur. In 1896, the line reached Thusis, in 1903, Celerina, and finally, in 1904, St Moritz in the Engadin. It was meant that this line ultimately would be extended across the Maloja Pass to the Italian town of Chiavenna. However, the onset of World War I unfortunately put an end to that idea. Eventually, though, a connection was made with the Valtellina Railway, albeit only as a tourist railway. From the Albula main line various spurs led off in all directions, the first being the Chur-Thusis section and a connection with the Davos line at Landquart was made. In 1903, the line to Illanz in the Vorderrhein valley was completed and extended to Disentis by 1912. The line to Scuol-Tarasp was created in 1913. It was intended that this line would link up with the Arlberg Railway at Landeck, but after 1914 with the impact of war in Europe, all such plans for an extension had to be abandoned. A key event in the history of the RhB was the electrification of the network. When the Albula line had been built between 1896 and 1904, electric traction had not been sufficiently developed that it could be considered feasible. At that time there were only electric streetcars, interurban tramways and a few mountain railways. Technology developed quickly in the first decade of the 20th century and the feasibility had changed favourably by the time the UnterEngadin line

An RhB service led by non-powered rail car Abt No. 1701 arrives at the beautiful Lüen station on the Chur-Arosa line on 3rd October, 2006. The descent by road down to the station from the main No. 28 road is definitely not for the faint-hearted!      *Author*

was constructed in 1910. Earlier trial runs between Seebach and Wettingen (1904-9) with the single phase low-frequency alternating current (AC) system had been found to be a success. Consequently, the RhB decided to operate the St Moritz-Scuol line which was opened in 1913 using single-phase alternating current of 11,000V 16.7Hz as the power source. This electric power system proved itself to be so successful that the RhB decided to introduce electrification to all its other lines between 1919 and 1922. This decision allowed RhB to provide an efficient and effective service in the canton even during the years when the other form of power – stocks of coal – were both extremely scarce to find and expensive. The next major event in the history of the RhB occurred 77 years later when the Vereina tunnel was opened (*see entry 107*).

### 102  Rhätische Bahn - Albula Car Transportation

*Location:*  Chur, 120 km south-east of Zürich and Bever near to Samedan, 6 km north-east of St Moritz.
*Canton:*  Both in Graubünden (GR).
*Michelin map reference:*  M5 and N6 respectively.
*Nearest main line station:*  Chur.
*Route:*  Chur to Samedan, a distance of 70 km.
*Journey time:*  2 hours 36 minutes.
*Gauge:*  Narrow (metre) by adhesion only. The maximum gradient negotiated is 4 per cent.
*Traction:*  Electric-powered (11,000V 16.7Hz).
*Rolling stock:*  Locomotives: Ge 4/4 III's and non-powered driving carriages. (*For more information see Rhätische Bahn Main Network at entry 101*).

*Places to see*: There are numerous viaducts/bridges of which probably the most famous are the Landwasser and the Wiesen. There are also many tunnels on this route of which the principal is the Albula tunnel with a length of 5.8 km.
*Contact details*: Rhätische Bahn, Bahnhofstrasse 25, CH-2002 Chur. Telephone: 081 254 91 04. E-mail: contact@rhb.ch
*Website*: www.rhb.ch (de fr it en)
*Operating dates*: Daily, with hourly services from 0815 to 1815 hours. (Information about car transportation can be obtained by telephoning 081 288 66 77 which delivers a pre-recorded message.)
*Tariff*: Road vehicles that do not exceed the maximum dimensions for a single journey cost CHF 145 and adults one way are charged CHF 24 for 2nd class and CHF 40 for 1st class (2007).
*Comments*: This road vehicle carrying train may seem expensive but it does make the journey considerably less arduous, especially in winter when road access either to Chur or St Moritz may be very difficult, if not impossible. Travellers are strongly advised to book well in advance, especially in winter. Doing so, also ensures that there are no delays in boarding.

### 103 Rhätische Bahn - Arosa Express sometimes referred to as 'The Blue Line'

*Location*: Chur, 90 km south of St Gallen.
*Canton*: Graubünden (GR).
*Michelin map reference*: M5.
*Nearest main line station*: Chur.
*Route*: Chur to Arosa, a distance of 26 km and rising in altitude by 1,157 m. In total there are 41 bridges including the outstanding Langwies viaduct which at the time of its construction in 1914 was the world's largest concrete and steel structure ever built. There are 21 tunnels. The maximum gradient on the route is 6 per cent.
*Journey time*: Chur to Arosa takes 1 hour 1 minute and the return journey 3 minutes longer.
*Gauge*: Narrow (metre) by adhesion only.
**Traction:** Electric (11,000V 16.7Hz).
*Rolling stock*: Electric-powered locomotives of the class Ge 4/4 II are mainly used to haul the trains on this line but occasionally class Ge 4/4 I 's can be seen. (*For more information see Rhätische Bahn Main Network at entry 101*).
*Places to see*: The train climbs the beautiful and at times dramatic Schanfigg Valley.
*Contact details*: Rhätische Bahn, Bahnhofstrasse 25, CH-2002 Chur. Telephone: 081 254 91 04. E-mail: contact@rhb.ch
*Website*: www.rhb.ch (de fr it en)
*Operating dates*: All year with one service running each day in each direction. Leaves Chur at 1008 and leaves Arosa at 1448 hours. There is also a regular service of local trains.
*Tariff*: Adult tickets are CHF 26.80 for a 2nd class return and CHF 44.40 for a 1st class return. Group discounts of 20 per cent for more than 10 people are available on advance booking (2006).
*History*: Prior to the opening of the Vereina tunnel in 1999 the Chur-Arosa line was the last major addition to the RhB narrow gauge network in the Grisons (Graubünden). Many different proposals were made for the construction of this railway line. One idea, for example, was a rack/cogwheel railway that would

The livery of the Rhätische Bahn's rolling stock usually comprises (Swiss) red panels with grey coloured roofs. However, a departure was made when the RhB introduced the 'Arosa Express'. Here is depicted one of the distinctive blue liveried carriages which is temporarily 'filling-in' on a regular RhB Chur-Arosa service on 3rd October, 2006. *Author*

A winter scene of the Langwieser viaduct being crossed by the 'Arosa Express'
*Rhätische Bahn/swiss-image.ch*

negotiate the first ascent from Chur to the valley of the Plessur river. However, the route eventually chosen by the founding railway company - Chur-Arosa (ChA) - began, as it does today, by following the streets of the upper part of the town. The merger with the RhB was the beginning of the modernisation of the ChA railway. State-of-the-art remote controlled signalling and shuttle trains were introduced to the Chur-Arosa line. Nowadays. to meet the needs of winter sports enthusiasts, this line has to cope with extraordinarily heavy traffic especially at weekends. The power supply was changed from 2,400V DC to 11,000V 16.7Hz in 1997.

*Comments*:  Panoramic carriages are available for 1st class passengers. A special attraction of the Arosa-Express is that the entire train (but not the locomotive) is liveried in a fashionable blue design instead of the usually predominant red colour of the normal RhB rolling stock.

### 104  Rhätische Bahn - Aqualino Scuol

Locomotive  Ge 4/4 III No. 648 in its Swisscom livery leads RhB Aqualino-Scuol train from Landquart on 3rd October, 2006.    *Author*

*Location*:  Landquart, 80 km south of St Gallen.
*Canton*:  Graubünden (GR).
*Michelin map reference*:  M5.
*Nearest main line station*:  Landquart.
*Route*:  Landquart to Klosters to Scuol, a total distance of 90 km.
*Journey time*:  1 hour 28 minutes.
*Gauge*:  Narrow (metre) by adhesion only.
*Traction & rolling stock*:  (*For more information see Rhätische Bahn Main Network at entry 101*).

The RhB Aqualino-Scuol service train crossing the 110 m high viaduct in the Val Tuol near Guarda in Unterengadin. *Rhätische Bahn/swiss-image.ch*

The carriages of an 'Engadin Star' train crossing the Val Mela viaduct near Sagliains. *Rhätische Bahn/swiss-image.ch*

*Contact details*: Rhätische Bahn, Bahnhofstrasse 25, CH-2002 Chur. Telephone: 081 254 91 04. E-mail: contact@rhb.ch
*Website*: www.rhb.ch (de fr it en)
*Operating dates*: All year with frequent services every hour between 0520 and 2145 hours from Landquart.
*Tariff*: An adult single fare is CHF 33 (2007).


## 105  Rhätische Bahn - Engadin Star

*Location*: Landquart, 16 km north of Chur.
*Canton*: Graubünden (GR).
*Michelin map reference*: M5.
*Nearest main line station*: Landquart.
*Route*: Landquart to Klosters to Zemez to St Moritz, a total distance of 108 km.
*Journey time*: 2 hour 9 minutes.
*Gauge*: Narrow (metre) by adhesion only.
*Traction & rolling stock*: (*For more information see Rhätische Bahn Main Network at entry 101*).
*Contact details*: Rhätische Bahn, Bahnhofstrasse 25, CH-2002 Chur. Telephone: 081 254 91 04. E-mail: contact@rhb.ch
*Website*: www.rhb.ch/
*Operating dates*: Daily from 20th May to 22nd October each year leaving Landquart at 0820, Klosters at 0903 and arriving St Moritz at 1018 hours. For the return journey, the train leaves St Moritz at 1637 and arrives at Landquart at 1836 hours.
*Tariff*: An adult single fare is CHF 45 (2007).


## 106  Rhätische Bahn - Railrider

*Location*: Filisur, 150 km south of St Gallen.
*Canton*: Graubünden (GR).
*Michelin map reference*: N5.
*Nearest main line station*: Thusis.
*Route*: Filisur to Bergün to Preda, a distance of 22.3 km.
*Journey time*: 49 minutes out and 44 minutes in.
*Gauge*: Narrow (metre) by adhesion only.
*Traction & rolling stock*: (*For more information see Rhätische Bahn Main Network at entry 101*).
*Places to see*: Twelve viaducts including the famous Landwasser viaduct (65 metres high) and the Albula viaduct (138 metres long).
*Contact details*: Rhätische Bahn, Bahnhofstrasse 25, CH-2002 Chur. Telephone: 081 254 91 04. E-mail: contact@rhb.ch
*Website*: www.rhb.ch (de fr it en)
*Operating dates*: Every Sunday from 2nd July to 3rd September and on 1st August (2006).
*Tariff*: Single tickets for adults cost CHF 16 and children (6-16 years) CHF 11, return tickets for adults cost CHF 27 and children CHF 17 (2006).

'Hang on to your hats' on the Rhätische Bahn's summer 'Railrider' service. Here the train is high above the Lago di Poschiavo on the Bernina Express route.     *Rhätische Bahn/swiss-image.ch*

Cars disembark at the Selfranga terminal at the Klosters end of the Vereina tunnel on 10th October, 2006. BDt No. 1742 had led the way.     *Author*

## 107 Rhätische Bahn - Vereina Line

*Location*: Klosters, 100 km south-east of St Gallen.
*Canton*: Graubünden (GR).
*Michelin map reference*: M5.
*Nearest main line station*: Landquart.
*Route*: Klosters (Selfranga) to Sagliains, a distance of 22.1 km. There are three bridges and three tunnels on this route of which the principal is the Vereina tunnel with a length of 19.042 km. The maximum gradient negotiated is 4 per cent.
*Journey time*: 30 minutes.
*Gauge*: Narrow (metre).
*Traction*: Electric-powered (11,000V 16.7Hz).
*Rolling stock*: Locomotives: Ge 4/4 III Nos. 650-652 and non-powered BDt rail cars.
*Contact details*: Rhätische Bahn, Bahnhofstrasse 25, CH-2002 Chur. Telephone: 081 254 91 04. E-mail: contact@rhb.ch
*Website*: www.rhb.ch (de fr it en)
*Operating dates*: Daily with frequent connections from 0520 to 1920 hours (half-hourly connections from 0720 to 1920 hours).
*Tariff*: For a single journey with a car up to nine seats including passengers, in summer costs CHF 27 and in winter CHF 35 (2007).
*History*: In 1999 Rhätische Bahn network was extended for the first time since 1914 with the opening of an additional 22 kilometres of track. This came about with the building of the 19.1 km long Vereina tunnel connecting Prättigau with lower Engadin. The line runs from Klosters (Selfranga) to Sagliains. The first thoughts about building of this connection go back to the 1970s. However, not until 1984 was it decided in the canton not to renew the deteriorating Flüela road but rather, in its place, build a railway tunnel allowing for car and other road vehicle transportation. However, after years of discussions and legal arguments, ground-breaking did not in fact occur until April 1991. The first project was to replace the old Landquart bridge in Klosters with a new double-track bridge, thus allowing the construction works at the Zugwald tunnel to begin without interrupting the regular rail services on the Klosters-Davos line. The building of the Vereina tunnel was managed from two locations - in the north at Selfranga near Klosters and in the south at Sagliains near Susch and Lavin. In March 1997, breakthrough of the tunnel was achieved six months ahead of schedule. After the breakthrough a 2 km-long central siding was constructed allowing for train passing on what would otherwise be in a single-track tunnel. After completion, extensive testing was made with the new car transportation trains and finally, on 19th November, 1999, the tunnel was opened by senior representatives of the Rhätische Bahn company and local politicians. On 22nd November, regular traffic began routine operations at 0545 hours. The Vereina tunnel is 19,042 m long and is double-tracked at the entrances and in the middle of the tunnel. Its cost, incidentally, was approximately CHF 800 million at 1999 prices. In normal operation, there are hourly pairs of trains between Landquart and Scuol via the tunnel as well as half-hourly car shuttle trains between Selfranga and Sagliains. In spring 2000, because of the opening of this route, the express train 'Engadin Star' (Landquart-Vereina-St Moritz-Albula-Chur) was able to be introduced (*see entry 105*). Not only is the tunnel used for passenger traffic but also for extensive goods traffic, thus reducing significantly the road haulage traffic on the roads in the region. For example, the 'Coop' chain of retail outlets now uses the Vereina line instead of taking heavy goods vehicles over the Julier and Flüela passes. The highest capacity carried on the auto trains is 186 cars per hour.

## 108  Rheineck-Walzenhausen Bergbahn [RhW]

There is only one rail car on the Rheineck-Walzenhausen Bergbahn, BDeh 1/2 No. 1, seen here passing a pretty Swiss cottage on its descent to Rheineck on 5th October, 2006.

*Author*

*Location*: Rheineck, 21 km east of St Gallen.
*Canton*: St Gallen (SG).
*Michelin map reference*: M3.
*Operated by*: Appenzellerbahnen.
*Nearest main line station*: Rheineck.
*Route*: Rheineck to Walzenhausen, a distance of 2 km.
*Journey time*: 9 minutes.
*Gauge*: Narrow (1,200 mm) operating all the way on a rack/cogwheel system of the Riggenbach design. The maximum gradient on this line is 25 per cent.
*Traction*: Electric-powered (650V DC).
*Rolling stock*: Just one powered rail car, BDeh 1/2 No. 1.
*Near to here*: Rorschach-Heiden Bahn (*see next entry*).
*Places to see*: A pleasure steamer trip can be enjoyed on nearby Lake Constance (Bodensee).
*Contact details*:  Appenzellerbahnen AG, Bahnhofplatz 10, CH-9101 Herisau. Telephone: 071 354 50 60 Fax 071 354 50 65. E-mail: via the Kontakt page of the website.
*Website*: www.ar-bergbahnen.ch (de)
*Operating dates*: Daily, with two services per hour in each direction from 0555 to 2050 hours. A bus service also operates for this route between 2000 hours and midnight.
*Tariff*: An adult single ticket costs CHF 3.80 (2007).
*History*: This railway started out life in 1896.

**Comments:** Walzenhausen, incidentally, is in the neighbouring canton of Appenzell Ausserrhoden (AR). Appenzellerbahanen (*see entry 98*) is now responsible for rail services between Altstätten-Gais, Gossau-Appenzell-Wasserauen, St Gallen-Appenzell, St Gallen-Trogen, Rorschach-Heiden, Walzenhausen and the bus services Speicherschwendi-Teufen.

## 109  Rorschach-Heiden Bahn [RHB]

Rorschach-Heiden Bahn's BDeh 3/6 No. 25 approaches Heiden station on 5th October, 2006.                                                                                    *Author*

**Location:** Rorschach, 14 km north-east of St Gallen on the shores of Lake Constance.
**Canton:** St Gallen (SG).
**Michelin map reference:** M3.
**Operated by:** Appenzellerbahnen.
**Nearest main line station:** Rorschach.
**Route:** Rorschach to Heiden, a distance of 7.1 km.
**Journey time:** 19 minutes.
**Gauge:** Standard operating rack/cogwheel of the Riggenbach design negotiating a maximum gradient of 9 per cent.
**Traction:** Electric-powered (15,000V 16.7Hz).
**Rolling stock:** Locomotives: DZeh 2/4 Nos. 21-22. Electric-powered rail cars: ABDe 2/4 Nos. 23-24 and BDeh 3/6 No. 25. Non-powered rail cars: Bt Nos. 4 & 31. Retained as being of historical interest is steam locomotive H 2/2 No. 3 *Rosa*.
**Contact details:** Appenzellerbahnen AG, Bahnhofplatz 10, CH-9101 Herisau. Telephone: 071 354 50 60 Fax 071 354 50 65. E-mail: via the Kontakt page of the website.
**Website:** www.ar-bergbahnen.ch

Rorschach-Heiden Bahn celebrated its 125 years of existence in the year 2000. Part of the celebrations was to use its older rail cars ABDeh 2/4 Nos. 24 and 25. Here No. 24 is seen behind Heiden station on 5th October, 2006.                                                                                          *Author*

Südostbahn's Re 456 No. 94 leads a Voralpen Express over the plateau near Sulgen on 7th October, 2006.                                                                                          *Author*

*Operating dates*: Daily frequent services every 45 minutes - consult local timetables or visit www.sbb.ch/en
*Tariff*: An adult single ticket costs CHF 5.40 (2007).
*History*: Railways in this region first ran in 1875.
*Comments*: Major investment was taking place in 2006 to improve the station at Heiden. Heiden is in the neighbouring canton of Appenzell Ausserrhoden (AR). Appenzellerbahanen is now responsible for rail services between Altstätten-Gais, Gossau-Appenzell-Wasserauen, St Gallen-Appenzell, St Gallen-Trogen, Rheineck-Walzenhausen and for the bus services Speicherschwendi-Teufen.


## 110 Südostbahn [SOB]

*Location*: St Gallen, 90 km east of Zürich.
*Canton*: St Gallen (SG).
*Michelin map reference*: M3.
*Route*: A regional railway offering various routes connecting St Gallen with the townships of Romanshorn, Herisau, Degersheim Rapperswil, Wattwil, Ebnat, Nesslau, Arth, Sattel and Einsiedeln. The network totals 115 km.
*Gauge*: Standard gauge operating by adhesion only for a maximum gradient of 5 per cent.
*Traction*: Electric-powered (15,000V 16.7Hz).
*Rolling stock*: Locomotives: Re 446 Nos. 015-018 and Re 456 Nos. 091-096. Electric-powered rail cars: RBDe 566 Nos. 071-076 & 077-080 and BDe 576 Nos. 048-049, 050-053, 054-1 & 055-059. Non-powered rail cars: Abt 50 48 38-03 Nos. 159-0 (ex RM), Abt 50 48 38-35 Nos. 171-176, Abt 50 48 38-35 Nos. 177-180, Abt 50 48 38-35 Nos. 141-9, 148-4, 149-2, 150-153 & 154-158 and BDt 50 48 Nos. 80-35 Nos. 191-195, 196-1, 197-198 & 199-5. Historic material includes: steam locomotives Eb 3/5 No. 9 & E 3/3 No. 4 *Schwyz* currently under restoration, and electric-powered Be 4/6 Nos. 011-5 & 014-9, Be 4/4 Nos. 11 (BT) & 14 (BT) - Ae 476 012-0, B2 50 48 93-15 Nos. 401-4 , 402, 403-0, 405-5 & 404-8 and Be 556 No. 043-8.
*Places to see*: St Gallen is Eastern Switzerland's largest town, its origins going back to 612 AD when an Irish monk called Gallus chose this location for his hermitage. St Gallen's cathedral is well worth visiting, especially for the paintings and ceiling frescoes.
*Contact details*: Südostbahn AG, Bahnhofplatz 1a, CH-9001 St Gallen. Telephone: 071 228 23 23 Fax 071 228 23 33. E-mail: info@sob.ch
*Website*: www.suedostbahn.ch (de)
*Operating dates and tariff*: All year round. Consult local timetables or go online to www.sbb.ch/en
*History*: This railway traces its origins back to 1870 with the establishment of the Toggenburger Bahn followed in 1904 by the Bodensee-Toggenburg Bahn.
*Comments*: Südostbahn also operates the Voralpen Express (*see entry 113*).

Two of Thurbo's 'Flirts' RABe 526 rail cars Nos. 757-0 and 706-7, built by Stadler AG, depart Wil station bound for St Gallen on 5th October, 2006.    *Author*

Departing Trogen for St Gallen is Trogenerbahn's Be 4/8 No. 32 on 5th October, 2006.   *Author*

## 111  Thurbo AG

*Location*:  Kreuzlingen, on the Swiss-German border near Constance (Konstanz) and the lake of the same name and also referred to as Bodensee.
*Canton*:  Thurgau (TG).
*Michelin map reference*:  L3.
*Route*:  A regional railway operating in the north-east of Switzerland and connecting Kreuzlingen, Winterthur, Frauenfeld, Weinfelden, Rapperswil, Wattwil and St Gallen. The network totals 470 km in Switzerland and 80 km in Germany.
*Gauge*:  Standard by adhesion only with a maximum gradient of 2.2 per cent.
*Traction*:  Electric-powered (15,000V 16.7Hz).
*Rolling stock*:  Locomotive: Re 416 No. 628-6 (ex 4/4 I No. 10039). Electric-powered rail cars RABe 526 Nos. 680-689 & 701-780, ABDe 536 Nos. 611-615, ABDe 566 Nos. 631-634 and Bm 596 Nos. 671-673. Non-powered rail cars: Bt 50 46 28-02 Nos. 231-232, Bt 50 46 29-33 Nos. 201-204 & 211-216 and Bt 50 46 29-35 Nos. 221-224.
*Contact details*:  Regionalbahn Thurbo, Bahnhofstrasse 31, CH-8280 Kreuzlingen 1. Telephone: 05 12 23 49 00, Fax: 0512 23 49 90. E-mail: hallo@thurbo.ch
*Website*:  www.thurbo.ch (de).
*Operating dates and tariff*:  Regional services all year round - consult local timetables or go online to www.sbb.ch/en
*History*:  The present company was formed on 15th December, 2002 as a result of a number of amalgamations including that of the Mittelthurgaubahn which had been taken over by Thurbo earlier in September 2001.


## 112  Trogenerbahn [TB]

*Location*:  Trogen, 10 east south-east of St Gallen.
*Canton*:  Appenzell Ausserrhoden (AR).
*Michelin map reference*:  M3.
*Operated by*:  Appenzellerbahnen.
*Nearest main line station*:  St Gallen.
*Route*:  St Gallen to Trogen, a distance of 10 km.
*Journey time*:  30 minutes.
*Gauge*:  Narrow (metre) by adhesion only for a maximum gradient on this line of 7.6 per cent.
*Traction*:  Electric-powered (1,000V DC).
*Rolling stock*:  Electric-powered rail cars: BDe 4/8 Nos. 21-25, BDe 4/4 Nos. 6-8 and Be 4/8 Nos. 31-32
*Contact details*:  Trogenerbahn AG, Hauptstrasse 19, Postfach 173, CH-9042 Speicher. Telephone: 071 343 70 10 Fax: 071 343 70 20. E-mail: info@trogenerbahn.ch
*Website*:  www.trogenerbahn.ch (de)
*Operating dates*:  Monday to Fridays from 0515 to 1900, Saturdays from 0555 to 1140 & 1310 to 1610 and Sundays from 0800 to 1140 & 1310 to 1710 hours.
*Tariff*:  Local fare structure applies.
*History*:  This railway first started its operations in 1893.
*Comments*:  Trogenerbahn is now part of Appenzellerbahnen (*see entry 98*) which is also responsible for rail services between Altstätten-Gais, Gossau-Appenzell-Wasserauen, St Gallen-Appenzell, Rorschach-Heiden, Rheineck-Walzenhausen and the bus services Speicherschwendi-Teufen.

## 113  Voralpen Express

Some distinctive liveried coaches of Südostbahn's Voralpen Express seen here on 7th October, 2006.                                                                                          *Author*

*Locations*:  Romanshorn is on Lake Constance (Bodensee) and Luzern.
*Cantons*:  Thurgau (TG) and Luzern (LU).
*Michelin map references*:  M3 & I4.
*Operated by*:  Südostbahn (*see entry 110*).
*Route*:  Romanshorn by Lake Constance to Luzern, a distance of 150 km.
*Journey time*:  2 hour 42 minutes each way.
*Gauge*:  Standard by adhesion only.
*Rolling stock*:  See entry for Südostbahn.
*Near to here*:  Rigi Bahn (*see entry 93*) to ascend the 'Queen of the Mountains' and the Pilatus Bahn (*see entry 92*) near Luzern.
*Places to see*:  Luzern is known as 'the city of lights' and where one can find the Swiss Transport Museum (*see entry 96*). Other places of interest to visit are Einsiedeln - the baroque monastery with the Black Madonna, Rapperswil - the 'rose town' with its castle and old town on the shores of Lake Zürich, St Gallen - a university and cultural town with a beautiful cathedral and excellent shopping and Lake Constance itself which is shared by Switzerland with neighbouring Germany and Austria. A ferry can takes one from Romanshorn to Friedrichshafen in Baden-Württemburg, Germany.
*Contact details*:  Voralpen Express, Postfach 2203, CH-9001 St Gallen. E-mail: info@voralpen-express.ch
*Website*:  www.voralpen-express.ch (de fr it en)
*Operating dates*:  Daily throughout the year with 13 services each way every hour commencing 0737 from Luzern and 0634 hours from Romanshorn.
*Tariff*:  An adult 2nd class ticket one way is CHF 42 with children travelling at half price (2006).

*Comments*: The Voralpen-Express is the most attractive railway route between Lake Constance and Lake Luzern. The region offers the visitor one of Switzerland's most attractive alpine mountain and lakeland scenes.

## Related Interest

### 114  Club 1889

*Location*: Samedan, 8 km north-east of St Moritz.
*Canton*: Graubünden (GR).
*Michelin map reference*: N6.
*Contact details*: Club 1889, Postfach 284, CH-7503 Samedan.
*Website*: www.club1889.ch (de) See also: Verein Dampffreunde der Rhätischen Bahn on www.dampfvereinrhb.ch and Freunde der Schmalspurbahnen on www.melchnauerli.ch
*Comments*: Club 1889 is directly related to the Rhätische Bahn (RhB). In recent years it has been necessary for RhB to invest in modernising its network originally with Swiss Federal Government help. However, as such subsidies have reduced so there has been less RhB money available for the preservation of historic rolling stock. This was why Club 1889 was formed in 1996 in order to fill what otherwise would be a void. The Club has over 350 members worldwide with about 40 locally active, many of whom are railway workers and craftsmen. Together with sponsors, Club 1889 volunteer members have not only saved historic stock but also have been able to restore some, the yellow-liveried 1908-built passenger carriage 'La Bucunda' being a good example. The current project is to restore a G 3/4 to active service. In 2003, Club 1889 joined forces with three other organizations to form an umbrella organization 'Historic RhB'. As a consequence, Historic RhB has a contract with the Rhätische Bahn which ensures the continuing preservation, maintenance, use, and in some cases, marketing of the historic rolling stock. There are three working groups for Historic RhB based in Samedan, Chur and Poschiavo.

### 115  Verein zur Erhaltung der Dampflok Muni [VDM]

*Location*: Ramsen, 10 km east of Schaffhausen and 23 km north of Winterthur.
Canton: Schaffhausen (SH).
*Michelin map reference*: K2.
*Nearest main line station*: Schaffhausen.
*Rolling stock*: Locomotives: steam locomotive Ed 3/3 *Muni* & diesel locomotive Tm 2/2 *Grizzly*. Passenger carriages: Nos. C 101, 102, B 104, 104, WR 201, 301 & 302. Postal carriage: No. X 401 and goods wagons: Tbks 501, DVZO 354 & MThB X 40 46 94 21 635-3.
*Contact details*: Verein zur Erhaltung der Dampflok Muni, Postfach 14, CH-8262 Ramsen. E-mail: info@muni-dampflok.ch
*Website*: www.muni-dampflok.ch (de)
*Comments*: For details about when viewing is possible, contact the organization direct. The president is Herr Willi Reichlin. This group is linked with Etzwilen-Singen project (*see entry 117*).

An example of an articulated rail car (GTW) manufactured by Stadler and delivered with three others to the Chemin de fer Veveysans now known as the Chemin de fer Legère de Riviere. Here is seen Be 2/6 No. 7003 at Blonay station.          *Author*

Stadler-built 'Flinker Leichter Innovativer Regional Triebzug' (FLIRT) operated by Thurbo. RABe 526 No. 757-0 is seen here at Wil station.          *Author*

## 116  Stadler Rail AG

*Location*:  Bussnang, 19 km east of Frauenfeld.
*Canton*:  Thurgau (TG).
*Michelin map reference*:  Bussnang is not shown on the map but the place where it is located is close to Weinfelden which is in L3.
*Nearest main line station*:  Bussnang.
*Manufacturing*:  Stadler AG manufacture eight main categories of rail vehicles which have been supplied to various locations in Switzerland, Manufactured are: a) articulated rail cars; b) FLIRTs; c) SPATZs; d) rack/cogwheel trains; e) commuter vehicles; f) trams; g) passenger carriages; and, g) urban shuttle vehicles. In more detail these are:

a) Articulated  rail cars (GTWs) Swiss customers being Biel-Taufelen-Ins Bahn (7 delivered), Chemin de Fer Veveysans (4 delivered), Mittelthurgaubahn (now part of Thurbo) (13 delivered), Regionaverkehr Mitelland (now part of BLS AG) (13 delivered), Yverdon-Ste Croix (part of Travys SA) (2 delivered), Chemin de Fer du Jura (4 delivered), Thurbo (80 delivered) and AareSeeland mobil (2 delivered).
b) Standard gauge FLIRTs (Flinker Leichter Innovativer Regional Triebzug - Fast Light Innovative Regional Train) have been supplied to SBB (54 delivered), TILO (19 delivered), Thurbo (9 delivered), Südostbahn (11 delivered) and Transports Régionaux Neuchâtelois (1 delivered).
c) Metre gauge SPATZs have gone to SBB-Brünig (now die Zentralbahn) (10 delivered) and the Matterhorn Gotthard Bahn (9 delivered).
d) Stadler has cornered the market as the largest supplier of rack railway vehicles and systems in the world. Swiss rack/cogwheel railways which have benefited from Sadler's products include the Gornergratbahn (GGB), the Matterhorn Gotthard Bahn (MGB) and the Wengeralpbahn (WAB).
e) Customized commuter vehicles have gone to die Zentralbahn (SBB-Brünig), Meiringen-Innertkitchen-Bahn, Trogenerbahn and Forchbahn.
f) Tango street trams have gone to Baselland Transport AG (BLT) and Basler Verehrsbetriebe (BVB).
g) Passenger carriages have gone to the Glacier Express, the Bernina Express, Transport Public Fribourgeois, Bern-Solothurn and the Rhätische Bahn.
h) The company also produces the Regio-Shuttle RS1 - a low-floored vehicle meeting the needs of regional and urban rail services, but none at this time to Swiss locations.
i) The Variobahn - a low floor tram, but none at this time to Swiss locations.

*Contact details*:  Stadler Rail AG, Bahnhofplatz, CH-9565 Bussnang. Telephone: 071 626 21 20. Fax: 071 626 21 28. E-Mail: stadler.rail@stadlerrail.ch
*Website*:  www.stadlerrail.ch
*History*:  Stadler traces its origins back to 1942 when Ernest Stadler founded an engineering office in Zürich. At the end of the World War II, the company began manufacturing battery-powered and diesel-powered locomotives. This was followed, 39 years later, with the production of passenger rail vehicles. In 1997, the company took over another Swiss company, the Schindler Works in Altenrheim and a year later acquired SLM's rack railway business at Winterthur. A joint venture followed in 1999 with ADtranz which lasted for two years before Stadler assumed total control. About the same time a new assembly plant and offices was constructed

'Schmalspur Panorama Triebzug' (SPATZ) is the model name given by Stadler AG to this class of rail car. One of Zentralbahn's SPATZs, No. 130 001-1 is seen here at Interlaken Ost station.
*Author*

Wengernalpbahn have benefited by the delivery of Stadler-built rack/cogwheel rail cars such as Bhe 4/8 No. 142 seen here at Kleine Scheidegg station on 9th October, 2006.    *Author*

Two of the beautiful and very practical panoramic coaches built by Stadler for the Glacier Express.     *Author*

at Bussnang. In 2005 the company took over Winpro AG at Winterthur which was renamed a year later as Stadler Winterthur AG.

**Comments:**   The Swiss Stadler Rail Group has three sites in Switzerland, i.e. Bussnang, Altenrhein and Winterthur; and four in other countries, i.e. Berlin and Weiden in Germany, Siedlce in Poland and Budapest in Hungary. The company focuses on meeting the needs of the regional and suburban service markets for light regional express railway services, streetcars and the rack railway vehicle market. Stadler Rail, an independent company, complements other rail vehicle builders such as Alstom, Bombardier, and Siemens. There is no doubt that Stadler have had and are continuing to have a significant impact on rail transport in Switzerland as well as many other countries in Europe and elsewhere in the world.

## Project

### 117  Die Bahnlinie Etzwilen-Singen

*Location:*  Etzwilen, 28 km north-east of Winterthur.
*Canton:*  Thurgau (TG).
*Michelin map reference:*  K3.
*Route:*  Etzwilen to Singen in Baden-Württemburg in Germany, a distance of 16 km.
*Contact details:*  Herr Franz Signer, Steigblickstrasse 389, CH-8262 Ramsen. Telephone: 052 743 1490. E-Mail: franz.signer@etzwilen-singen.ch
*Website:*  www.etzwilen-singen.ch (de)
*Comments:*  This is an ambitious project to re-build this railway line by an enthusiastic band of local volunteers. On the route to Singen the old railway line crosses the River Rhine into Germany on a magnificent iron girder bridge.

The beautifully restored 1916 SLM-built C5/6 (4-cylinder compound) No. 2965 is seen here in all her glory at the Swiss Transport Museum. One of her sister locomotives, No. 2969, is in the course of restoration at the Ballenberg-Dampfbahn's depot at Interlaken (*see entry 47*). *Author*

Krokodil Be 6/8 II No. 13254 on display at the Swiss Transport Museum (*see entry 96*). *Author*

# Appendix
# Preserved Swiss Federal Railway Locomotives

**Rolling Stock including Electric Traction:**

A 1 ex-SNB
X 10 85 94 00 No. 228-0
X 10 85 94 00 No. 702-4
X rot m 100 (Schneeschleuder)
Re 4/4 I Nos. 10001 & 10044
RAe 2/4 No. 1001 *Roter-Pfeil*
RAe 4/8 1021 *Churchill-Pfeil*
Ae 3/5 No 10217
Ae 3/6 III No. 10264
Ae 3/6 II No. 10439
Rae TEE II No. 1053
Dr No. 10112
WR No. 10225
Ae 3/6I Nos. 10650, 10664 & 10700
Ae 4/7 Nos. 10905, 10949 & 10976
Ae 8/14 Nos. 11801 & 11852
Be 4/6 Nos. 12320, 12332 & 12504
'Krokodils' (Crocodiles):
  Be 6/8 II No. 13254 & Be 6/8 III No. 13302
  Ce 6/8 II Nos. 14253 & 14270
  Ce 6/8 III No. 14305
  Ce 6/8 I No. 14201
BFe 4/4 No. 1643
BDe 4/4 No. 1646
De 4/4 No. 1679
ABt No. 1715
D3 No. 18275
Bm 4/4 I No. 18451
Fe 4/4 No. 18518
F3 No. 18542
BDt No. 1990
Ce 4/4 No. 2 *Marianne*
RCe 2/4 No. 203
B 22 ex-SNB
A 2252 (Leichstahl)
As 2301 (Salon-Wagen)
J3 No. 23074
AB4 Nos. 2856 & 2671
A4 No. 2763 (Leichstahl)
Ass Nos. 2801 & 2802 (Salon-Wagen)
X 30 85 94 25 No. 032-3
KRC1 No. 3031
K2 No. 3109
BC4 No. 321 ex-SCB
C Nos. 33, 41 & 42 ex-SNB
AB No. 3721
X 40 85 94 02 Nos. 010-017, 013-8, & 015-8
X 40 85 94 05 No. 074-7
X 40 85 94 21 No. 009-3
X 40 85 94 22 Nos. 218-9, & 219-7
X 40 85 94 25 Nos. 049-5 & 050-3
X 40 85 94 29 Nos. 013-7 & 026-9
X 40 85 94 45 No. 200-0
Xs 40 85 95 22 Nos. 220-4, 227-9, 228-7 & 229-5
As 40 85 95 25 No. 035-037

**Rolling Stock including Electric Traction:**

Xs 40 85 95 25 No. 043-7
Xs 40 85 95 29 Nos. 024-025, 030-0 & 031-8
Xs 40 85 95 44 No. 153-1 (Magazinwagen)
X 40 85 96 27 No. 028-5
X 40 85 96 48 No. 316-9
K3 No. 43686
Tm No. 464
Tm I No. 475
K4 Nos. 49361, 50081 & 50610
Z4 50 85 00-33 No. 813-4 (Postwagen)
A 50 85 18-33 Nos. 229-3 & 235-0
EW I, WR 50 85 88-33 Nos. 700-8 & 702-4
SR 50 85 89-33 No. 611-6 (Salon-Wagen)
DZt 50 85 92-33 No. 915-6
BC4 No. 5043
ABm 51 85 30-70 No. 009+023
Am 51 85 19-70 No. 005-9
C4 Nos. 5301, 7802, 8754, 8809 & 9574
P No. 534471
B Nos. 5466 & 5560 (Leichtstahl)
L6 No. 57186
M6 No. 57581
WRm 61 85 88-70 Nos. 000-4, 004-6 & 006-21
(Verkaufswagen)
C2 No. 6138
C 66
LR1 No. 7488
C3 Nos. 7727 & 8395
F No. 94
Z4i No. 961
Ta 971

**Steam Locomotives:**

A 3/5 No. 705
B 3/4 No. 1367
CZm 1/2 No. 31 (Dampftriebwagen)
D 1/3 No. 1 *Limmat*
E 2/2 No. 3 *Zephir*
Eb 2/4 No. 5469
Eb 3/5 No. 5813
Ec 2/5 No. 28 *Genf*
Ec 3/3 No. 5 (Kastendampflok)
Elefant C 5/6 No. 2965
Elefant C 5/6 No. 2978
Mallet Ed 2x2/2 No. 196
Tigerli E 3/3 No. 8487

Many of these items can be viewed at the Swiss Transport Museum at Luzern (*see entry 96*).

# Glossary of Swiss Railway Terms

| German | French | Italian | English |
|--------|--------|---------|---------|
| Autowagen | train auto | carico d'automobli | vehicle carrier |
| Bahn | reseau | ferrovia | railway |
| Bahnunternehmen | enterprise ferroviaire | ferovia impresa | railway company |
| Bahnhof, station | gare | stazione | station |
| Betriebslänge | longueur exploitée | lunghazza escercita | route length |
| Doppelstockwagen | voiture à deux niveaux | carrozza a due piani | double-deck coach |
| Eigentumslänge | longeur du proper réseau | lunghezza della propria rete | length of line owned |
| Eurospaische Bahnen | réseaux européens | ferrovie europee | European railways |
| Fahrplan | horaire | orario | timetable |
| Fahrzeuge | véhicules | veicoli | rolling stock |
| Fahrleitung | igne de contact | linea di contatto | catenary |
| Gleis | voie/quai | binario | track / platform |
| Gepäckwagen | fourgons | bagaglia | baggage car |
| Güterwagen | wagons | carri merci | goods wagon |
| Güterzug | train merchandises | treno merci | freight train |
| Lokomotiven | locomotives | veicoli motori | locomotives |
| Neigezug | train pendulaire | treno ad asserto variabile | tilting train |
| Normspur | voie normal | a scartamento normale | standard gauge |
| Niveauubergang | passage à niveau | passaggio a livello | level crossing |
| Personenwagen | voiture | carroze viaggiatori | passenger carriage |
| Personenverkehr | voyageurs | traffico viaggiatori | passenger traffic |
| Rangierfahrzeuge | locotracteurs | veicoli motori di manovra | shunting locomotives |
| Reisezug | train voyageur | treno viaggiatori | passenger train |
| Rollmaterial | matérial roulant | materiale rotabile | rolling stock |
| Schmalspur | voie étroite | a scartamento ridotto | narrow gauge |
| Steuerwagen | voitures de commande | veicoli di comando | (steering) rail car |
| Trasse | sillon | traccia d'orario | train path |
| Triebwagen | autorail | automotrici | (powered) rail car |
| Unfälle | accidents | infortuni | accidents |
| Unterhalt | entretien | manutenzione | maintenance |
| Weiche | aiguillage | scambio | points |
| Zug | train | treno | train |

Meiringen-Innertkirchen Bahn's snowplough at Innertkirchen station on 3rd February, 2007.  *Author*

# Bibliography

## Books and Journals

All publications are in the English language unless indicated otherwise.

*Bahn-Jahrbuch Schweiz 2006* edited by Peter Hürzeler and Hans-Bernard Schönborn, Edition Lan AG, Zug 2006. ISBN 3-906691-28-4 (de).

*Bernina Express Travel Guide* by Photoglob AG 2001. ISBN 3-907594-01-0.

*Die SBB Brunigbahn*, by Bear Moser and Thomas Küstner, Eisenbahn Journal, Fürstenfeldbruch 1996. ISBN 3-922404-85-5 (de).

*Die Rhätische Bahn macht Dampf* by Christian Müller, Foto Geiger Flims, Davos 1998. ISBN 3-9520828-5-6 (de).

*Glacier Express - from St Moritz to Zermatt* by Klaus Eckert and Ilona Eckert, Travel House Media (Merian Live!) Munich 2005. ISBN 3-8342-9505-1.

*Great Railway Journeys of Europe* edited by Tom Le Bas of Insight Guides, London 2005. ISBN 981-234-720-8.

*Les chemins de Fer Rhetiques*, published by Eisenbahn Journal, Fürstenfeldbruch undated. ISSN 0986-6663 (fr).

*Les 'Mountain' de l'Est* by Oliver Constant, Le Train-Editions Publitrains eurl, Betshdorf 1996/7. ISSN 1267-5008 (fr).

*Les trains du Jura*, published by Oliver Constant, Le Train-Editions Publitrains eurl, Betshdorf 1996. ISSN 1267-5008 (fr).

*LGB Journal 2005*, published by Ernst Paul Lehmann, Nurnberg 2006.

*Mountain Rack Railways of Switzerland* by J.R. Bardsley, Oakwood Press, Usk 1999. ISBN 0-85361-511-X.

*Schweizerferien 2006 mit Dampf un Nostalgie* published for SBB-RailAway by Dek-Verlags, Seltisberg 2006. ISSN1421-8631 (de).

*Switzerland - Eyewitness Travel Guides*, by Adriana Czupryn, Malgorzata Omilanowska and Ulrich Schwendimann, Dorling Kindersley, London 2005. ISBN 13-978-4055-0292-0 & 10-1-4053-2092-5.

*Swiss Express - Quarterly Journal of the Swiss Railways Society (UK)* Issues: March 2003-December 2006 inclusive.

*Swiss Museum of Transport - Highlights Guide* published by Verkerhshaus der Schweiz, Luzern 2006.

*The Complete Encyclopaedia of Locomotives* by Mirco de Cet And Alan Kent. Rebo International, The Netherlands 2006. ISBN 13-978-90-366-1505-1 & 10-90-366-1504-4.

*The Encyclopedia of Trains and Locomotives*, edited by Davis Ross, Amber Books, London 2003. ISBN 1-85605-792-5.

*The History of Trains* by Colin Garratt, Octopus Publishing, London 1998. ISBN 0-7537-0630-X.

*The Essential Guide to French Heritage and Tourist Railways* by Mervyn Jones, Oakwood Press, Usk 2006. ISBN 0-85361-648-5.

*The Swiss Railway Saga - 150 Years of Swiss Trains* by Hans Peter Treichler *et al*. AS Verlag & Buchkonzept, Zürich 1996. ISBN 3-905111-16-0.

*Trains alpines*, marketing brochure published by Schweiz Tourismus (MySwitzerland.com) 2006.

*Trains du massif du Mont-Blanc* by Beat Moser, Le Train-Editions Publitrains eurl, Betshdorf 2000. ISSN1267-5008 (fr).

## Maps

*Michelin Map No. 729* – Switzerland published by Michelin Travel Publications, Watford 2006. ISBN 13: 978-2-06-7111701-3 & ISBN 10: 2-06-711701-7.

*Carte Routiere officielle Automobile Club de Suisse* published by Kümmerly & Frey, 2006. ISBN 3-259-01001-7.

# Interesting Websites

**www.srpc.ch** – photographic catalogue of Swiss railway companies operating on narrow and standard gauge tracks (de).

**www.photos-trains.ch** – another interesting photographic album (de fr).

**www.seak.ch** - a long standing Zürich Club (formed 1933) which publishes the Eisenbahn Amateur - see also their website www.eisenbahn-amateur.ch (de fr en nl).

**www.railclub.ch** - website of the Rail club of Montreux (fr).

**www.lok-remise.ch** - website of 'Kreissegment-Lokomotiv-Remise der Schweiz' - an organization focused on railway architecture including locomotive sheds and roundhouses (de).

**www.dampfschleuder.ch** - website dedicated to the Xrotd R 12 snow blower (de).

**www.ag2.ch** - website for enthusiastic supporters of Appenzellerbahnen (de).

**www.trittbrett.ch** - website dedicated to Bern transport of yesteryear (de).

**www.rheinschauen.ch** - website for a museum at Lustenau on the Austrian side of the Rhine 2 km from the Swiss town of Au which portrays some items of railway history (de).

**www.sbb.ch** – website of the Swiss Federal Railways (de fr it en).

**www.swisstravelsystem.ch** – website addressing most travel needs in Switzerland (de fr it en).

**www.swiss-rail.ch** – another website written by rail enthusiasts (de).

**www.rail-info.ch/index.en.html** - a very useful website written by Stefan Dringenberg, Klaus P. Canavan and Manfred Luckmann and which was particularly helpful to the author in his early research (de en).

**www.myswitzerland.com/de/loco/lok.cfm** - a webcam mounted on a train with continously changing views of the tracks, stations, and landscape. This site also links to another useful source of images and information - www.ferrosteph.net/ferrosteph/sbb/ (fr en).

**www.swissworld.org/eng** - a very useful website about all aspects of Swiss life. To learn more about Swiss Railways and save time finding the link the following URL will help - www.swissworld.org/eng/swissworld.html?siteSect=907&sid=5385230&rubricId=17145 (en).

**www.x-rail.ch** – another superb photographic gallery with a wealth of useful information (de).

**www.stadlerrail.com** - website of the Swiss engineering company, successor to SLM at Winterthur and other companies (de en).

**www.railfaneurope.net** - This most comprehensive website provides information about the European Railways for railway fans as well as for travellers who wish to explore Europe by train.

**www.oakwoodpress.co.uk** – publisher's website listing their UK and European titles (en).

**www.rail-guides.eu** – website written by the author to support this book and others he has written (en).

# Useful Addresses

**Switzerland Embassy**, 16/18 Montagu Place, London W1H 2BQ. Telephone: 020 7616 6000 Fax: 020 7724 7001. Website: www.swissembassy.co.uk

**Swiss Railways Society**, c/o Membership Secretary, 28 Appletree Lane, Redditch, Worcestershire B97 6SE. E-mail: membership@SwissRailSoc.org.uk

**Switzerland Tourism**, 30 Bedford Street, London, WC2E 9ED. (Opening hours are Monday to Friday 9am-5pm except Thursday 10am-5pm.) Telephone: 00800 100 200 30 (free-phone) or 020 7420 4900 Fax: 00800 100 200 31 (free-fax). E-mail: info.uk@myswitzerland.com Website: www.myswitzerland.com/handler.cfm/home

**Rail Europe** is located at the French Travel Centre, 178 Piccadilly, London W1. Telephone: 08708 371371. Website: www.raileurope.co.uk E-mail: reservations@raileurope.co.uk

**The Railway Touring Company**, 14A Tuesday Market Place, King's Lynn PE30 1JN. Telephone: 01553 661500 Fax: 01553 661800. Website: www.railwaytouring.co.uk e-mail: enquiries@railwaytouring.co.uk British company which frequently runs excursions in Switzerland, France (and elsewhere) often using heritage locomotives.

**Railtrail Tours Ltd**, 43 St Edward Street, Leek, ST13 5DN. Telephone: 01538 38 23 23 Fax: 01538 38 25 25. Website: www.railtrail.co.uk E-mail: enquiry@railtrail.co.uk Another British company which runs excursions to France and elsewhere.

**Travelsphere Ltd**, Compass House, Rockingham Road, Market Harborough, Leics LE16 7QD Tel: 0870 240 2426. Website: www.travelsphere.co.uk/website/intros/rail-intro.aspx

**Venice-Simplon Express Ltd**, Sea Containers House, 20 Upper Ground, London SE1 9PF. Telephone: 020 7805 5060. www.orient-express.com

**The Oakwood Press**, PO Box 13, Usk, Mon., NP15 1YS. Website : www.oakwoodpress.co.uk E-mail : sales@oakwoodpress.co.uk

*Above:* A RhB service train making its descent from Piz Bernina towards St Moritz on 6th October, 2006.                                                                      *Author*

*Left:* No. 9 *Gletschhorn* of the Dampfbahn Furka Berstrecke (*see entry 53*) begins its descent to the village of Gletsch passing the Rhône Glacier on the way.                    *Author*

Map showing locations

50 km